CHASING THUGS, NAZIS, AND REDS

CHASING THUGS, NAZIS, AND REDS

Texas Ranger Norman K. Dixon

Kemp Dixon

Texas A&M University Press
College Station, Texas

First edition

Manufactured in the United States of America
This paper meets the requirements of ANSI/NISO, Z39.48-1992 (Permanence of Paper).
Binding materials have been chosen for durability.

LIBRARY OF CONGRESS CATALOGING-IN-PUBLICATION DATA

Dixon, Kemp, author.
Chasing thugs, Nazis, and Reds: Texas Ranger Norman K. Dixon / Kemp Dixon.—First edition.
pages cm
Includes bibliographical references and index.
ISBN 978-1-62349-256-4 (cloth: alk. paper)—
ISBN 978-1-62349-260-1 (ebook)
1. Dixon, Norman, 1908–1992. 2. Texas Rangers—Biography. 3. Crime—Texas—History—20th century 4. Law enforcement—Texas—History—20th century. I. Title.
F391.D59D59 2015
363.2'09764092—dc23
[B]
2014032567

Dedicated to the three men whose influence on N. K. Dixon was beyond measure and whom he admired above all others:

Frederick W. Dixon
M. T. "Lone Wolf" Gonzaullas
Col. Homer Garrison

CONTENTS

Preface ix

Chapter 1: Yankee Ranger 1

Chapter 2: Oil! 18

Chapter 3: Bits and Bullets 30

Chapter 4: Slots and Goats 43

Chapter 5: Goldthwaite 53

Chapter 6: The Sheriff and the Socialite 64

Chapter 7: Home Front 76

Chapter 8: Rape and Race 91

Chapter 9: Red River Ranger 101

Chapter 10: Bad Men 113

Chapter 11: The Phantom and the War Hero 125

Chapter 12: Aggies Revolt! 134

Chapter 13: Gays and Reds on Campus 150

Chapter 14: A Lone Ranger 162

Chapter 15: The Chief 172

Chapter 16: The Fall 182

Chapter 17: An Old Ranger Lets Go 193

Notes 197

Bibliography 215

Index 219

PREFACE

One day years after my father, Norman Kemp Dixon, had passed away, my mother asked me to search for something in his file cabinet. I no longer recall what I was trying to find, but what I discovered was stunning: thirteen diaries laying out his daily activities as a Texas Ranger—morning, afternoon, and evening—from 1938 through 1950. He considered his work confidential, and his rigid sense of integrity prevented him from discussing his cases with his wife or his sons, or anyone else, even decades later.

In those diaries are many fascinating stories that begged to be told, such as his role in breaking up the largest oil-field theft ring in Texas history, his efforts to solve the most infamous cold case in Texas history (the murder of a socialite and her lovely daughter on a lonely West Texas highway), his attempt to catch the Phantom Killer in 1946 (the number-one story in Texas that year), his investigations of a near-mutiny by cadets and veterans on the campus of Texas A&M and of charges that Communists and a "nest of homosexuals" were on the University of Texas campus, and the story that began with a 4:00 a.m. phone call from a desperate rural sheriff asking that Dixon help him find the "unknown Negro" who had just raped a seventeen-year-old white girl. White farmers were beginning to roam the countryside, determined to carry out quick justice. There was no time to waste.

Along with the diaries was folder after folder containing newspaper clippings of his investigations; correspondence with everyone imaginable throughout his life, including his father, his brother, FBI agents, military-intelligence officers, and his two supervisors (and role models) during most of his career—M. T. "Lone Wolf" Gonzaullas and Col. Homer Garrison; plus countless documents, such as his elementary-school report cards, Army Air Corps cadet transcript, ID card for his clown-diving act at the Texas Centennial Exposition, Ranger commissions, and so on. Although his Ranger diaries ended in 1950—by which time he was the top security officer in the state, responsible for protecting Texans from the perceived threat of Communism—he continued saving items. One remarkable document is a 105-page transcript of a report by an informant inside a Communist cell in Austin. It reads like a novel.

Digesting all the materials in his files left me with many questions that could be answered only through research. Thank goodness wonderful resources were available. I wish to thank the very helpful archivists at the Texas State Library and Archives in Austin, with special thanks to Donaly

Brice for his always-cheerful support; to the staff at the Center for American History, the University of Texas at Austin, for their quick response to my research needs; to Tela Mange at the Texas Department of Public Safety for taking the time to search through several boxes to find materials I had requested, and offering me a workstation in her office to go through them; to Sherlynn Kelley at the Sheriff's Association of Texas in Austin for providing work space to review copies of the association magazine, a valuable source for anyone researching law-enforcement history in twentieth-century Texas; and to Christi Smith and others at the research center of the Texas Ranger Hall of Fame and Museum in Waco for their assistance, especially on the vast collection of newspaper clippings and photographs donated by Gonzaullas, who, as chief of the Bureau of Intelligence, hired Dixon in 1937 and then, in 1942, selected Dixon to serve with him in Company B.

I thank Leona Dixon, my mother, for directing me to my father's file cabi-

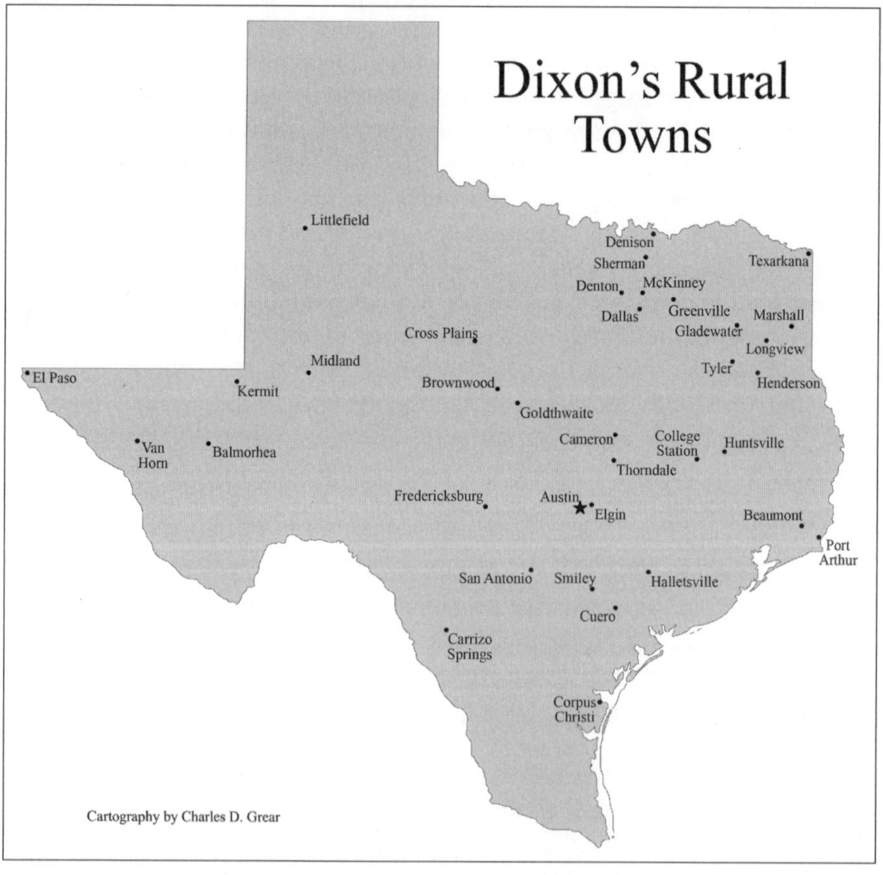

The towns on the map indicate the locations of many of the cases Texas Ranger Norman K. Dixon investigated. *Map courtesy Charles D. Grear.*

net, telling me many stories about their life together, keeping a valuable diary along with her husband during his first two years in the Ranger force, and, of course, simply being my mother. I also thank Tommie Spellman Bullock, my aunt and my mother's surviving sibling, for answering many questions about family events that occurred long ago. Special thanks to my brother, Ken, and his wife, Judy, for reading each chapter as it was written and providing me with their memories of events. Finally, but far from least, I thank my wife, Lea Ann. For more than two years of afternoons and evenings she quietly tolerated her husband's disappearance into an untidy mess of boxes, books, and materials.

Chapter One

YANKEE RANGER

One spring day in 1932, Nora and Christian Spellman watched from their front porch as a car bearing the new boarders drove up the dirt road to their farmhouse. Nora barely noticed Carl Mull or his three seedy wildcatters as they climbed out of the car. Instead, she focused on the remaining passenger, who had bounded from the vehicle and was taking great, confident strides toward the house. He exuded energy and athleticism. He was young and handsome. He was, Nora hoped, a possible match for her barely seventeen-year-old Leona, who, watching from the back porch, had not missed a single stride.[1]

This remarkable new boarder was Norman Kemp Dixon. Nora and Leona soon learned that he had been born during a thunderstorm early in the morning of June 30, 1908, in the township of Weathersfield, Vermont. His mother was Annie May Elsdon Dixon, a quiet, very religious woman. His father, Frederick William Dixon, was an all-around athlete who coached several major sports. He had served in the Spanish-American War, and during World War I he was in charge of organizing sports and recreation for allied forces in England. He made headlines at various times saving people's lives, as he did on March 25, 1913, when the Olentangy River flooded and drowned more than seven hundred people in Ohio and Indiana. In the town of Delaware, Ohio, where the Dixons were living, Frederick, a coach for Ohio Wesleyan University at the time, jumped into a boat with two students and rowed to a second-floor window, where three women climbed into the boat. Overloaded, the boat capsized in the raging current. Each man grabbed a woman and seized a branch as they were swept under a tree. Annie, blissfully assuming her husband was safe on campus, had her tranquility destroyed when a young man rang her doorbell and announced, "I just wanted to tell you that 'Prof' Dixon is perfectly safe in the tree, and we hope to get him soon." The three men and three women perched in the tree for hours, each man holding a woman in a waterlogged fur coat until they were rescued.[2]

Norman's athletic, heroic father was his first role model. As a boy, Norman strove to emulate him, enthusiastically participating in all kinds of sports and, whenever possible, roaming through woods and along beaches. One

Frederick W. and Annie May Dixon with sons Ronald and Norman. *Author's Collection.*

day in Bradley Beach, New Jersey, when the boys in his sixth-grade classroom were too boisterous, the teacher kept the entire class after the bell until everyone had stayed silent for ten minutes. One ten-minute detention led to another and then another as one boy after another acted up. The students were becoming restless, and at one point Norman threatened a classmate. When the teacher dismissed the class, she took Norman by the arm and told the boy he had threatened that she would not turn Norman loose until the boy had reached the school's main entrance. The boy took off running as the class cheered, and when the teacher let Norman go, he gave chase. Catching up, he challenged the boy to a race, but instead the boy began swinging his fists. Norman, who had been taught to box, blocked and dodged the blows as his classmates (and their teacher) formed a ring around the combatants. But then the principal showed up and separated the boys, sending them home.

One of the witnesses was Ruth Woodbury, Norman's cousin. The Woodburys were living with the Dixons, and Ruth reached home first, telling her aunt Annie about Norman's "beating up a boy." When Norman entered the house, he saw his gentle mother sitting in a straight chair across the room, her face as white as a sheet. Fearing she was ill, he rushed to her. "What did you do to that poor boy?" she asked, adding that she would have to go see the boy and his parents. It took some time, but when Norman finally convinced her that the boy was not hurt, the color slowly returned to her face. Norman loved his mother so much that when he did misbehave, her method of punishment was to simply sit down with a hurt look on her face. It always worked.

Tragedy struck when Norman was in the ninth grade in Asbury Park, New

Jersey. His mother became quite ill and was confined to her bed for weeks. Because their father was on the road much of the time as a community organizer, trying to provide for his family on a lower salary than he had made before the war, Norman and his brother, Ronald, prepared the meals and washed the dishes and clothes. On the few occasions when Frederick made it home for a short visit, Annie would force herself out of bed and downplay her health problems. When Norman wrote his father a letter explaining the seriousness of Annie's illness, Frederick rushed home, fired their doctor, and hired another, who quickly diagnosed the problem as intestinal cancer. It was too late. On February 23, 1923, Annie died.

After living with friends through the following school year, Norman moved to Brooklyn to live in a boardinghouse with his father, who now was running a boys camp. The next year his father remarried and moved to Florida, where he and his bride established a dancing and bathing pavilion on Anna Maria Key, between Tampa Bay and the Gulf of Mexico. When Norman, who was living with relatives in Cleveland, Ohio, finished his senior year, he moved to Florida to help his father in his new venture. But in September 1927 he bought a new pair of slacks and a railroad ticket to Gainesville, where he entered the University of Florida on an athletic scholarship. For the first two days, with no cash on hand as he waited for scholarship funds to come through, he had nothing to eat but a package of Fig Newtons. On the third day, assured he would have his money the next day, he borrowed a dollar from a student and spent it all on food. "In those days," he recalled, "that bought plenty."[3]

Norman joined the freshman football team and, after the season ended, made the boxing team as a welterweight. In March 1928 the university sent him to Mobile for the Southeast American Athletic Union Olympic Tryouts. After his first bout, the *Mobile Register* reported, "Norman Dixon, representing the University of Florida, put his team off to a good start when he laced Cecil Lee of Spring Hill, in a bout that took four rounds for the judges to reach a decision." Norman won, "rocking Lee with a bombardment of rights and lefts to the face and midsection." He finished the tryouts as runner-up for All-Southern as a boxing welterweight. After the boxing program ended in 1929, the student newspaper reported it a great success and singled out several for special comments, including the following: "Norman Dixon, possessor of worlds of stamina and nerve is going to carve himself a niche in Southern welterweight circles next year."[4]

During that summer, while Norman worked as a lifeguard at the Larchmont Shore Club, on Long Island Sound, C. Paul Jennewein, a well-known sculptor, ran into a problem. The American Battle Monuments Commission, which planned to erect a monument in Tours, France, to commemorate the support services for the American Expeditionary Forces during World War I, had commissioned Jennewein's proposed sculpture of an Indian and eagle.

Jennewein, wanting a real Indian to pose for him, located a prospect who claimed to be a cross-country runner and to be in excellent physical condition. Jennewein paid to fly him sight unseen from Arizona, but when he arrived, the sculptor was stunned. The Indian had no muscle definition at all. Jennewein put him back on a plane to Arizona.

An artist friend told Jennewein that his club had the best Indian one could want. He was somewhat dark-skinned and had great muscle definition. On a visit to the club, Jennewein took a good look at the lifeguard. Pleased with what he saw, he offered Dixon the job as a model, saying he could pose at his studio during his spare time from lifeguard duties. Curious and interested in this different kind of challenge, Dixon accepted. In the evenings the novice model took a short train ride from Larchmont to the Bronx, where Jennewein had his studio.

According to Shirley Reiff Howarth, editor of the *International Directory of Corporate Art Collections*, among the more than two thousand Jennewein models, drawings, and medals housed in the Tampa Museum, *Indian and Eagle* "is one of the most successful of Jennewein's bronze monuments." In 1932 it won the George D. Widener Memorial Gold Medal at the Pennsylvania Academy of Fine Arts. A review stated, "It is a heroic figure of an Indian and an eagle, a work of monumental character which will top a high column." The memorial was unveiled in Tours on August 5, 1937. A photograph of the statue that Jennewein sent to his model shows a twenty-one-year-old Norman Dixon with one knee on the ground, his left arm raised and bent at the elbow, and an eagle perched on his forearm ready to take flight. Beneath the photograph the sculptor had written, "To my model Norman Dixon, gratefully C. P. Jennewein."[5]

In September 1929, his modeling career over, Dixon was back at the University of Florida, where he had been elected to the student council for his junior year. But there had been an oversight: no scholarship money had been allocated for him. He was in debt to the school; he had no money to pay tuition or board; and his father, whose venture had suffered following the collapse of the Florida land boom, could not help. There was no choice but to leave. Dixon hitchhiked to Houston to enroll at Rice Institute, where he had understood he would be accepted, but he arrived too late for the current year. He headed to the Houston shipping channel, where he found employment, shipping out on the SS *Glenpool,* a Standard Oil tanker.

In port at New Orleans on November 26 he enlisted in the U.S. Army, hoping to be appointed to the Army Air Corps Flying School. He had dreamed of flying since the third grade. Sitting in class one day he heard a roaring. He rushed to a second-floor window but, unable to see the source of the sound, jumped to the ground. There he saw a biplane, its pilot seated on the center of the wing,. hedge hopping, barely clearing the trees and flying over the school playground. The thrill was unforgettable.

Photograph of "Indian and Eagle" sculpture, mailed by Paul Jennewein to his model, Norman Dixon.
Author's Collection.

Dixon was stationed at Fort Sam Houston, San Antonio, Texas. Within six months of enlisting, he received his appointment as a flying cadet in the Army Air Corps, an accomplishment made exceptional by the fact that, whereas he lacked a college degree, some cadets with college degrees waited two years for an appointment. The transcript of his flying records, dated May 14, 1931, shows that he completed better than 151 hours of flight training and had excellent flight-school grades but states, "Failed to meet the standard required in flying at the ACPFS." Two days later he signed honorable-discharge papers indicating that he had been "disqualified as Fl. Cadet." His character was listed as "Excellent." As he later wrote in his personal papers, he had "washed out." What happened?[6]

Several months earlier, in hospital for an appendectomy and a tonsillectomy, Dixon had met Gene Ellen Mull. She was cute and flirtatious, and like other cute, flirtatious young women in San Antonio, she spent time with the flying cadets. Then, in May 1931, an officer made a pass at Gene—when she and Norman were a couple and might even have been married. The boxer in Norman took charge, and he slugged the officer. His military career was over. A married man (or married soon thereafter), he needed a job. He arranged to fly mail and conduct other flight business in Honduras, but the Honduran government switched contracts to another company. Leaving Gene with her family, he headed north, seeking flying jobs at every airport en route. Unsuccessful, he went on to Mamaroneck, New York, where he found work as a lifeguard, and in the fall he was hired as floor manager at the newly established New York Physicians Club, in Manhattan.

By the spring of 1932 Dixon's brief marriage to Gene was in name only, but because her father, Carl Mull, was willing to add him to his wildcat crew, Dixon returned to San Antonio. From there he rode eastward with his father-in-law and the other crew members to Smiley, in Gonzales County, where they turned southward on the dirt road to Yorktown. After about six miles they turned onto a two-rut dirt lane that meandered to Nora and Christian Spellman's farmhouse, where Mull's crew would board while drilling a well in a pasture adjacent to the Spellman farm. Leona's life was about to change forever.[7]

Earlier that year Leona had been boarding at a home in Smiley while attending high school. Living in town gave her access to a life very different from that on the farm. She was playing cards, going to dances and ball games, and riding around with friends. It was a good life, but it was about to end, abruptly. One night in February she rode with a boy and another couple to a dance in Westoff, which among Smiley churchgoers had a reputation as a bad place, probably because of its dance halls. While the foursome sat in the car in the parking lot, Leona and her date in the backseat, he pulled out a bottle of whiskey and took a drink. Leona did not approve of drinking, and she began to cry. As luck would have it, Nora's brother, Roy Smith, was also in the parking lot, and he saw Leona crying. Misunderstanding what he saw, and not one to keep a secret, he told Nora that Leona had been molested by a boy in Westoff.

Nora, a strong-willed farm wife who did not trust her seventeen-year-old daughter living away from home, drove immediately to the Smiley school, pulled Leona out of class, took her to her boarding room and gathered her things, and drove her home, all without saying a word. That night the bewildered Leona slipped outside the house and hid in a grapevine arbor in the yard, where she cried through the night. Her good life was over, and she did not know why. She had not been molested in Westoff, nor had she seen Roy Smith there, so she had no reason to put the blame on that evening. It would be years before she learned why she had been yanked out of school and away from all her friends. She would never fully get over it. She was embarrassed and hurt at having infuriated her mother without knowing why, at having lived her life without a high-school diploma, and then, when she learned that it was all a misunderstanding, at knowing it was far too late to rectify.[8]

Neither Nora nor Leona expected that the arrival of the new boarders a few weeks later would give Leona a new lease on life. But while Norman drew their attention, he provoked Leona's brother, Clyde. Among the Spellmans' six children, eighteen-year-old Clyde was the competitive one, always seeking a challenge, especially to his physical prowess. Throughout his childhood, Clyde had loved taking on bigger boys, and here in his midst was this Yankee who talked a little too fast to understand, who appeared to be very sure of himself, and who was lithe and agile. But when he did backflips across the yard, the last one over the fence, that was too much! In front of the family, Clyde challenged Dixon to a boxing match. What Clyde did not know was that his opponent was a trained boxer, and as Clyde flailed away, Dixon easily fended him off while landing his own blows again and again, until Nora and Christian stepped in to stop the fight. It was clear to the entire family that this newcomer had bested Clyde.[9]

Norman Dixon did enjoy showing off. Leona's cousin, Louis Spellman, watched him scamper up the side of the oil derrick rather than climb the rungs. And when a part broke, he climbed down into the well even though red ants were swarming in it. The ants bit his arms, legs, and face, but he repaired the part and climbed back out, blithely brushing off the attackers, and returned to his normal tasks. Like Clyde, he took great pride in his ability to withstand pain.[10]

Leona was Nora's main worry, and much to her satisfaction, this attractive young Yankee began paying attention to her daughter. He looked like a gift from heaven. One day, however, Norman's wife, Gene, very attractive, with beautiful skin and wearing a lot of makeup, came to the Spellman farm-

At the rear is Christian Spellman. Standing in front are Gladys, Tommie (in front of Nora), Ethel (married to Audley), Audley, and Clyde Spellman. Seated are Elna and Leona Spellman with Norman Dixon. 1932 Photograph. *Author's Collection.*

house. But she was not a threat to Nora's plan. When she entered the house, she walked straight to Leona and handed her a handkerchief of Norman's, as if to say, "He's yours now."[11]

On Tuesday, June 28, 1932, the District Court of Bexar County granted the plaintiff, Gene Ellen Dixon, a divorce from the defendant, Norman Kemp Dixon. Later that day, Gene's attorney, McCollum Burnett, mailed the divorce papers to Norman at the Spellman home. The envelope, postmarked 3:30 p.m., probably reached him through rural delivery on Thursday or Friday. On Monday, Nora drove Norman and Leona to the Gonzales County courthouse to purchase a marriage license. The county clerk and the deputy clerk filled out the license and signed it—on July 4, a national, state, and county holiday. Nora was wasting no time. On Thursday, July 7, not one minute beyond the required seventy-two hours, Nora drove Norman and Leona to a preacher's house to be married. The preacher, a relative of Curtis White, Leona's sister Elna's husband, certified that he joined in marriage as husband and wife "Norman Kent Dixon" and "Leona V. Spellman," misspelling Norman's middle name. In rural Texas during the Great Depression, and at other times, couples married without announcements, bridal showers, wedding dresses, bridesmaids, or even a gathering of relatives to witness the ceremony. Money was always scarce. Even so, considering that no scandal was involved, Nora's haste was remarkable.[12]

After the quick ceremony, Nora drove the newlyweds back to the farmhouse. Norman borrowed Christian's brother Frank's horse from an adjacent farm, Leona borrowed her sister Tommie's horse, and they rode into the countryside for a night under the stars. Norman was at home in the outdoors. He loved wandering the woods in the Rocky Mound area, tracking coyotes, once sighting a lobo wolf, trapping rattlesnakes, watching hawks and vultures, and examining South Texas plants, trees, and foliage that were new to him. For Leona, lying on a quilt on the hard ground was not particularly comfortable, but they had the one thing they were seeking: privacy.[13]

When Mull's oil well came up dry, Norman followed him to Karnes County, where he tried again. The new well was within driving distance of the Spellman farm, allowing Nora and Leona to visit the site at least once. When it too failed, Dixon spent the next few months working for Christian on the farm. For a few days he also substituted for Rudolph Spellman, one of two teachers at the nearby Rocky community school.[14]

Norman was a proud man, and working as a farmhand was not a goal of his. And Christian really could not afford to pay him any wages. In May 1933, convinced he could find work in his part of the country, Norman took his bride to Philadelphia. There Ronald, Dixon's only sibling, and his wife, Isabel, met them at the bus station. Leona stayed in their New Jersey home while Norman became one of thousands hitchhiking or riding the rails out of Philadelphia to find work. After only a short time, perhaps because of his youth, vigor, and confidence, he was able "to talk [his] way into a job at the Higbee Company," a large department store in Cleveland, Ohio. For almost two years he worked there, setting up window displays and performing other tasks at a salary of sixteen dollars a week, four of which went for rent, four for groceries, four for entertainment, and the rest for clothing and other needs.

One night in June 1935, Dixon came home and told Leona it was time to move back to Texas. They had few belongings—everything in the apartment was rented—so the next day they were hitchhiking their way to Smiley. Partway home, out of money and famished, Norman traded his fountain pen to a café operator for lunch. Leona, a twenty-year-old farm girl who had never traveled out of Texas before marrying, experienced not even a moment of concern or fear during their journey. She had complete faith in Norman's ability to handle any situation. And he never let her down. Back in Texas, he left Leona at the Spellman farm while he looked for work. Once again, despite the Great Depression, he talked himself into a job, this time with the Associated Detective Service, a private company in Dallas. By November 1936 he carried the title of assistant manager, conducting investigations, designing and writing advertisements, and sending letters to prospective customers.[15]

Norman and Leona lived in Dallas near the entrance to Fair Park, where the annual state fair had been held since 1886, and where the Texas Centennial Exposition would be held in 1936, celebrating one hundred years of independence from Mexico. The exposition was the first world's fair in the Southwest. On October 12, 1935, Gov. James V. Allred appeared on the exposition site to launch the largest several-month building program in state history. With the grounds closed and the fair canceled, seven thousand men soon were working three shifts. By April 1936, ten thousand men were at work, trying to meet the June 6, 1936, opening date. Among the men was Norman Dixon, still employed with the detective agency but also working as a landscaping foreman at the fairgrounds, doing his part to help Texas prepare for its big celebration.[16]

At 8:00 a.m. on June 6, 1936, every factory and train whistle in Dallas blasted to announce the opening of the Texas Centennial Exposition. From July to late November, Norman performed a diving-clown act in a swimming pool at the Days of Real Sports concession. Leona worked in the concession kitchen for about a month and then left her job. She was pregnant, and the Dixons were happily looking forward to their first child. Even though Norman was working two jobs, the expenses of Leona's pregnancy led him to spend his last two dollars wiring his father and brother for temporary financial help. He could not reach his father, but Ronald wired eighteen dollars.[17]

The health care expenses paled in comparison to the joy Leona and Norman experienced on Tuesday, December 1, 1936, when Velma Ruth was born. "Velma" was Leona's middle name, and "Ruth" was in honor of Norman's

Norman and Leona Dixon on their wedding day, preparing to ride to Rocky Mound for their honeymoon night. *Author's Collection.*

cousin, Ruth Woodbury. She weighed 6¾ pounds and appeared to be well-formed and perfectly healthy. On Thursday morning, however, doctors notified Norman that they had ordered X-rays and wanted him for a blood transfusion, which was quickly done. Velma Ruth was not breathing correctly, the doctors said, and her color was not good. That afternoon they told Norman that the X-rays showed a collapsed right lung and an enlarged heart. Two specialists were called in, and with three other doctors and several nurses, they worked to save the baby. After a bronchoscope operation, in which the doctors opened the lung, a nurse was assigned to monitor her continuously, but the assignment lasted only one hour. At 6:45 p.m. on December 3, 1936, two-day-old Velma Ruth died.

The loss was devastating. Leona had dreamed and planned for a baby for years. Born alive and to all appearances healthy, Velma Ruth suddenly was gone. The next day Norman wrote to Ronald: "I can't tell you the crush it was to Leona; nor of how bravely she took it. She's truly wonderful, Ronald, and knowing as well as anyone else might, how she was suffering, and yet was fighting to take it just about broke me. I can't stand to see her hurt anyway—she's got too much spunk and stuff to her." But not only was Velma Ruth gone. So was most of the money Ronald had sent. Wiring Ronald and his father about losing the baby cost two dollars, a gown for Leona "which she sorely needed but was going to do without, as I know it will help ever so little to brighten her up" cost two dollars, and burial expenses were ten dollars. Costs of the doctors and operation were yet to come. Norman promised Ronald he would try to swing a loan to consolidate everything and send the eighteen dollars back to him.[18]

The Texas Centennial Exposition had closed on Sunday, November 29, 1936, two days before Velma Ruth was born and four days before she died. Continuing his work as assistant manager at the detective agency, Norman took on a second job—pruning trees in Dallas parks—to help cover his debts and make ends meet. He was twenty-eight years old and married, with two years of college. He had washed out as a flying cadet and served briefly as a merchant marine. He had worked for two years in a department store in Cleveland, Ohio, and for a few months drilling dry oil wells in South Texas. He had worked as a farm laborer for his father-in-law, as a landscape foreman on the state fairgrounds, and as a diving clown for the centennial celebration. Now he was a tree pruner for the City of Dallas and in his second year with the Associated Detective Service. He was not satisfied.

Dixon was a newspaper reader all his life. As a reader of the *Dallas Morning News* he would have been acquainted with the newly established Texas Department of Public Safety, and with the most famous members of the department—the Texas Rangers. During the months leading up to the centennial exposition, a nationwide advertising campaign had emphasized the image of Texas with "ten-gallon hats, six-shooters, high-heeled boots, Texas Rangers, bluebonnets, and sex." Beginning April 26, 1936, Governor Allred with 125 Texans, including the University of Texas Longhorn Band and Texas Ranger Capt. Leonard Pack with his horse, Texas, embarked on a highly publicized ten-day, seventeen-city cross-country tour to promote the centennial, a tour that included a visit to Pres. Franklin D. Roosevelt in the White House. Captain Pack garnered a lot of attention wearing a .45-caliber six-shooter on each hip as he rode Texas into a posh hotel in Detroit and a new municipal auditorium in Kansas City.[19]

Dixon would have been aware of all these events, and they might have been a factor in his decision in the midst of all the publicity—in May 1936—to meet with Homer Garrison, assistant director of the new Texas Department of Public Safety (DPS), to inquire about becoming a Texas Ranger (the Ranger force had recently been folded into the new agency) or finding work in some branch of the department. Garrison suggested he write a letter around the first of the year. The world's fair began the next month with the centennial parade. One of its highlights was the twenty-five Texas Rangers who rode their horses from downtown Dallas, where Dixon worked at the detective agency, through the entrance of the exposition, a block from where the Dixons lived, and into the fairgrounds, where Dixon worked as a landscaping foreman and would perform his diving feats. Their destination inside the exposition was a rustic two-story log cabin that would serve as a Ranger exhibit during the world's fair, and afterward as headquarters for Company B of the Texas Rangers.[20]

Dixon was one of more than a million visitors to the Ranger exhibit, but few others, if any, would one day find themselves wearing a Ranger badge and headquartered at the log cabin. In charge of the exhibit was Manuel Trazazas "Lone Wolf" Gonzaullas, who enthralled visitors, and possibly Dixon, with stories about the 250 guns on display that had been taken from criminals. The exhibit also contained a crime lab, where Dixon might have listened to Gonzaullas explain how they were able to identify hair and blood, and how they could put a bullet under a microscope and determine the murderer. Gonzaullas was chief of the Bureau of Intelligence, and one of the most famous Rangers of the twentieth century. By the summer of 1936, Norman Dixon—private eye and clown diver—had met the two men who would serve as his immediate bosses for most of his law-enforcement career and who, along with his father, he would admire above all others: Col. Homer Garrison and Lone Wolf Gonzaullas.[21]

In August, Gonzaullas, more than fifty former Texas Rangers, and most of the current force gathered at the Rangers' log cabin at the exposition for a three-day session—the largest gathering of Rangers in history—climaxed by the unveiling of a bronze statue of a Ranger. Present at the event was noted film director King Vidor, whose movie *The Texas Rangers* had its world premiere in Dallas after the unveiling, with the same former and current Rangers in attendance. Norman and Leona Dixon, who loved going to the movies, very likely saw the film while it played in Dallas.[22]

On January 16, 1937, following Garrison's suggestion that he send a letter after the first of the year, Dixon wrote and mailed a two-page effort to gain an appointment to the Texas Rangers or, at least, to a branch of the DPS. Garrison referred Dixon's letter to Horace H. Carmichael, the department director, whose January 18 response was not encouraging. Dixon, however, did not give up. On April 26 he wrote to Governor Allred regarding his interest in a position in the Bureau of Identification and Records, which was part of the DPS. The governor's office referred the letter to Director Carmichael, who on April 29 responded that the bureau had no vacancies but suggested he write C. G. McGraw, chief of the bureau.[23]

On April 30 Dixon wrote to Chief McGraw stating that "a life long interest in science has equipped me with a fundamental background for adaptation," that "my ultimate aim is directed towards the scientific efforts of the State Department," and that to meet that aim he had extended his studies into such identification systems as anthropometry, handwriting, fingerprinting, poroscopy, Bertillon, and anthropology, "to include friction skin, bones, hair direction, dentology, facial restoration." He had done his best to impress McGraw—it is doubtful many of the chief's job applicants referred to the "poroscopy" and "Bertillon" identification methods—and on May 4 Chief McGraw responded that Dixon's application was on file for any future vacancies. On May 13 Dixon wrote to L. G. Phares, chief of the Texas Highway Patrol, which was also part of the DPS, expressing his interest in state police work, and asking for application forms that he could fill out and submit. The next day Dixon attended the monthly meeting of the Dallas Claim Men's Association to hear "important Committee reports" and news about the annual round-up picnic. But his thoughts were elsewhere.[24]

On May 30 Dixon met with Lone Wolf Gonzaullas, seeking a position as a criminal investigator in his bureau. After a long interview, in which Gonzaullas questioned Dixon about his character, experience, and qualifications, the chief suggested Dixon submit a letter of application to Colonel Carmichael. On May 31 Dixon typed his letter, referring to his meeting with Gonzaullas, giving his background, and listing his height (5 feet 8¼ inches) and weight (137 pounds). He said he did not drink alcohol or use narcotics and had never been convicted of a felony. In his current job, he wrote, he investigated criminal and civil cases and performed general office work. At the same time, he "had been studying modern scientific crime detection methods."[25]

On June 18 Dixon received a form letter from Phares, chief of the Texas Highway Patrol, instructing him to take a competitive exam in Dallas on June 28 at the North Dallas High School. He was told to bring three lead pencils, a fountain pen full of ink, and ten or twelve sheets of scratch paper the exact size of the form letter. He took the test, and waited. It all paid off. On July 26 the persistent applicant received a second form letter from Chief Phares notifying him that he had been "tentatively" selected as a member of the Texas Highway Patrol at a salary of $125 per month. The appointment was "tentative" in case something in his record but not mentioned in his application would embarrass him and the department. If he had failed to mention such a fault, he should decline the offer of employment. Otherwise, he was being selected for trial—a seven-week training course beginning August 2 at Camp Mabry in Austin. Dixon was told he would have to pay one dollar per meal during the training period plus one dollar for a physical exam and would be required to purchase two suits of work clothes. He should bring one pillow, toilet necessities, and two pairs of shoes. To accept the appointment, he needed to send a wire immediately. Dixon complied with alacrity.[26]

When Norman Dixon arrived to start his training, Camp Mabry was being transformed from an old National Guard encampment, with "dilapidated barracks and sun-baked grounds," into a permanent home for the two-year-old DPS. From a veranda, one could look out on the hills to the west. To the east were the state capitol and the University of Texas tower. On the site were machine shops, in which state cars and motorcycles would be repaired, and training facilities, including a rifle range and a "crime city"

Norman Dixon's application photograph for acceptance in the fifth Texas Highway Patrol training school. *Author's Collection.*

training site, where state police officers would enact real-life encounters with criminals.

Dixon was enrolled in the fifth Texas Highway Patrol training school, overseen by Homer Garrison and his staff. Training began before sunrise and ended at eight or nine at night. The recruits marched in formation to meals and classes. One instructor, Capt. Jimmy Dikes, a veteran army officer, lectured the recruits "in table manners, dining room deportment and military drill." Dikes also supervised the canteen and was responsible for the cafeteria menus. Instructors in the miniature hospital trained the recruits in first aid.[27]

From Capt. O. L. Canady, who was in charge of motorcycle classes, Dixon and the other recruits learned to ride, make emergency stops, and perform skid turns. From Capt. E. M. Wells, in charge of the rifle range, Dixon learned how to handle different kinds of situations when pursuing criminals. He learned to fire a submachine gun from a moving car. He practiced driving a car to force vehicles off the road and, more dangerously, to leap from one moving car onto another and from a motorcycle onto a moving car. He even learned to stay balanced on his motorcycle while standing straight up on its seat. In gym class, Dixon—who barely met the height requirement for the highway patrol—learned how to subdue larger, stronger men through wrestling and jujitsu maneuvers. He was taught some boxing techniques (which for him would have been a refresher course). In addition, he was taught how to handle tear gas. Training also included instruction in fingerprinting and other identification methods, lectures on safety, and the geography of Texas.[28]

When Norman Dixon completed his training on September 11, 1937, he did not join the highway patrol. On August 2, his first day of training, he had been offered a choice between becoming a highway patrolman or a junior criminal investigator for the Bureau of Intelligence under Gonzaullas in the Texas Ranger division. Both paid $125 per month. It was one of the easiest decisions of his life. Before a notary public he signed his oath of service, swearing among other things that he would not engage in a political campaign, that he had not fought any duels with deadly weapons or acted as a second in any duels, and that he had not bribed anyone to gain this appointment.

On September 1 the three DPS commissioners, the DPS director, and Chief Gonzaullas signed a document appointing Dixon a "Junior Criminal Investigator in the Bureau of Intelligence." On the following day the commissioners, the director, and Ranger Quartermaster and Captain R. W. Aldrich signed a document appointing Dixon a "Private in the Texas Ranger Force." Because the Texas Legislature, always notoriously stingy with money, never adequately funded the Ranger force, DPS stretched its funds by using the lower-paying title "junior criminal investigator" for new hires. Chief

Gonzaullas assigned Dixon to partner with Robert (Bob) Austin Crowder, a senior criminal investigator, in Tyler, Texas. Dixon's chief was one of the greatest Texas Rangers of the twentieth century. His partner was destined to become one of the great Ranger captains. Norman Kemp Dixon could not have chosen a better way to begin his career with the Texas Rangers.[29]

OIL!

IN 1823 STEPHEN F. AUSTIN CALLED FOR VOLUNTEERS "TO ACT AS RANGERS for the common defence." That was the beginning of the world-famous force that would become known as the Texas Rangers. More than a hundred years later, in 1935, the Ranger force was incorporated into the newly established Texas Department of Public Safety (DPS), with two mounted companies and a headquarters company. Department policies required that new hires in the Ranger force be 5'8" (Norman Dixon was 5'8¼"); sound in mind and body; instructed in the latest techniques in fingerprinting, communications, ballistics, and records; and excellent marksmen. By 1937 (the year of Dixon's employment), the Ranger force had been divided into six districts, each with a Ranger company, and with each Ranger assigned to a separate duty station in towns spread through the district.[1]

On September 11, 1937, when Norman Dixon completed his training at Camp Mabry, M. T. "Lone Wolf" Gonzaullas, chief of the Bureau of Intelligence, assigned him as a junior criminal investigator to work with Robert (Bob) Austin Crowder, senior criminal investigator, in Tyler, in East Texas. On September 13 Dixon rented a garage apartment at 303½ West Phillips in Tyler, and Leona, who had stayed at her parents' farm near Smiley during the weeks when Norman was in training, arrived the next day. On September 15, Dixon began his new job by working on his first case in nearby Gladewater. Between September 15 and December 31, he worked on eleven cases. He also attended the first Texas Peace Officers Training School conducted by the DPS Bureau of Police Training, completing the course on December 17. On Saturday, January 1, 1938, he made an initial entry into his first Ranger diary, listing the cases he had been assigned since September 15, 1937, and their status. With few exceptions, he would continue to record his Ranger activities on a daily basis for the next thirteen years, using his entries to prepare his weekly and monthly reports.[2]

Leona also began keeping a diary on Saturday, January 1, 1938, though she made entries only until mid-October 1939. In her first entry, she noted that it was her brother Clyde's birthday, that she rose late that Saturday morning, and that at two in the afternoon, she and Norman went with Bob Crowder

Bob Crowder holding Norman and Leona Dixon's son Kemp ca. 1941. *Author's Collection.*

and his stepdaughter to see a movie, *The Last Gangsters*, in downtown Tyler. That evening the Dixons played cards until midnight with Bob and his wife, Lucille. Leona's diary records contacts with one or both of the Crowders on at least forty-three separate days between January 1 and May 31, 1938, the Dixons' last day in Tyler. On many of these occasions, the Dixons and the Crowders visited socially, usually to play cards, bridge being a favorite game. At other times Leona and Lucille had lunch, shopped together, or talked by phone. On several occasions when Norman was out of town overnight, Leona spent the night at the Crowder home. Yet, in her diary, she invariably writes "Bob" but never "Lucille," referring to her as "Mrs. Crowder" or "Mrs. C," perhaps because she was an older woman with two children. Whatever Leona's reason for not writing Lucille's given name in her diary, the Dixons and the Crowders became close friends.[3]

Bob Crowder, thirty-seven years old in 1938, stood 6'3" and weighed about two hundred pounds. Ranger Lewis C. Rigler wrote that Crowder "reminded me of John Wayne, James Arness, and Jimmy Stewart, all rolled into one." Crowder, who grew up on a farm in East Texas and joined the U.S. Marines in 1921, met Lucille in Dallas after leaving the military, married her, and adopted her two children. He served as a Dallas police officer for five years before being selected for the first highway-patrol training class, in 1930, and after seven years as a patrolman, he was invited by Lone Wolf Gonzaullas to join the Bureau of Intelligence. The answer was as easy for him as it was for

Norman Dixon. Without hesitating, he said, "Hell, yes," and went to work as a criminal investigator in Tyler a few months before the arrival of his junior partner.[4]

As a senior investigator, Crowder was assigned a state vehicle, but Dixon, a junior investigator, was not, although his investigations would take him over much of East Texas. Nor did he own a personal car. However, the two men usually rode together, working jointly on most investigations. When Dixon was not riding with Crowder, he rode with a highway patrolman, a sheriff or a deputy sheriff, or, sometimes, an oil-company investigator. For longer trips, such as from Tyler to Dallas or Austin, he took a bus or a train.

At about 9:00 p.m. Monday, January 3, 1938, Crowder phoned his partner to tell him that a Mrs. Capps had pleaded with Sheriff William McMurray of Rusk County to find her husband, George Dillard Capps, 46, a Henderson oil worker who had been missing since his abandoned automobile was found near Jacksonville three days earlier. At the sheriff's request, the criminal investigators left Tyler in Crowder's state vehicle at 9:15 the next morning and drove the thirty miles to Henderson to meet with McMurray and Capps's son and son-in-law. From Henderson they drove to Wright City for a 10:40 meeting with Capps's Hunt Oil Company supervisor, and at 11:15 they set out on a trip of about thirty miles to the pond near Jacksonville where Capps's car had been found. After reviewing the scene, they traveled to Jacksonville for a noon lunch at the Palace Café, and after lunch they borrowed grappling hooks from the fire department, returned to the scene, where a sizable crowd had gathered, and dragged the pool near where the car was found, looking for evidence that might shed light on Capps's disappearance. Leaving the pool, they drove to a constable's house where Capps's car had been taken and searched through the car. They then drove back to Jacksonville to return the grappling hooks and review Capps's wallet and other papers that the sheriff's department had secured from the car earlier. At 6:30 p.m. Crowder and Dixon were at a home near the scene interviewing the occupants; by 7:30 they were at the Tyler jail interrogating a prisoner for information unrelated to the Capps case; and by 8:30 they were home. At 10:00 the Anderson County District Attorney called Dixon regarding a trial date on another case.[5]

Almost all the information in the preceding paragraph comes from Dixon's entry in his diary for Tuesday, January 4, 1938. It is a typical entry, so thorough in detail that a reader can know the hour of any work-related activity he performed that day. The entry is also typical in showing that Dixon had no work-hour limitations whether as a criminal investigator or as a Texas Ranger. Historian Robert M. Utley writes, "I have examined enough weekly reports . . . to confirm that typical Ranger weeks involved more than sixty hours and sometimes one hundred."[6]

At the Tyler courthouse on Saturday morning, January 8, Dixon and Crowder met with Capps's brother and his son, who had new information

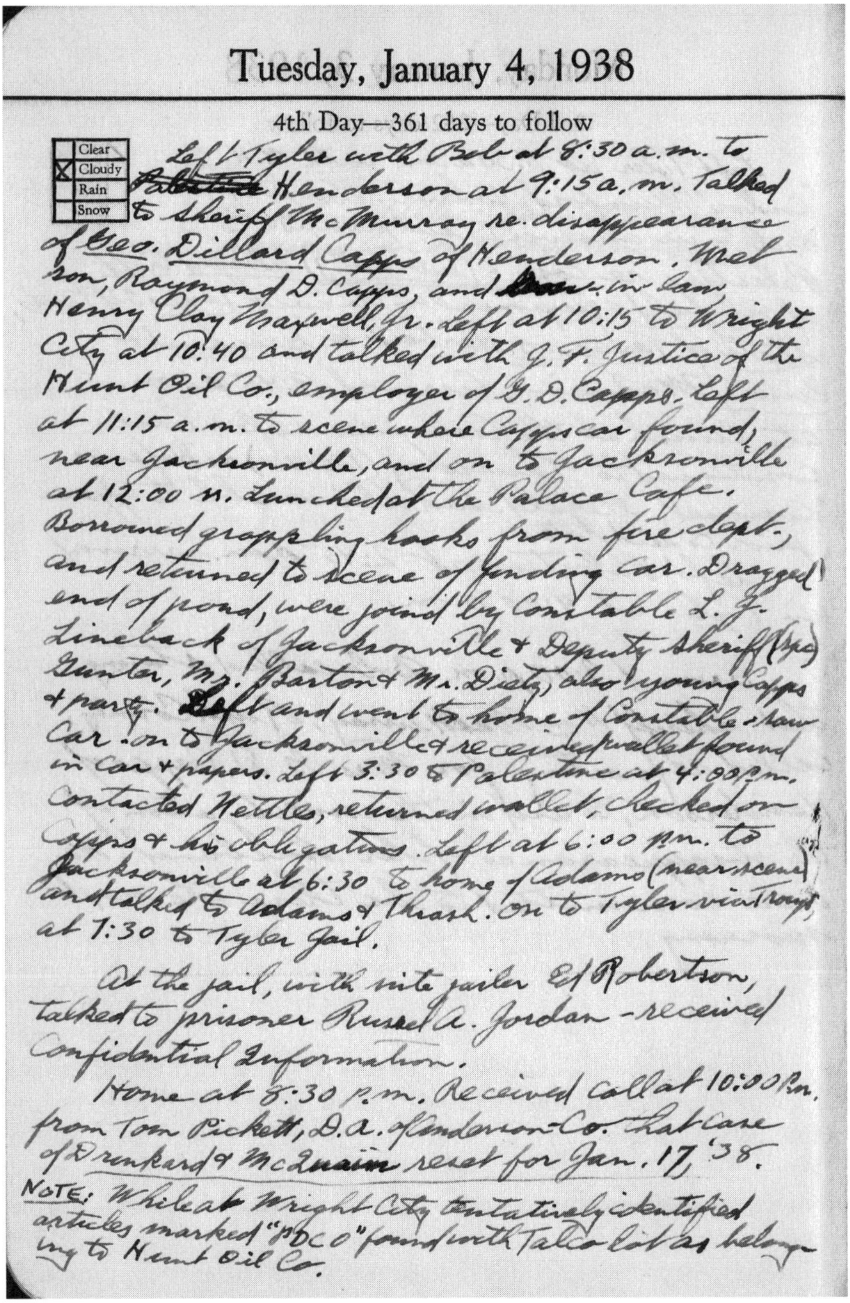

Tuesday, January 4, 1938

4th Day—361 days to follow

	Clear
X	Cloudy
	Rain
	Snow

Left Tyler with Bob at 8:30 a.m. to ~~Palestine~~ Henderson at 9:15 a.m. Talked to Sheriff McMurray re. disappearance of Geo. Dillard Capps of Henderson. Met son, Raymond D. Capps, and ~~son~~-in-law Henry Clay Maxwell, Jr. Left at 10:15 to Wright City at 10:40 and talked with J. F. Justice of the Hunt Oil Co., employer of G. D. Capps. Left at 11:15 a.m. to scene where Capps car found, near Jacksonville, and on to Jacksonville at 12:00 M. Lunched at the Palace Cafe. Borrowed grappling hooks from fire dept., and returned to scene of finding car. Dragged end of pond, were joined by Constable L. J. Lineback of Jacksonville & Deputy Sheriff (Spec) Gunter, Mr. Barton & Mr. Dietz, also young Capps & party. Left and went to home of Constable - saw car. On to Jacksonville & received wallet found in car & papers. Left 3:30 to Palestine at 4:00 p.m. Contacted Nettles, returned wallet, checked on Capps & his obligations. Left at 6:00 p.m. to Jacksonville at 6:30 to home of Adams (near scene) and talked to Adams & Thrash. On to Tyler via Troup at 7:30 to Tyler Jail.

At the jail, with nite jailer Ed Robertson, talked to prisoner Russel A. Jordan - received Confidential Information.

Home at 8:30 p.m. Received call at 10:00 p.m. from Tom Pickett, D.A. of Henderson Co. that case of Drunkard & McQuain reset for Jan. 17, '38.

NOTE: While at Wright City tentatively identified articles marked "PDCO" found with Talco loot as belonging to Hunt Oil Co.

Norman Dixon's diary entry for January 4, 1938. *Author's Collection.*

about the last people to see Capps. The investigators took the information, drove to Jacksonville, interviewed the named individuals, checked out their stories, and verified that on the long, busy previous Tuesday, when Crowder, Dixon, the sheriff, deputy sheriffs, a constable, and countless others were searching for the missing husband, he—Capps—sauntered into a Jacksonville store and bought a coat for Myrtle, his girlfriend. As Dixon wrote in his diary, "Case closed."[7]

Another case was about to close with a trial scheduled for January 13. E. H. Sojourner, a thirty-five-year-old oil-field worker, had been indicted for the November 3, 1937, murder of his sixty-nine-year-old neighbor, J. B. Massengale, a farmer, five miles south of Hallsville, between Longview and Marshall. Active in civic affairs and popular in the community, Sojourner, who had never had a brush with the law, rented his farm from an "old maid" schoolteacher. Eccentric and crotchety, Massengale, who often carried a pistol while working his farm so he could chase off anyone found on his property, owned the farm adjacent to Sojourner's.

The teacher had given Massengale permission to cut down a tree on her property that leaned over the fence onto his, but Sojourner told him not to cut it down. When Massengale removed the tree, Sojourner drove to Massengale's house and confronted him. After a fierce argument, Sojourner returned home, retrieved a shotgun, put it in his pickup next to a .22 rifle, and returned to Massengale's. In the meantime the schoolteacher, driving down the road, was hailed down by Massengale and informed about the argument. Sojourner pulled up next to the schoolteacher's car, and as he stepped out of his pickup with the shotgun, she reached out through her window and took it from him. Sojourner then retrieved the .22 rifle, stepped to the front of his truck, and fired seven shots into Massengale, killing him.

As the Massengale's family members, who were in the front yard, watched the confrontation, a young boy ran across the pastures to a neighbor, who telephoned for help. When a justice of the peace (JP) arrived, he found Massengale's body on its stomach with the head toward the house, away from where Sojourner was standing. Sojourner turned himself in to the JP. At the request of the district attorney, Crowder and Dixon undertook an investigation to help determine if Sojourner had murdered Massengale or shot him in self-defense. The district attorney had taken a rubber doll to the funeral home and, with the help of the undertaker, had marked on the doll in red the entrance wounds and in black the exit wounds.

Studying the markings on the doll, Crowder and Dixon determined that the first shots entered Massengale's back, and the others hit him as he whirled toward Sojourner, perhaps pulling his pistol out, completing the turn, and pitching forward toward the house, with his face on the ground. It was, they concluded, murder. Continuing the investigation, Dixon interviewed the JP, asking him a series of questions about the crime scene. Were there any signs, such as damp spots or grass pressed down, suggesting that the body had been moved? The JP had not noticed. In fact, he had done none of the basic checks of the crime scene. Another witness, the teacher, proved too excitable during an interview to be considered a reliable witness.[8]

On the morning of January 13, Dixon sat in the courtroom in Marshall as Sojourner pleaded self-defense, testifying that he saw Mrs. Massengale come out of her house carrying a shotgun and a pistol. During the lunch break, Dixon overheard Sojourner's attorney instruct him to change his testimony by saying he had been wrong about the pistol, that Mrs. Massengale had only a shotgun. Apparently, Dixon thought, the attorney believed that the image of her carrying two weapons to her husband might appear unlikely to the jurors. At the beginning of the afternoon hearing, Sojourner changed his testimony as instructed. That evening Dixon talked to a character witness subpoenaed for the defense and learned that he had met Sojourner only about a year and a half earlier, had seen him only a couple of times, and had not seen him at all in about a year. Dixon testified the next morning and left Marshall in the late afternoon, when the jury began its deliberations. Early the following morning, the jury acquitted Sojourner.[9]

While Norman was staying overnight attending the Sojourner trial in Marshall, which was about fifty-five miles east of Tyler, Leona was feeling ill at home. In her diary on January 13, she wrote, "Feeling sickish for about a week. Worse today." Her condition did not improve. On January 16 she "ate nothing all day till supper." On the next day, "Ate practically nothing." On the day after that, "Sicker—fruit & juices. Heaves." One day later, "Worse. Nothing to eat all day. Canned pears just before going to sleep." She was pregnant. On February 14, a Dr. Brown conducted a thorough exam, found that she weighed one hundred pounds, and pronounced her "OK." As she limped home with hip pains, she decided she liked her new doctor.[10]

Norman was at home on Sunday, March 13, when the Dixons decided to go to church for the first time since their arrival in Tyler. With Marvin Gordon, a sergeant in the highway patrol, and his wife, they attended Sunday school and services at the Methodist church. Leona had been raised a Methodist and Norman a Baptist, but Leona's ties to her faith were much stronger than Norman's were to his. That evening they went to the Crowders', where at 9:30 Bob received a call asking that he join a blockade being set up to capture Harry Wells, an escaped Arkansas convict suspected of robbing the Luling bank of nearly three thousand dollars.[11]

Bank robberies were nothing new for Texas. In fact, between 1924 and 1927 forty-three banks had been robbed, including fifteen in the first six months of 1927. In response, more drastic measures were employed. Thus in December 1927, following the Cisco Bank robbery in Eastland County, Lone Wolf Gonzaullas flew the area for two days in a canvas-winged biplane, the first instance of a Ranger using an airplane in a manhunt. And at about the same time, the Texas Bankers Association posted a sign at each bank offering a $5,000 reward for each bank robber killed while robbing a bank. As a result, some drunks were killed and framed as bank robbers.[12]

Paroled from an Arkansas penitentiary in 1933, Harry Wells kidnapped and robbed a physician in Camden, Arkansas, and was sent back to prison for fifteen years. He escaped on January 14, 1938, and on March 2 he married a South Texas college girl under an assumed name. After a brief honeymoon, he drove to Westoff, where he bought license plates for his car from a junk dealer, and went to Luling on the pretext that his father was going to give him and his bride money to live on. He did bring back money—from robbing the Citizens State Bank of Luling. That weekend he returned his bride to her college in Kingsland, telling her that he had to take a business trip to Wichita Falls and that when he returned he would bring her a diamond ring. But he did not come back. Eventually she learned he was not "Harry Northcutt" but the wanted desperado Harry Wells.

When law enforcement identified twenty-six-year-old Wells as a suspect in the Luling bank robbery, he found himself in a desperate flight. After wounding three officers in a gun battle in South Texas, he maneuvered his way into East Texas, abandoning his car on the highway between Marshall and the Louisiana border. The discovery of his abandoned car led to a massive manhunt and the 9:30 p.m. phone call to Crowder on Sunday, March 13. At 1:30 a.m., as Crowder went to Waskom, near the border, Dixon and a patrolman headed to Jefferson, north of Marshall. All local highway patrolmen and various other law-enforcement officials were involved in the search.

Every rumor was checked out. At 4:45 a.m., Dixon traveled to Longview, between Tyler and Marshall, to continue the search, and that afternoon, following up on a tip, he went to Gladewater, where he participated in raids on the home of Wells's parents and other places in the area. At 6:00 p.m. he was home, but an hour later, he, Crowder, and Marvin Gordon were on the road to Gladewater, where they arrested Wells's mother, sister, and brother. Next, in Longview, they raided a service station and a rooming house. Then a relative revealed that Wells was hiding in a shack on the north edge of Gladewater just off the Gilmer highway.

At 1:30 a.m. twenty-one officers raided the shack. Dixon was with Capt. Lee Miller at the front corner of the house while Crowder was with the detail tossing tear-gas bombs into the shack. As tear gas filled the shack, the officers yelled for Wells to come out with his hands up. According to the *Tyler Courier-Times,* Wells "displayed a cool attitude and limping on his left foot, came out with his hands up without saying a word." The bank robber had a bullet wound in his left foot from the South Texas gun battle. It had not been treated, and red streaks indicating blood poisoning were running up his leg from the wound. Dixon gathered with other officers in the Longview sheriff's office, where Wells, as Dixon wrote in his diary, "voluntarily told of bank robbery and hi-jackings & battles." After taking notes on Wells's verbal statements, Dixon returned to Tyler, arriving home at 6:00 a.m. on Tuesday—forty-eight hours without sleep. In April, convicted of robbery by firearms, Wells was sentenced to ninety-nine years in prison.[13]

But in spite of bank robberies and missing husbands, most of Norman Dixon's time between September 1937 and June 1938 was spent on assignments related to the oil industry. The black gold that gushed from the ground, changing hardscrabble farmers into wealthy men and tiny communities into boomtowns, attracted every criminal element imaginable and occupied many Rangers from dawn till dusk. The biggest oil boom began in East Texas in late 1930 with Dad Joiner's gusher in Rusk County. That oil field, which covered six hundred square miles in four counties, was one of the world's largest and soon was pumping one-third of the nation's total production.

Following the oil booms, the General Land Office, which maintained mineral rights to millions of acres of public lands, including seven million acres that had been sold, was transformed from a routine agency into one of the most important in the state. Among the Land Commissioner's most difficult responsibilities was setting fair prices for mineral leases on the six million acres set aside for public schools, the university, and the state eleemosynary institutions. Offers for leases included bids based on cash and royalties, and the commissioner had to decide whether to accept a high-royalty bid or a high-cash bid. Accepting a high-cash bid could cost the schools a considerable amount of money if drilled wells proved successful, but accepting a high-royalty bid could mean little or no income if the wells were unproductive.[14]

A number of agencies, including the General Land Office, were led by elected officials who owed no allegiance to the governor. On January 3, 1938, Gov. James Allred refused to approve a land sale, accusing Land Commissioner W. H. McDonald of not receiving full value and of altering the records. The next day, Sen. T. J. Holbrook, chairman of the Senate General Investigating Committee, said his committee would look into Land Office leasing policies. McDonald quickly canceled the riverbed lease, explaining that the "alteration" was simply a notation of the sales price.[15]

On January 9, Governor Allred ordered the attorney general and the state auditor to investigate the General Land Office. Two days later he called W. E. "Dub" Naylor (a criminal investigator in the Bureau of Intelligence) into his office and ordered him to conduct a "thorough investigation" of the alleged irregularity committed by McDonald and other Land Office employees. The governor handed him two letters and told him to interrogate the writer.

The next morning Naylor called Norman Dixon, who rode with Bob Crowder to Longview to meet Naylor at the Hilton Hotel. There they interviewed the man who had written the letters to the governor. W. E. Jones, a surveyor, told them that the application for the first lease McDonald granted

Governor James Allred. *Author's Collection.*

as land commissioner was stalled until two men from Tyler, B. A. "Jerry" Adams and Mead Eldred "said they could get the lease granted. . . . They got the lease in forty-eight hours." That afternoon the investigators interviewed another land surveyor, who gave a similar account, stating that Adams and Eldred told him that the application was good and that the Land Office knew it was good, "but that I couldn't get it acted on unless it went through their hands." They signed a contract, and the lease was quickly issued.

On January 18 Dixon and Crowder received a message from Naylor that the governor wanted the credit, character, and general reputations of Adams and Eldred investigated. After conducting investigations in Tyler, Kilgore, and Longview, Dixon teletyped a report to Naylor stating that Eldred's credit was satisfactory and that nothing came up negative about his character or reputation except his association with Adams, who "appears of bad repute—known as one who will 'do anything.'"[16]

After he sent the report, Dixon received a call from Gonzaullas to come to Austin as soon as possible for special work for Governor Allred regarding the oil-lease scandal. The next morning Crowder drove Dixon to Jacksonville, where he took the Missouri Pacific to Austin, meeting first with Chief Gonzaullas and then with Naylor, who gave him detailed information about his assignment. At 12:50 a.m. he boarded the Missouri Pacific, arriving at 7:00 a.m. in Houston. There, during the next two days, he investigated two individuals. Back in Austin on Sunday morning, January 23, Dixon met with Naylor and A. R. Stout, an attorney and former judge from Ennis hired by Allred for the investigation. At Stout's request, Dixon and Naylor checked hotel registrations and telegram and telephone records on several individuals.[17]

On each of the next three days, Governor Allred held meetings with Naylor and Dixon. At the third meeting he told them to take their orders from Stout, who would serve as special prosecutor for the state. Stout's first order to them was to serve summonses, signed by Senator Holbrook, to twenty-two men. Over the next several days they would be given an additional twenty-four summonses to serve. Dixon also took on another assignment for the governor. On January 28, he wrote to H. W. Fowler in St. Joseph, Missouri, ordering a "spring shoulder holster of plain black leather to be worn on the left side, with a forward break. This holster should be designed for a .38 caliber Colt's revolver with a two inch barrel. I would appreciate a rush order on this holster, as it is for the Governor of the State of Texas." At the end of the letter, he identified himself as "N. K. Dixon, Texas Ranger," ignoring his payroll title of "junior criminal investigator." Of course "Texas Ranger" sounded much better, but Dixon was part of the Ranger force, and his understanding was that the lower title was used simply because of lack of adequate funding to pay bureau staff at the Ranger pay level.[18]

For the next ten days, Dixon remained in Austin on assignment for the governor. Working with Naylor he served summonses by phone, helped prosecutors, attended senate committee hearings, and kept in contact with witnesses who came to Austin to testify. He also responded to a letter Senator Holbrook had received from someone saying he had information to give but was afraid he would be killed. After contacting the person, Dixon got his story. His last two days in Austin, Friday and Saturday, February 4–5, he spent mostly with Chief Gonzaullas before boarding the Missouri Pacific for Jacksonville at 10:55 p.m. From Jacksonville, he took a Greyhound bus to Tyler, arriving at 9:15 a.m.[19]

The Dixon's dog, Honeyboy, a gift to Leona after Velma Ruth died, was Leona's alarm system. On February 6 she wrote in her diary, "About ten a.m.

heard H.B. raising Cain on front porch & in walked Norman. Were we surprised, & pleasantly!" Norman had been gone seventeen consecutive nights. Leona, twenty-two years old and pregnant, had Honeyboy for company, but the Ranger's wife had trouble adjusting to being alone, and especially staying by herself at night. After sleeping alone the first two nights Norman was gone, she spent two at the Crowders'. On January 24 Leona walked to downtown Tyler and went to a movie by herself for the first time in her life. On January 26 she wrote in her diary, "Getting used to being alone. Not scared at nite." But alone at home on January 29 Leona read a mystery novel, and as she prepared for bed she wrote in her diary, "Will probably have nightmares if I sleep at all." With Norman and Bob both gone, she stayed with Lucille the nights of February 2, 3, and 5. On each of those days, Leona received letters from Norman. The first contained a check. She walked to town, cashed the check, paid their bills, and saw a movie, *Tovarich*, starring Claudette Colbert and Charles Boyer. After reading the second letter, she wrote in her diary, "He wants to come home." In the third letter, Norman said he still could not come home. Weary of being alone for a sixteenth consecutive day, Leona considered going to her parents' home but changed her mind after learning that boarding Honeyboy would cost $3.50 a day.[20]

In mid-February, after his lengthy stay in Austin, Dixon finally returned home. The governor and Stout were not finished with him, but the alleged rape of a minor under fifteen years of age occupied him in Marshall for three days. On the second day of this investigation, en route from a trial in Sulphur Springs back to Marshall, Dixon and Crowder encountered a man lying on the highway, seemingly dead. He was alive, but the two criminal investigators reached different conclusions: "Investigated and determined either under influence of (Liquor—Bob) or (Marijuana—Dick)." On the morning of the third day, Dixon took a statement from the alleged rape victim. That afternoon, Dixon interviewed her again and finally discovered that the rape charge was her mother's scheme to defraud the "perpetrator" by lawsuit. Three months later, after Dixon had testified to the grand jury, the mother was indicted.

Arriving home on February 18, Dixon found a letter from Stout asking him to interrogate twenty-six men in East Texas and a phone message from Naylor to interrogate two other men for Governor Allred. Stout requested quick action. He told Dixon, "If you should run across anything that looks real good, get in touch with the writer or the Governor here."[21]

Dixon worked on Stout's assignment from Saturday, February 19, through Tuesday, February 22, conducting interviews in Kilgore, Henderson, Gladewater, Longview, Marshall, Jefferson, Linden, and Texarkana. While in Longview, he accompanied the chief of police to 446 S. Fredonia with a "Lunacy Warrant" for Mrs. L. U. Perry, who, "crazed" with dope, was armed, and "had driven all from house & threatened to kill all." They entered the house at 11:05 a.m. and found her dead. She had shot herself "with .38 S&W blue, 5 in barrel, 5 load in left temple holding gun in right hand and pulling trigger with right thumb."[22]

On February 22 Dixon wrote to Stout, attaching a two-page report on his interrogations, stating "no information of irregularities" or "no knowledge of irregularities" for most of them. On the same day, Dixon and Crowder sent copies of all their reports and communications on the "confidential investigation of alleged irregularities of W. H. McDonald, Land Commissioner, and other employees of the General Land Office" to Chief Gonzaullas, who on March 5 sent a detailed report to his superior, Col. H. H. Carmichael, director of the Texas Department of Public Safety. On March 7 Carmichael forwarded the report to the Honorable James V. Allred, governor of Texas.[23]

In the meantime the political charges between Governor Allred and Commissioner McDonald had escalated, with the governor seeking to cancel several leases accepted for high-royalty instead of high-cash bids and McDonald insisting that high-royalty leases would generate an additional $100 million dollars for the permanent school fund. The governor's effort to widen a lawsuit against the Land Office created a rift with the attorney general, who said, "We are not going to risk the State's interest with an ill-advised and untimely suit."

Stout's claims in Senate committee hearings that McDonald's decisions benefited his friends were countered by McDonald's insistence that he always took the highest bid, which would be a high-royalty bid only if seismograph pictures showed oil would be found. Charges and countercharges led to friction between senate committee members as they switched back and forth between investigating the land commissioner and looking into the attorney general's bank accounts as the attorney general prepared to run for governor. On March 4, having been accused of degenerating into a political body, the senate committee abruptly ended its inquiry, leaving Norman Dixon free to focus on one of the biggest oil-field theft rings in history.[24]

Chapter Three

BITS AND BULLETS

An oil scout named Paul Davis witnessed the result of the oil well drilled by Columbus Marion "Dad" Joiner in Rusk County in 1930: "Here comes the oil, over the derrick, and all the pine trees downwind from us for several hundred yards were just soaked with oil." The great East Texas oil boom was under way. The Great Depression also was under way, and the oil fields offered jobs "to prepare drilling sites, to build rigs and tanks, to drill wells, and to lay pipes." Long hours were required, the work was dangerous, and the weather could turn nasty, but the only skills needed were physical strength and the ability to keep at it. The workers built wooden oil rigs with saws and hammers, dug ditches with pickaxes and shovels, and assembled drill pipes with tongs and ropes. It was a chance to get ahead, and they worked hard, building oil rigs so close together that there was barely any space between them. They packed into the nearby oil boomtowns after work to have a good time gambling, drinking, and visiting the red-light districts. They got into fights with one another in the saloons and in the streets, but the rowdiness was mostly tolerated because oil workers were good for business.[1]

Not good for business were oil-field thieves. Typically a thief took a job as a roustabout, or he drove around the field locating materials and equipment. In 1937 and 1938 hundreds of thousands of dollars in goods—tongs, drilling bits, mercury, and so on—were taken from poorly guarded oil fields at night, loaded into vehicles with extra-heavy-duty springs to handle the weight, and driven by thieves across county lines, across the state, and at times across state lines to a "fence." Often a thief and his fence worked close together, with the fence telling the thief which items he needed.[2]

Oil-field theft occupied much of Dixon's time throughout the eight and one-half months when he was stationed in Tyler. He left no record of his daily activity from September 15 through December 31, 1937, but on January 3, 1938, he was in Palestine, Texas, for a trial regarding the theft of equipment from the East Texas oil fields; on January 4 he was in Wright City, where he found stolen Hunt Oil Company equipment in the Talco oil lot; and on January 5 he spent the night on watch at a Sun Oil Company lease.

By May 31, 1938—Dixon's last day in Tyler—more than thirty East Texas oil-field thieves had been apprehended and had signed confessions, and better than $100,000 worth of stolen property had been recovered. One confession, nineteen pages in length, detailed thirty-six oil-field thefts. Criminal cases had been filed in Texas, New Mexico, Oklahoma, and Louisiana. Three fences had been arrested, and two convicted. The third was killed before his trial was held.[3]

One fence was particularly notorious. He had operated in several Texas oil fields through the years, costing the oil industry more than $5 million. In the *Theft Prevention Handbook*, which Dixon helped prepare for the oil industry, and in an unpublished article about the East Texas oil-field theft ring, he describes in detail the rise of this fence. First purchasing small amounts of stolen property, he began working with increasing numbers of thieves and eventually developed contacts who dealt with other thieves. By 1938 he owned a prosperous, though illicit, business protected by a shrewd and successful criminal lawyer whom he kept on retainer. He owned four automobiles, several large trucks, various bank accounts, a nice home, and a separate home for his paramour. His oil-field supply house—by all appearances a legitimate business—was on a highway near Gladewater, a few miles northeast of Tyler.

Oil-field thieves pulled their car off the road to the rear of the fence's building, where his young assistant opened the large back door. The thieves backed their car into the building and there unloaded their stolen goods. The fence, a rather large man, gave them a price and wrote a check. He might pay $200 for goods worth in excess of $2,000. The thieves left with their money, and the assistant quickly washed the tools with lye, removed serial numbers and other identifying marks using a power emery wheel, and applied a fresh coat of paint. Thus the goods were protected from the prying eyes of any officer looking for stolen property, and they were ready to sell at a large profit.[4]

Catching thieves and fences was difficult. Thieves became adept at stashing their goods safely in rural areas around oil fields and, once their vehicles were loaded, transporting the property far from the field where it was stolen. Missing equipment was seldom reported promptly and sometimes not at all. Many reports lacked adequate descriptions, stolen property was often poorly marked for identification, people in the oil industry seldom reported evidence of stolen goods being offered for sale, and few law-enforcement officers knew much about oil-field equipment.[5]

On February 7, 1938, following seventeen days in Austin on the Land Office investigation, Dixon and Crowder drove to Gladewater, where they arrested Walter "Curly" Radliff for possessing stolen oil-field property, took him to Longview, where they fingerprinted and photographed him, and then delivered him to the jail in Tyler. On February 8 they transported him to

Sulphur Springs, where, on February 17, Dixon testified at his trial. Seven witnesses testified on behalf of the prosecution, including those whose property was stolen, but thirteen witnesses testified in support of Radliff, and the jury acquitted him. Lester "Dutch" Orr, who was charged with Radliff for the same burglary, pleaded guilty and was sentenced to two years in prison. Radliff and Orr may have been the fence and his assistant that Dixon wrote about in the *Theft Prevention Handbook*.[6]

On March 10 Crowder and Dixon raided "Dad" Trower's house in Tyler, seizing roller bits stolen from Hughes Tool Company and Reed Bit Company. Alerted on March 17 that Trower would be coming into Tyler from Wichita, Dixon staked out the incoming highway and Crowder checked a tourist camp, where he found Trower and arrested him at 12:30 a.m. The criminal investigators interrogated him in the Smith County Jail, in Tyler, and then moved him to the jail in Henderson.

Three days later, investigating an oil theft, the criminal investigators interrogated Payne Snow in the Smith County Jail, and then they transported him to Henderson, where they talked to both Snow and Trower. That afternoon they took an "old negroe" to the state asylum in Rusk, where they stayed longer than expected, breaking up a planned jailbreak. They spent the next day investigating oil thefts allegedly committed by Payne Snow and his brother, Dewey, and by the end of the day they had fingerprinted and mugged the brothers at police headquarters. On March 17 Dixon interrogated V. C. "Cotton" Wofford, an oil thief from Oklahoma, and on March 29, he took Wofford's signed confession of oil thefts in Fannin County.[7]

Leona Dixon spent the morning of March 29 packing, and that afternoon a "highway boy" helped move her and Norman's belongings to a duplex at 633 S. Augusta in Tyler. The "boy" was probably the same patrolman Norman had brought home to supper a week earlier "without notice," as Leona lamented in her diary. After supper the three went to the movies. On April 3, when Norman was out of town, the Dixons' new landlady told Leona that the woman across the street was threatening to shoot Honeyboy if she found him on her lawn. Leona also had problems with the landlady's plumber, who had done unsatisfactory work and kept promising to come back to fix it. When Norman finally returned after several days, she wrote in her diary, "Norman home about five, thank goodness, & all my troubles ceased." He talked to the neighbor, resolving the issue with Honeyboy, and to the plumber, who finally came and fixed the problem.[8]

During the first part of April, Dixon was gone from Leona chasing down oil-field thieves. On April 1 he was in Longview with Tom Mobley, an investigator for Hughes Tool Company, who, working undercover, arranged to purchase a stolen pump and generator from oil-field thieves. As planned, Dixon intercepted the thieves on the highway and arrested them. A few days later, Dixon and Mobley were in Weatherford, where they worked with

Law officers being honored for breaking up the largest oil-field theft ring in Texas history. Norman Dixon is at the far left. *Author's Collection.*

local officers and received a search warrant for Lee Burns's home. In the early afternoon they raided the house for stolen oil-field tools and captured Burns. They also laid a trap to snare oil-field thief Jess Shipley, and the next morning he was arrested near Weatherford. Dixon took a statement from Burns and deposited Shipley in jail in Dallas, where he interrogated him.

On April 11 Dixon received a $50 money order, which he passed on to "Dad" Trower, who now was cooperating with him. A day later he arrested oil thief Buster Nichols, jailing him in Jefferson, and oil thieves Blackie Young and Butch Jarrell, jailing them in Longview. On April 27 he raided George Pitcock's supply house in Longview, which would lead to eleven theft indictments against Pitcock and a fifty-five-year sentence in the penitentiary. He was home by 2:00 a.m. but up early to take the bus back to Longview, where he would stand proudly alongside several other officers in front of a stack of stolen oil-field tools and equipment as newspaper photographers took their picture and reporters wrote down the big news of the day: the break up of the

East Texas oil-field theft ring. The story that twenty-two organized oil-field thieves had been arrested and more than $50,000 in stolen goods recovered appeared on the front page of newspapers all over the state. Chief Deputy Sheriff Stanley Dean proclaimed it the largest gang of oil-field thieves ever to operate in Texas, and he credited two oil company investigators, Ranger R. W. Holliday, and Department of Public Safety officers Bob Crowder and N. K. Dixon with breaking up the ring and making all the arrests. He added that they were still on the case.[9]

Indeed they were. On Saturday, April 30, Dixon, Tom Mobley, and "Dad" Trower met at Dixon's home until midnight, discussing how to recover stolen bits Dixon had traced to L. E. "Red" Merritt's oil rig a few days earlier. On Sunday Trower made initial contact with Merritt to express interest in purchasing rock bits. The plot had begun. On Tuesday, Dixon secreted himself in Longview, where he watched as Trower met with Merritt, rode off with him to pick up the bits, and returned a half hour later. Dixon and two other officers followed them into a wooded area in Gregg County, where they confronted Merritt and confiscated the stolen rock bits. Merritt was indicted, but in late August, prior to the trial, while he was boating on Caddo Lake near Marshall, he was shot in the back by a .22-caliber rifle fired from another boat. He died the next day. Two Marshall men were charged with his murder. Merritt was the one fence in the East Texas oil-field theft ring who evaded prison, but he did it the hard way.[10]

"Dad" Trower's work of contrition was not finished. A few days after Merritt had fallen into their trap, Dixon received another $50 money order for Trower. The new target: a West Texas oil-field theft ring. After eating lunch at home with Leona, Norman left with Trower for West Texas via Austin, where he conferred with Chief Gonzaullas on the assignment. During the meeting, Gonzaullas offered Dixon a position in the crime lab in Austin, effective June 1. It was an opportunity to work directly with the famed Ranger. Dixon had an easy and quick answer to the offer, and he immediately prepared a letter to the chief referring to their conversation, stating that unless told otherwise, he would report to him in Austin around June 1 to begin work in the "Scientific Crime Detection Laboratory."[11]

From Austin, Dixon and Trower traveled to Kermit, forty miles west of Odessa, where Dixon, using the name "Dick Edwards" and representing himself as a hot-bond salesman, arranged to buy stolen drilling bits from a Charlie Harris. The next morning Dixon and Trower met with Harris and followed him to his stashes, where they paid $180 for ten bits that had been stolen new.[12]

Four days later they were in Midland to make another purchase from Harris. Still using their assumed identities, Dixon and Trower conducted the transaction with Harris, who had ridden to the scene with an associate named Dowdy. When Bob Crowder and other officers suddenly appeared to make arrests, Harris sped off in Dowdy's car with Dixon, who had jumped into the car with him. While Crowder and the other officers took Dowdy to jail, Dixon took Harris to a hotel, where he registered him under the name "George Kelley" and said he would register as "George Wilson" at a different hotel to make it harder for the authorities to find them. Convincing Harris not to leave his room, Dixon left and called Crowder, who, with other officers, soon arrived and arrested Harris.[13]

Later that day, as Dixon drove a borrowed pickup south of Midland looking for stashes of stolen oil-field tools, Crowder and Mobley were driving to Kermit with Dowdy. Along the way the prisoner spotted an oil-field thief known as "Rabbit" Bell. Crowder stopped the car, found a stolen bit in Bell's possession, and arrested him. When Dixon and Crowder subsequently interrogated Dowdy and Bell, both agreed to make statements. The West Texas oil-field theft ring had been broken.[14]

The next week Dixon worked with the sheriff on terms of the settlement with "Dad" Trower and wrote his final reports, closing out thirty-eight cases in Tyler. On Monday, May 23, he took a bus to Weatherford, testified to a grand jury on charges against Jess Shipley, and then went to Dallas for a meeting at Ranger headquarters. After supper with Leona and friends, he rode a train to Ft. Worth, where he booked a Pullman car on the Missouri Pacific and rode to Austin, arriving at 5:47 a.m. the following day. At Camp Mabry he submitted his reports to Chief Gonzaullas and discussed his new assignment in the crime lab. That afternoon he searched for a place to live, renting a duplex at 3410 Bailey Lane for $29.50 a month. (As he would do frequently to meet immediate needs, he borrowed money against his next paycheck.) On Thursday at 12:50 a.m. he boarded the Missouri Pacific for Dallas, arriving at 7:47 a.m. With Leona, who had been caring for a sick friend in Dallas, Norman returned on the Sunshine Bus to Tyler, where "Dad" Trower paid them a visit. On the following day he and Crowder drove to Longview, where they received reward money for their role in breaking up the East Texas oil-theft ring. On May 18, after picking up Honeyboy from the animal clinic, where he had been all week, Norman and Leona had the Crowders over for supper.[15]

On Sunday, May 29, Dixon and Crowder conducted their last raid together. In the garage at the home of W. E. Stewart, president of Stewart Oil Company, in Tyler, they found $585 worth of stolen bits from Hughes Tool Company. Several months later, when Crowder testified before the Smith County grand jury, the jury foreman said he had known Stewart all his life and did not believe the allegations. The jury no billed Stewart, ruling the evidence insufficient to warrant prosecution. Some time later, when Crowder ran into Stewart in Wichita Falls, the oil man ridiculed him, mimicking his testimony before the grand jury.[16]

On Monday the moving company loaded the dishes and furniture from the Dixon duplex in Tyler. On Tuesday, Joe Thompson of the Bureau of Intelligence arrived to load his car and take the Dixons to Austin. Before leaving, however, they drove to the Crowders' home to say good-bye. According to Leona, the trip to Austin was smooth, Honeyboy was good, and their new duplex on Bailey Lane in the capital city was cute. Norman reported to Camp Mabry in the late afternoon. On the same day he had the water and lights connected, and on the next day, while Leona arranged for milk and ice to be delivered, he had the phone and gas turned on.[17]

More than a year earlier, when he was working for Associated Detective Service, Dixon had indicated, both in letters to DPS officials and in an interview with Chief Gonzaullas, his interest in crime detection. To show he was serious, he explained in one letter that he had extended his studies into a wide variety of identification systems. This was no exaggeration. He was intellectually curious throughout his life. Walking the pastures of his father-in-law's farm, he would ask Christian Spellman the names of plants, trees, and grasses on his land, and he was astonished when, as often happened, Spellman did not know. Every few years Dixon would purchase an encyclopedia set and follow up with their annual yearbooks so he could satisfy his curiosity on any question that arose while he was reading newspapers, magazines, or books, listening to a radio, watching television, or talking with friends and relatives. He regularly subscribed to daily morning *and* afternoon newspapers and multiple magazines, and he purchased *three* sets of Great Books. They were not for decoration; he read them. So it was with his new job as "laboratory technician." He did not consider it a come-down from his work as criminal investigator. He threw himself into learning everything about it. His first few days were a period of orientation: meeting with various staff members, such as chief chemist and toxicologist J. H. Arnette (with whom he would work closely on several assignments), and spending hours with Chief Gonzaullas, learning from the master.[18]

Under Gonzaullas, the Bureau of Intelligence Scientific Crime Detection Laboratory was responsible for gathering and analyzing information on criminal activity in Texas. Gonzaullas was ideally suited to be the first chief, owing not only to his record as a Texas Ranger but also to extensive training he had received as an investigator for the U.S. Department of the Treasury during and after World War I. As much as anyone, Gonzaullas brought Texas to the forefront nationally in crime control and prevention. In the bureau's first annual report, dated September 1, 1936, Gonzaullas wrote that he had a staff of ten men and one woman (his secretary), and five on temporary assignment. He discussed the success of the crime lab exhibit at the Texas Centennial Exposition (which Dixon had visited between his performances as a clown diver). He focused on identification of and forensic ballistics on firearms, bullets, cartridges, and cartridge cases. For identification purposes, the lab had more than a hundred types of firearms, fifteen hundred kinds of cartridge (each of which the staff had dismantled and referenced), and 920 types of tire-tread impression. He explained how the lab detected bloodstains, inks, erasure marks, and the like and listed thirty-one items subject to scientific examination, including blood, hair, tissue, bone, poison, fabrics, dirt, fuel, and chemicals.[19]

In his first full week on the job, Dixon worked with colleague Joe Thompson on several bullet cases. On Tuesday, June 14, he conducted research on fabrics and worked on a bullet case. That evening, Gonzaullas and his wife, Laura, drove to the Dixons' duplex, picked them up, and took them to their house, where Norman worked with the chief on a speech Gonzaullas was scheduled to give in El Paso. Dixon wrote the speech on Wednesday at Camp Mabry, rewrote it at home that evening, and on Thursday put it into final form. On Saturday, traveling with Colonel Carmichael, Gonzaullas left for El Paso carrying the speech with him. The new man had become the chief's speechwriter.[20]

In his speech, Gonzaullas said that the crime laboratory had conducted 4,036 examinations of evidence in felony criminal cases, that laboratory staff had testified as expert witnesses 176 times in courts, and that in every one of these 176 cases the accused were convicted. The sentences included a total of 3,750 years in prison and 14 death penalties, and none of the cases had at that time been reversed on appeal. Equally important, laboratory results often "absolved innocent parties."[21]

On Wednesday, June 22—the chief's last day in El Paso—two sporting events made it into Leona's diary: Joe Louis knocked out Max Schmeling in the first round, and she watched Norman play baseball. After working Saturday morning, Norman took Leona downtown to visit Dr. H. L. Klotz, her new doctor, to watch Mickey Rooney in *Judge Hardin's Family,* and to shop at a dime store, where they ran into the Arnettes, who gave the Dixons a ride home. A few days later, on the way to Camp Mabry, Dixon dropped in on Governor Allred, who gave him an autographed photograph and, much to Dixon's pleasure, "was very friendly & remembered me—calling me 'Dick.'"[22]

Nora and Christian Spellman arrived for a visit on July 15. At 1:00 p.m. Norman came home with Arnette to take everyone to the Paramount Theater downtown to watch a preview of a Popular Science film on the Texas Rangers, which included a segment on the crime lab. In her diary, Leona wrote, "We only saw side of Norman's face once." That night they left Honeyboy with the vet and rode with Leona's parents to the farm near Smiley to spend a two-week vacation. One day later Leona wrote that Norman was looking better already; a week later she noted that he was "looking grand."

Norman thoroughly enjoyed the vacation, but his mind was never far from his job. When he returned to the lab, he brought fibers from a cotton boll and corn silk, and hairs from "pigs, sows, horses, cows, calf, mules, cat, dog, jackrabbit, cottontail." Back on the job, he spent the first week of August building a card file of 350 firearms and bullet markings with the help of Edward Kelley, a criminologist and firearms-identification expert from the St. Louis Police Department and a week long guest of Chief Gonzaullas. On the afternoon of August 5, Dixon traveled with Arnette to a funeral home to make diphenylamine tests for gunpowder residue on the hands of Benjamin Joe Crane, an eighteen-year-old boy who died of a gunshot wound, an apparent suicide, near Jollyville. They found gunpowder around the wound and on both hands, but mostly on the left hand, concluding that the youth cocked the .45 automatic by holding it in his right hand, pointing it toward himself, grasping the front of the slide with his left hand, and then pushing it back.[23]

Ten days later, at about 6:15 a.m., a twenty-seven-year-old service-station operator named Adolph Laake was awakened by a knock on the door. He and his wife of four months lived in the rear of the station two miles west of Paige and about forty miles east of Austin. As he answered the door, his wife went back to sleep—only to be awakened by a shot. She screamed and leaped out of bed in time to see a car speed off and to find her husband dead. It was an apparent robbery attempt, but when she screamed the killers left without taking any money. At 10:00 a. m. Norman Dixon left Austin driving a state vehicle. Chief Gonzaullas and criminal investigator Wick Fowler were riding with him. In the car were a plaster kit, a fingerprint kit, and Fowler's photographic equipment. At the funeral home in Giddings, Dixon noted "the entrance wound just below left molar, appearing downward ½"x ⅝." A Giddings physician X-rayed the wound and removed the bullet about one inch below the "occipital bone, center cervical, anterior to spine." It was a .32-caliber bullet. At the service station, an *Austin Statesman* photographer followed Dixon and Gonzaullas around the murder site, and the next morning the story of the murder, including a photograph of the two men searching for clues in front of Adolph's Place, dominated the newspaper's front page.

Two armed ex-convicts from Georgia caught in a stolen car in Dallas became the primary suspects. One was identified by a Paige witness who, a few minutes before the murder, had talked to two men looking for gas and sent them to Adolph's Place. During the rest of the week, Chief Gonzaullas and Dixon worked with the murder bullet and the bullets and firearms found in the possession of the suspects, and by midweek the evidence appeared conclusive that a test bullet fired from one of the suspect's weapons matched the bullet taken from Laake's body. Norman called Leona to tell her "he had definitely found bullets to be fired from suspect's gun," and Chief Gonzaullas gave the same information to the Bastrop County sheriff, who had the two suspects brought from Dallas for questioning and then filed murder charges against them. But by the end of the week—on the day when the chief drove Dixon home by way of the house he was building (two days later Dixon drew up plans for his own house)—Dixon said that although the lab evidence was strong, there was room for doubt, and a few days later the suspects' alibis appeared solid. The next month, a Bastrop County grand jury no billed the suspects.[24]

During the first two weeks of September 1938 Dixon worked on several bullet cases, including bullets that killed a night watchman in Houston, a cow in Wharton, and Red Merritt in his boat—the last brought by Louis Grigsby, an associate in breaking up the East Texas oil-field theft ring. On Sunday, September 11, the chief told Dixon he had asked two men who worked for the state highway department to meet him at the lab. They had dived into Onion Creek ten miles southeast of Austin to retrieve a gunnysack after seeing two men toss it into the creek from a car. The sack was filled with bones, and they were concerned that the bones might be human. Arnette analyzed the traces of blood, and Dixon put hair fibers under a microscope. Their finding: three kittens or puppies.[25]

With Leona nine months pregnant, Norman was bringing home a state vehicle each night. She weighed 129½ pounds on August 27, suffered gas pains and cramps four days later, received an enema on September 1, suspected labor pains two days later, and took another enema on September 6. On Labor Day, Camp Mabry's cafeteria being closed, she still had the strength to prepare a lunch for Norman, Chief Gonzaullas, and Joe Thompson. On September 10 she weighed 134½ pounds. At the beginning of her pregnancy, she had weighed 100 pounds. After supper on September 13, she began feeling cramps, and at 10:35 she called Dr. Klotz. At 11:00 Norman drove her to the hospital and called Nora, in Leona's words, "to let her know the party started." The next morning, September 14, 1938, Norman sent his brother, Ronald, a wire: "Eight one-half pound boy this morning. Everything fine = Norman." On Sunday, September 18, he wrote to Ronald and Isabel in more detail: "What with my job tied down with an unidentified skeleton mixed with shot and shotgun wad brought to me, washing and ironing gowns, and buying more diapers etc., I am busy—and due back at the hospital in short order. . . . Frederick Kemp Dixon is the newcomer. . . . Leona had no difficulty. . . . She labored nine hours. . . . She is doing splendidly, the baby nursing like a pig, sleeping all the time it isn't nursing or howling for it. . . . She is happy and proud—me, well I'm getting headaches from wearing too small hats, and popping all the buttons off my shirts."[26]

Leona spent nine days in the hospital—not unusual at the time. During her stay, Nora and Leona's sisters, Tommie, Gladys, and Elna, visited. They were undecided on what to call the baby but were not happy with "Frederick." The Arnettes visited, as did Laura Gonzaullas, bearing a gift. Before Leona left the hospital, at 3:30 p.m. on September 23, Dr. Klotz instructed her on care of the baby, and the nurses gave her some notes on baby care. Three hours later, Leona had a visit from Dr. Klotz, who dropped by to see how the first baby he had delivered was doing at home. The little one was doing fine, with Nora staying for several days to help with her wealth of experience. A few days later Leona wrote in her diary, "He loves his bath, never cries, thank goodness."

The first morning after Leona was brought home from the hospital, Norman carried her to the breakfast table and to the bathroom, brought Honeyboy home from the vet, and—despite a special assignment involving a suspicion that Governor Allred's phones had been tapped—returned home for lunch and for supper. At 4:30 p.m., DPS Director Carmichael, only fifty-three years old, suffered a heart attack while driving down Austin's Barton Springs Road. When his car crashed into a post at a service station, the attendants rushed to the car and found him dead. Two days later, Rangers and highway patrolmen from all over Texas came to Austin for the funeral. Afterward Dixon brought Crowder home for supper, then went to a hotel to visit with others before their trains departed.[27]

Thirty-seven-year-old Homer Garrison Jr., assistant director since the formation of the department, was quickly named as Carmichael's replacement. A native of Lufkin, Texas, Garrison had become a deputy sheriff when he was only nineteen years old. Prior to becoming assistant director, he had risen through the ranks of the highway patrol. He would serve as director for the next thirty years, and in the words of historian Robert M. Utley, "Colonel Homer Garrison has no peer." According to Utley, Garrison had an imposing physique and an engaging personality. "Soft-spoken, smiling, quietly gracious, unpretentious, authoritative but not authoritarian, his easy manner put people quickly at ease." During his tenure, he upgraded the crime lab, increased the size of the Ranger force, and put Rangers and patrolmen in high-powered automobiles with modern radio equipment. Nationally and even internationally his reputation grew through the years. Rangers lionized Garrison, none more so than Norman Dixon, who would work directly for the colonel beginning in 1948.[28]

The shot-up skeleton Dixon referenced in his September 18 letter to Ronald had been brought in by Ranger Stuart Stanley from Red River County. Dixon determined that the victim, whom he named "Oscar," was a 5'6" male Caucasian of slight build, perhaps 130 pounds, who had been shot in the back of the head by a 12-gauge shotgun. He decided to try to restore Oscar's face and spent considerable time on it while, at the same time, conducting tests on the hair and on clothing fibers and stains. He almost lived with the skeleton for nearly three months, working on it at every opportunity. Finally, on November 7, he shipped Oscar back to Red River County.[29]

All Dixon's experimental work on Oscar may have paid off, at least for one young college student. Michael Charney, an anthropology student at the University of Texas at Austin, walked into the crime lab one day to ask for help on determining the blood type of five-thousand-year-old bones. He was so fascinated with the lab that he stayed for a year without pay (though occasionally he was given a free meal at the cafeteria) to help solve forty murder cases. As he explained to a newspaper reporter in 1984, he was at the lab one day when a skeleton was brought in, and he watched with fascination as Norman Dixon used clay to reconstruct the face, restoring its features. As a result, Charney began studying facial-reconstruction methods, and in time he became a nationally recognized forensic anthropologist and leading expert in facial reconstruction, specializing in helping police identify crime and disaster victims. Someone forwarded the article to Dixon, who then wrote to Charney. In his response, Charney wrote, "I well remember that skeleton that came in from the west Texas desert, the crease on the right frontal bone, a deep, healed gash that meant you had to put a 'scar' on the clay." Responding to Dixon's expression of surprise that Charney remembered his name after so many years, Charney wrote, "I have known hundreds and hundreds of officers but one never forgets the professionals like you."[30]

On October 30 Leona noted in her diary that while Orson Welles's realistic radio production of *War of the Worlds* was panicking its listeners, who thought the world was being invaded by hostile aliens, the Dixons were calmly enjoying the "Edgar Bergen and Charlie McCarthy show." November 3, however, was not a good day for Leona. It was rainy, Honeyboy came into the house with "40,000,000" fleas and ticks, and the coffee man, whom Leona detested, came by and sold her two pounds of coffee. "When we move, I hope to get rid of him," she wrote in her diary. Her wish was fulfilled. Within three weeks the Dixons moved from their small duplex on Bailey Lane to a five-room house with two backyards at 3709 Cedar St.[31]

Between the *War of the Worlds* panic and Honeyboy's acquisition of forty million fleas and ticks, a doctor was found shot dead, sitting upright in the driver's seat in his automobile three miles from San Antonio on the highway to Kerrville. David H. Carson, a physician at the veterans' hospital in Kerrville, had been shot above the right eye. He appeared to have powder burns on his right hand, his hat was crushed between the steering wheel and his body, and a .32-caliber pistol was at his feet. A few hours before his body was found, Carson had borrowed $100 from a Kerrville bank and was seen leaving the bank in his automobile with Olen C. Ireland, an ex-convict and patient at the hospital, identified by witnesses as wearing a patch over one eye.[32]

Chief Gonzaullas ordered Arnette and Dixon to San Antonio to perform a paraffin test on Carson's hands. At the funeral home, they were joined by Rangers Johnny Klevenhagen and Lee Miller and Kerrville's chief of police. The test showed traces of nitrate, which could have come from the powder in a bullet. When the county physician removed the brain and recovered the .32 caliber bullet, Dixon noted that the bullet was badly distorted with its head flattened. After removing the stomach, the doctor found that it contained a quantity of alcohol.

The next day the *San Antonio Light* displayed, beside its headline story about Dr. Carson's death, a large photograph of Dixon working on the paraffin test. The article correctly stated that the test revealed nitrates on both hands, but what bothered Arnette and led him to call Dixon that evening was a United Press article in the *Austin Statesman* falsely stating that Arnette had told Ranger Captain Lee Miller that the paraffin test "proved conclusively" that Dr. Carson had fired the gun. That same evening Olen C. Ireland was found hanging in a hotel in San Antonio, his wrists and forehead slashed. Near him was a note: "I can't get on like this. No money, love to all. Olen." His death was ruled a suicide. In late December, Justice of the Peace Raymond Gerhardt issued an inquest verdict on whether Dr. Carson's death was a murder or a suicide: "This fact is unknown."[33]

In December, with baseball season long over, Dixon took up playing basketball. Bob and Lucille Crowder spent a few days in Austin, staying with the Dixons in their five-room house. J. H. Arnette ate supper at their home on December 19 while his wife was in the hospital with their newborn son, Jay. On Christmas night, Dixon left on the Missouri Pacific for Texarkana to meet his father (whose second wife, Agnes, had died) and his girlfriend, Ethel, who had taken the train from the East. The three rode a train to Austin, arriving at 3:00 a.m. on December 27. Leona's reaction to her father-in-law's girlfriend: "Surprised Ethel not attractive. Nice figure, tho, & pleasant." Ethel stayed one week, Frederick two weeks.

Four months earlier, Frederick had once again saved lives. Living in Syracuse, New York, as an investment specialist and counselor, he was on Oneida Lake in his forty-six-foot cabin cruiser when from its bridge he saw two men clinging to an overturned sailboat and waving for help. When he reached them, they were almost totally exhausted, but they insisted that he save their dog first, which he did. As reported on the front page of the *Syracuse Post-Standard*, the two men were so tired from floundering in the lake that Dixon had great difficulty lifting them from the water onto the deck of his cruiser. But the "yachtsman" succeeded, just as he had in the past, in saving the lives of those in peril.[34]

For Dixon his father's visit was a pleasant end to 1938 and a nice beginning for 1939, a year in which he would see less work as a lab technician and more as a criminal investigator. Instead of analyzing bullets, blood, and skeletons, he would be investigating white slavery, gambling, prisoner abuse, hijackings, bank robberies, murders, swindles, narcotics, bigamy, burglaries, and forgeries—not to mention writing speeches for the chief and tracking down a hound thief.

SLOTS AND GOATS

FREDERICK DIXON LEFT FOR THE EAST ON JANUARY 4, 1939. NORMAN had devoted much of their time together to showing his father the sights—Camp Mabry, Marshall Ford Dam, Lake Buchanan, and San Antonio. But upon returning to work after having seen his father off on the train, Norman soon found that his evenings had not been freed up. Honeyboy had become a homebody, staying in the backyard at the Dixons' newly rented house and insisting that Norman play with him when he came home. Leona noted, "I don't have a chance." Norman also continued to play basketball one or two evenings a week. After he returned from basketball one night, Leona wrote, "Stiff, sore, & skinned, but victorious. Says he's getting good. Ha!" A few days later, a new governor, W. Lee O'Daniel, was inaugurated, and instead of playing basketball in the evening, Norman walked the packed streets of Austin to help keep the peace. It had been a wild day, with thousands, including Norman, attending O'Daniel's inauguration at the University of Texas football stadium. Leona had gone downtown to see Dr. Klotz and stayed for the governor's parade. Her observation: "Some mob!"[1]

On Friday, May 13, Norman returned home for a brief weekend respite in the midst of a Galveston murder investigation. To Leona, Norman was "looking tired and sleepy" when he arrived around 8:00 p.m., but their friends, Mary and Forest Wray, came by to visit, and resting had to wait. Two days later Leona lamented, "Now he's gone again for goodness knows how long." When Norman returned at the end of his investigation a week later, he again faced the presence of Forest and Mary Wray, leaving Norman, in Leona's word, "irritated." The next night the Wrays visited again, to play cards. Leona wrote: "Norman still irritated at outside interference. Tired of the 'social whirl.'" Part of his frustration may have arisen from his failure, after such an exhaustive investigation, to solve the Galveston murder. But there was a bank robber to go after, and perhaps this chase would meet with more success.[2]

Several weeks earlier, at noon on April 18, a small, black-haired man about twenty-five years old and wearing a light-colored shirt but *not* a hat (men routinely wore hats in those days), walked into the Thorndale State Bank and said to Alvin Heintze, the bookkeeper, who was alone: "This is a matter of life and death. I need money quick." He pistol-whipped Heintze and helped himself to more than a thousand dollars in cash—although he overlooked four hundred dollars in bills lying nearby. He put Heintze in the bank vault, though he left it unlocked, and escaped in a black 1935 or 1936 Ford sedan, heading west on the road to Thrall and Taylor. Within minutes, Dixon was on the road with Ranger Captain R. W. Aldrich looking for the culprit. The next day authorities learned that the getaway car had been stolen in Houston on April 17. Earl Wilson had stopped to buy cigarettes when a man shot at his car, jumped into it, and forced him to drive out of town, where he had Wilson stop and ordered him out of the car. Asked if he had any money, Wilson said he had two or three dollars. The robber said, "Aw, keep it," and drove off.[3]

That evening, armed with a license-plate number possibly tied to the suspect, Dixon rode with Dub Naylor to search the area. Over the next week, Dixon checked out and exhausted all his leads, including a suspect who fit the bank robber's description and had treated several cab drivers to a restaurant dinner, peeling $20 bills off a thick roll of money. A month later, Dixon and Naylor had another suspect, Harold Oldham. They interrogated from ten in the morning until three in the afternoon, but he would not confess. The next day they drove him to Houston and Earl Wilson, but Wilson shook his head. Oldham was not the car thief, and therefore not the bank robber. That evening Dixon and Naylor enjoyed a barbecue dinner in Houston.[4]

During the next ten days, Dixon investigated a series of cases involving swindlers, hijackers, and narcotics dealers. On June 12, at Colonel Garrison's request, he cleaned a new lever-action Model 94 Winchester .30 and checked its sighting for Speaker of the House R. Emmett Morse. On that same day, a young man drove a coupe into a Hallettsville service station, eighty miles southeast of Austin, and asked for directions. Also at the service station was Ben Appelt, a barber, who watched as the young man left the station and circled his car slowly around the People's State Bank. Thinking it a bit odd, he wrote down the car's license-plate number on the service station's telephone directory.

Two days later at 10:30 a.m. a jittery young man entered the bank, pointed a shaking pistol at the cashier, and demanded the contents of his cash drawer. Within minutes after he stuffed $895 into his pockets and fled in a coupe, everyone in Hallettsville, including the barber, knew the bank had been robbed. Appelt rushed to the service station and delivered the telephone directory to officers, who sent out an alarm that included the license-plate number. Deputy Sheriff Buck Flournoy received the alarm in Wharton, sixty miles southeast, and upon checking the license number, discovered that he knew the suspect—Ralph Gresham. Thinking Gresham might stop in Wharton, where he had relatives, Flournoy waited for him on the main street.

State vehicle wrecked by Norman Dixon en route to Hallettsville to take Ralph Gresham's confession. *Author's Collection.*

He later told a reporter, "I watched him park the car, then nabbed him." Flournoy took Gresham to Hallettsville, where Dixon, who was interviewing witnesses, took his statement.[5]

The next day Dixon and J. O. McGuire of the Bureau of Intelligence returned to Hallettsville with fingerprint evidence that Gresham had committed the Hallettsville *and* Thorndale bank robberies. Six miles out of Austin, Dixon accidentally crashed his state car into a bridge. When another car was provided them, they drove on to Hallettsville, where, with Tom Sisk of the Federal Bureau of Investigation, they took Ralph Gresham's full confession. Gresham told them that prior to the Thorndale bank robbery, he had held up a motorist (Wilson) in Houston and driven his car to Conroe, where he robbed a service station of $6.50. That $6.50 would prove costly to Gresham. On September 4, after Dixon and the service-station operator testified as the only witnesses at the Conroe trial, Gresham pleaded guilty and received a five-year prison sentence.

In his confession to Dixon, Gresham explained how he eluded officers chasing him between Conroe and Huntsville. At Thorndale, he delayed robbing the bank until 12:20 p.m. because there were "too many people around." He spent part of the morning hanging around a barbershop. He held up the bank with a toy pistol, escaped through Taylor and Round Rock to Austin, left the car in front of a wholesale building, and took a train to Houston, using his family's railroad pass. On the train he counted his money. He had $1,351. He took a train from Houston to Wharton and hitchhiked to his home in nearby Boling. A week later, he threw his pistol into the Colorado River and left for Los Angeles, where he spent $500 in four days. On his return, a girl in Tucson took $150 from him. In Albuquerque he bought a pistol. Then, having lost around $600 gambling in Houston and Galveston and having spent $75 on clothes and jewelry in Wharton and Houston, he was down to $1.50. That was when he decided to rob the Hallettsville bank.[6]

Dixon had his confession, the Hallettsville bank's money was recovered, and Gresham was charged with both bank robberies. While in Houston on June 19 to remove the bullet Gresham had shot into the car he had stolen from Earl Wilson, Dixon paid his respects to the former governor, "Jimmy" Allred, who was serving as federal judge in the Southern District of Texas. Although Dixon would work directly with several governors, none would impress him more than the genial Allred.[7]

Dixon returned to Austin later that day, bringing Ranger E. M. "Pappy" Davenport with him to spend the night at his home. Leona fixed them breakfast the next morning, and that evening the Wrays were over for a hash supper. Leona does not indicate if Norman was irritated yet again at "the social whirl," but at 10:50 p.m. he left with a Dictaphone for Tyler on a Pullman sleeping car on the Missouri Pacific. At 6:50 a.m. he arrived at Troup, eighteen miles south of Tyler, where he was met by Patrolman Joe Hubbard, who drove him into Tyler. At the Tyler jail he set up the Dictaphone in the reception room, wiring it to the office lavatory. In the 1930s these devices recorded sound using a wax cylinder, and Dixon may have had an electric microphone to capture the sound.

Will A. Hergesheimer was brought in for questioning. A former worker for the depression-era federal Works Progress Administration, Hergesheimer had confessed, but then denied, that he had murdered his fourteen-year-old stepson, Leroy Higgins, for $1,000 in insurance money by putting strychnine in a jar of jam. The boy had eaten a jam sandwich and died. Upon analyzing his internal organs, the state crime lab had found a quantity of poison. After questioning Hergesheimer for more than half an hour, Dixon brought in the suspect's wife, Leroy's mother, ostensibly to question the two together. Ten minutes later, Dixon and the other officers left the two alone for a half hour with the hidden Dictaphone recording their conversation. The Dictaphone recording revealed nothing, but Hergesheimer was indicted and put on trial in December. The prosecutors presented testimony by a physician that Leroy Higgins had died from poison in a jam sandwich, a conclusion supported by chemists in the state crime lab. After deliberating for four hours, the jury found Hergesheimer guilty and sentenced him to thirty years in prison.[8]

While Norman was in Tyler, Ranger B. F. Spain called Leona to tell her that he had seen Tommie in San Marcos. He also "spilled beans" that Norman had wrecked the state vehicle on the way to Hallettsville. When Norman returned from Tyler the next day, she confronted him, and he "had to admit to accident, said he totally demolished 1938 Ford. Whew!" Over the next few weeks, Dixon looked for a missing son from Skiatook, Oklahoma, thought to be in Texas; delivered letters dismissing three guards at the governor's mansion; investigated accusations against two highway patrolmen; tended to a brush fire near Austin; worked on a bigamy case; and, among other things, investigated burglaries of Mutual Lumber Company and a service station in Jarrell, including processing fingerprints found on a fence post where the burglars had climbed over the fence, and making casts of footprints on the road. On his return to Austin from Jarrell, Dixon stopped and gave assistance at the scene of a car wreck. He would encounter many car wrecks throughout his career, always stopping to render aid and to assist officers.[9]

On Saturday night, July 22, Fred A. Pointer, a forty-six-year-old stock farmer and employee of the state highway department, was plowing by moonlight at his farm eighteen miles south of Carrizo Springs in southwest Texas, near the border with Mexico, when he was shot dead with two bullets in his back. On Sunday, Dixon, with Sheriff A. J. Knaggs and Ranger Alfred Allee, was at the crime scene taking statements from three prominent cattlemen who had argued with Pointer over a disputed cattle range: Roe McRorey, his adult son Elwin, and a relative, Worth McRorey. The officers photographed the suspects and performed paraffin tests on their hands, photographed the deceased and the crime scene, and searched for cartridge cases and other evidence. By the end of the day, twenty-seven-year-old Elwin McRorey was under arrest.[10]

On Monday District Attorney Philip Kazan joined Dixon and the other officers as they questioned nine individuals, visited the crime scene again—this time finding the cartridge cases—and searched the McRorey premises, including wading through a cow tank looking for the murder weapon. On Tuesday Dixon returned to Austin with evidence for the crime lab, where he conducted the tests with Arnette. That evening he returned to an angry Leona, who had expected him home Sunday. "I told him a thing or two," she wrote in her diary. "I think next time he'll [telephone] if delayed long." On Wednesday Norman Dixon returned to Carrizo Springs with A. L. Barr, who conducted a lie-detector test on Elwin McRorey. On Thursday, Roe and Worth McRorey underwent lie-detector tests, and as a result, sixty-one-year-old Roe McRorey was arrested for murder. Dixon set up the Dictaphone and operated it through the evening at the jail, secretly recording conversations between Roe and Elwin. On Friday Elwin was released.[11]

Barr returned to Austin on Saturday. Dixon remained in Carrizo Springs but, having learned his lesson, asked Joe Thompson to tell Leona he would not be back until Tuesday. "Blue," Leona wrote in her diary. In the meantime Dixon worked the brush country near the crime scene and searched a well looking for the murder weapon. He continued his investigation through Sunday, and at 10:45 a.m. on Monday, he testified at an examining trial. At Camp Mabry the next day he called Leona with exciting news. He had received a letter from Homer Garrison informing him that he was being promoted to senior criminal investigator with a twenty-five-dollar salary increase to $175 a month. "Was he tickled," Leona wrote. To celebrate, she baked a cake, fried chicken, and had the Wrays over for supper.[12]

On Sunday, February 11, 1940, Dixon rode to Carrizo Springs with Thompson and Arnette for the trial that was to begin on Monday. During the first two days, however, the special venire (jury pool) of one hundred men was exhausted with only six jurors selected. Another hundred were ordered to appear the next day. Once the jury was selected, the state presented the testimony of twenty witnesses before a packed courtroom. With emotions high and support divided between the dead Pointer and the accused McRorey, a strong Ranger force was present to ensure the peace. On Saturday, February 17, after deliberating only one hour, the jury returned a verdict of not guilty.[13]

By August 1939, after nearly two years in the Ranger force, Norman Dixon finally had a state car assigned to him. On August 23, however, he left his car at home and drove a state truck to Dallas, where he helped load it with fifty-three confiscated slot machines, the result of an antigambling crusade in the city. By late September most Dallas gambling establishments were back in business, but Sheriff Pleas Porter of Grayson County, north of Dallas, announced that he would continue his antigambling campaign, and on Tuesday, September 26, Dixon arrived in Sherman to help him. By the end of the day, Dixon had placed horse-race bets over the telephone and been invited to a poker game. On Wednesday, placing bets on horse races at the Leizure Lodge, five miles northwest of Sherman, he uncovered evidence connecting the bets to a location in Dallas that relayed horse-race results to the lodge. Driving to Dallas with a deputy sheriff, he turned over his evidence.

On Thursday Dixon arrived undercover at the Leizure Lodge at 2:15 p.m., and at 3:00, the sheriff and his deputies stormed into the lodge in a surprise raid. Six men, including the operator of the tavern and dance hall "bookie shop," were arrested on the basis of the four bets Dixon placed on horse races. Dixon, still undercover, was also "arrested." At the moment of the raid, the bookies were receiving racing returns from Dallas and posting them on racing forms next to the telephone. Even though Dixon had told the Dallas authorities about the Dallas operators, they were still in business.[14]

On October 2 Dixon was back in Sherman to testify before the grand jury against the proprietor of the Leizure Lodge, and he was not happy. The sheriff had outed him. His undercover role in placing the bets was on the front page of the Friday issue of the *Denison Herald.* Even so, two days later he was undercover at a café in Giddings. His gambling winnings: a free hamburger.

On November 10 he climbed aboard a Greyhound bus heading to El Paso, and he arrived the following day. That evening he played dice. He spent the next three days checking out suspected gambling sites. After a week he was back in Austin. He completed a report, accompanied by a chart of gambling spots he had uncovered in El Paso, and delivered it to Captain S. O. Hamm, DPS assistant director. On December 4 an Associated Press article gave an account of the raids: "Gamblers hit the ground running Monday as Texas rangers, their guns cocked for business, cleaned out gambling dens. Most of El Paso's faro dealers, croupiers, dicemen and card sharks ducked over to Juarez, Mexico, or headed out of town." According to the article: "The rangers sauntered into the town's most exclusive club first. Play was at its height. Men and women patrons were held two hours, then freed. Big shot operators were told gambling complaints would be filed. Roulette wheels, dice and blackjack tables, keno boards, croupiers' sticks, slot machines and marble tables and punch boards were seized."[15]

Antigambling campaigns were not always popular among city officials or even in police and sheriffs' departments, partly because community leaders were not interested in antagonizing powerful forces in town. Dixon wrote in his diary that he had "received word" that the city of Austin was "trying to get on coop. [cooperative] basis with us, aftermath of our raid in Austin and that [Detective Captain] Rex Fowler resents me." Dallas officials also seemed ambivalent about gambling raids, although on December 10 Dixon drove the state truck to Dallas again and loaded it with eighty-six pieces of confiscated gambling equipment, which he took to Camp Mabry and burned on December 12.[16]

Few Rangers were happy to be enforcing antigambling laws. They believed there were more serious infractions of the law than entertaining oneself by wagering on card or dice games, horse races, or slot machines. There were, for example, knobknockers to contend with. On December 22 Dixon investigated a safe burglary in Centerville, east of Houston, and on December 23 he did the same in Yorktown, in South Texas. On February 6, 1940, at the request of the mayor, he was in Cuero investigating a series of safe burglaries. Two days later he was back in Yorktown investigating a safe burglary at a lumber company. On March 2 he was in Llano, where safecrackers had removed a grocery store safe, blown it up, and taken nine cases of cigarettes (two cases of Chesterfields, four of Lucky Strike, three of Camels). He inspected the remains of the safe, the tool marks on the knob and the door, and a piece of the blasting cap. He also examined a footprint and tire tracks, identifying them as from a 6:00 x 16 Ford. Two days later he examined a safe burglary at the Alamo Theater in Bartlett and determined it to be an inside job. Three days after that he drove to Cameron, where someone had broken into the post office safe and stolen two mail pouches.

These knobknockers were safecrackers who typically used a sledgehammer to knock the knob (or dial) off a safe, breaking the locking mechanism. Knobknocking was a common and fairly quick method of safecracking. Others used crowbars, hammers, or chisels to peel a side of the safe open, but that was noisy and time-consuming. Another approach, used on the Llano grocery-store safe, was to blow it up with dynamite. This, however, was very noisy—and dangerous unless one knew how to use explosives.[17]

On several occasions during the winter of 1939–1940, Dixon escorted a state treasury messenger to the bank. He also investigated the character and reputation of drugstore operators seeking federal permits to carry and sell narcotics. He also chased down a hound thief and recovered the hound. At Colonel Garrison's request, he spent three days gambling undercover in San Angelo, and at the request of the Bell County sheriff he looked into concerns about marijuana use in Temple. By March 1940 Lone Wolf Gonzaullas had transferred to Dallas as captain of Company B. Ranger Royal G. Phillips became head of the Bureau of Intelligence, but Ranger Sgt. Ernest Best would issue most of Dixon's orders.[18]

On March 18 Dixon had an assignment requested by a state representative, Alfred Petsch of Kerrville, in the Texas hill country, who was a director of the Texas Sheep and Goat Raisers Association, to investigate a sheep-and-goat theft ring. Dixon drove to Kerrville, met with Petsch, the sheriff, and a prisoner, Chester Ellebracht, who had received a two-year prison sentence for embezzlement and claimed to be part of the theft ring.

Except for brief trips to Austin, Dixon staked out a wide area of the hill country. He conferred with county sheriffs and ranchers and with Representative Petsch, and he observed the primary suspects, roamed the country roads, visited ranches, and rounded up and examined sheep and goats. On April 17—one full month after starting the assignment—Dixon, along with Ranger Fred Olson and Inspector Dan Westbrook, examined four hundred goats on the Buie Ranch, held his last conference with Representative Petsch, in Fredericksburg, and returned to Austin. Later that same day, Representative Petsch wrote to Homer Garrison praising the work of "Rangers N. K. Dixon and Fred Olson" on behalf of "the sheriffs of this part of the country and a great many property owners of our parts." Dixon may have made no arrests during the month, but he gathered considerable information for law-enforcement officers in the region.[19]

On May 22 Dixon drove from Brownwood (where he had been assisting witnesses in a grand-jury gambling inquiry) to San Antonio, where he went undercover to gamble during the next two days at the Kit Kat Klub, a swank nightspot. He returned to the Kit Kat Klub at 11:00 p.m. on June 8. At about 11:10, he began playing craps, and at about 11:35 he stood up, announced that he was the law, and said no one should move. For the next five minutes he held the players and the operators at bay and kept the equipment from being hidden until Rangers Phares and Olson and city detectives entered the club. They arrested Everett G. Bass, the operator, and J. M. Taylor, the croupier, and they seized the equipment. Bass was charged with exhibiting and operating a gaming device, and Taylor with loitering around a gaming house.[20]

At the end of June, Dixon participated in raids all over Austin, seizing marble tables. About thirty-eight officers took part, each assigned to one establishment. At 9:00 a.m. on June 29 Dixon entered Mickey's Drive-In, and at 10:30 the illicit machines at that location were picked up by the state truck. Dixon followed the truck, loading his car with officers waiting at the next five stops, and taking them back to Camp Mabry. In late August he was in San Antonio raiding club after club with other Rangers and members of the San Antonio vice squad. A few days later, the San Antonio Committee on Law Enforcement commended the Rangers' raids, with a slap at their local officers, stating, "Until officers are steadily actuated by their oath of office to enforce the law without fear or favor, rangers are still necessary." That local officers were not "steadily actuated" was apparent when, during the same period as the San Antonio raids, Dixon raided a bookie shop in Seguin, brought charges against four players and two operators, and confiscated equipment. This is the same bookie shop in which Dixon had wagered three bets on September 8, 1939, and which he had reported to local authorities, who never took action.[21]

One day during the San Antonio raids, Bob Spellman, Leona's cousin, walked into a "colored joint" on the east side of San Antonio with a group of friends. It was not uncommon for white youths in the 1940s to go into nightclubs that catered to black clientele. The entertainment was good, and the atmosphere was quite different from that in the upscale nightclubs for whites. But on this occasion Dixon was working undercover in that club. Their meeting was brief. Dixon looked at Spellman and said, "What are you doing here? Get out!" Bob and his friends left quickly, but the encounter became part of Spellman family lore. Many years later Bob's brother Laurance would recall, "We younger kids were thrilled with the idea that Norman was on an undercover job, with possible great danger to his life."[22]

There was more undercover work to come—so much so that Dixon and his fellow state raiders incurred the wrath of a major city mayor. More painful, Dixon's closest raiding partner died of a heart attack in the midst of the crusade. But there was good news. On August 20, 1940, Leona gave birth to the Dixons' second son, Kenneth Ray. However, she made no diary entry about the event. On October 15, 1939—one month before her pregnancy began—

Leona had written in her diary her "pleasant surprise" when "at 11:00 p.m. the Crowders popped in" to stay with them for a couple of days while Bob attended court. Two days later, thirteen-month-old Kemp cried when the Crowders prepared to depart, so they rode around the block with him in the car before leaving. That was Leona's last diary entry. Her last words that day were, "Honeyboy hasn't coughed lately." With that she was through keeping a diary. Norman, however, would continue for the next eleven years.[23]

Chapter Five

GOLDTHWAITE

On September 2, 1940, Ranger Sgt. Ernest Best led Rangers R. F. Rohatsch, B. F. Spain and N. K. Dixon, along with two San Antonio Police Department vice-squad members, in a two-and-one-half-hour raid of the Labor Temple, a union building, seizing fourteen slot machines, which the raiders called "automatic payoff devices." As the more than one hundred people caught up in the raid began threatening the Rangers, someone called for ten policemen to be sent to the scene. Mayor Maury Maverick, who was at a movie theater when he learned of the raid, rushed to police headquarters, refused the request for the policemen, and ordered that the vice-squad members leave the scene. He also ordered two traffic patrolmen who were directing the trucks hauling away the slot machines to leave. "I have had enough trouble with riots," he said, adding that although the police department would not tolerate "commercialized, professional gambling," he was not interested in raiding private clubs or parties.

Displeased with Police Chief Ray Ashworth's role in this and past gambling raids, the mayor held a tense and heated conference with him. Ashworth made it clear that he intended to enforce the law regardless of political consequences, but the mayor said the Labor Day raid was an attempt to turn organized labor against him. The Texas Department of Public Safety announced that it would "continue its policy" of using Rangers to enforce antigambling laws, and the *San Antonio Express* gave its support, noting the "astounding presence" of slot machines after the police and sheriff's departments "made so much ado" about having cleaned the city of gambling machines.

On Friday, September 27, Ranger Sergeant Best told Dixon to go to Corpus Christi and work on an antigambling campaign with Ranger Davenport. On Saturday evening, Dixon and Davenport, with Corpus Christi Police Chief George Lowman and Detective Capt. Earl Dunn, raided both a Mexican pool hall, where they arrested seven caught playing poker in a back room, and a tourist camp on the north side of town, where they broke up a poker game but filed no charges.[1]

"Pappy" Davenport had been the sheriff of Jackson County before joining the Rangers in 1931. Because the Rangers had no official uniform at that time, he dressed like a country sheriff—and continued to do so throughout his Ranger career, routinely wearing a wide-brimmed hat, cowboy boots, a black suit, and a string tie. As a Ranger he had handled twenty-nine cases in which the accused received the death penalty, but he was best known for his aggressiveness in investigating illicit gambling. One newspaper estimated that during his career he had arrested ten thousand individuals on gambling charges and that most were convicted. This was theoretically possible because, like most Rangers, Davenport worked tirelessly days, nights, and weekends, living off coffee and cigarettes. One of his famed comments was: "Twenty-four hours is not enough for a day; when I get control of the universe I'm going to make the day thirty-five hours long so I'll have time enough to get my work done and drink a cup of coffee now and then."

Davenport's stature was not typical of Rangers. He stood barely five feet, was slight in build at about 120 pounds (but known for his wiry strength), and looked years beyond his actual age. Hence his nickname "Pappy." Dixon, at five feet eight inches, now had a partner he could look down on. In reality, though, he looked up to Pappy. Davenport's gambling raids were legendary, and Dixon had the privilege of tagging along with him. Davenport was newly transferred to Corpus Christi from Houston with orders to suppress gambling, a growing problem in the city, partly because large numbers of construction workers had been hired to build the naval air training station.[2]

Davenport and Dixon continued their raids day after day and night after night, arresting gamblers and operators and seizing slot machines, marble tables, and punchboards. During the campaign they raided a poker game at the Thomas Model Pharmacy in Corpus Christi, arresting nine men (who paid a total of $180 in fines) and seizing tables, chairs, cards, chips, and such. They raided the house of Polita Gonzalez, arresting fourteen playing "panguinge." At Uncle Lonnie's Place, finding four men playing dice and card games, they seized the dice and cards and fined each player five dollars.[3]

Occasionally the antigambling campaign was interrupted by other law-enforcement activities, such as on October 8 when Dixon helped two police officers disarm an inebriated U.S. customs agent who had drawn his pistol on one of the officers. Dixon also took an occasional break, as he did on Sunday, October 12, driving to Smiley, where Leona and the boys were staying with her parents. The day before, he and Davenport had raided the Roosevelt Bar, seizing eighty-four punchboards, poker chips, nine pairs of dice, two "chuck-a-lucks," two slot machines, and a craps table.

Dixon returned to Austin on Monday, October 14, on a special assignment for Colonel Garrison to track down a sexual pervert bothering female employees in the office of the secretary of state. On Wednesday a suspect was identified; on Thursday Dixon interviewed several employees; and on Friday he arrested the suspect, took his fingerprints, photographed and jailed him, and called in a doctor to observe him. Later that day he returned to Corpus Christi in time to spend the night "prowling with Pappy." On Sunday, October 20, Pappy and "Dick" (Dixon's informal name) hit the Oso Beach Club, seizing slot machines; broke up a game in a private residence in the black section of town; stopped a bingo game at Elliot's Modern Trailer Camp; and visited a funeral home, where they examined the wounds on the body of Leonard Griffin, killed by Officer Tommy Mathews while resisting arrest.

On Monday, October 21, Dixon, Davenport, and Captain Dunn searched the home of suspected marijuana dealer John Henry Owens. At first they found nothing, but as they looked through items piled high on a table, an officer looked under the table and found three matchboxes, each with ten marijuana cigarettes, glued there. After his arrest, Owens told the officers he had been selling the cigarettes for about five months, mostly to taxicab drivers, for twenty-five cents each. Twice a month he bought two or three dollars' worth of marijuana from a "wholesaler" and rolled about eighty cigarettes. The cab companies quickly complained that their drivers had been put under a "blanket" accusation, and Dunn responded by telling the press that there had been an increase in narcotics traffic but that his main interest was in finding "the 'wholesaler' and his agents" and "in stopping the weed at its source."[4]

With the exception of a short visit to Smiley, a day spent in gambling raids in San Antonio, a quick return to Austin, and a couple of brief assignments, Dixon continued conducting gambling raids in the Corpus Christi area throughout November. In December he worked with assistant attorney generals Alex Cason and Ben Woodall, FBI agents, and other officials on an antitrust case that took him to San Antonio, Alice, and Corpus Christi. On December 11 he and Spain joined Davenport for a raid on the residence of H. E. Stumberg, owner of a considerable amount of real estate in Rockport and possessor of 103 slot machines, forty-five marble tables, and three punchboards, all confiscated from his residence and warehouses in Rockport and Tivoli. It was the largest seizure of gambling devices in any part of Texas in several months, and it was Davenport's last raid.

On December 15 Norman was in Smiley with Leona, the boys, and Leona's parents when he received a telephone call from Ida Mae Davenport that her husband, Pappy, was sick with indigestion but still planned to meet Norman in Corpus Christi the next evening. At 8:00 a.m. the next day, after having conducted interviews on the antitrust case in Gonzales, Dixon arrived in Corpus Christi, where he learned that E. M. "Pappy" Davenport had died of a heart attack. On December 17 state highway patrolmen escorted Davenport's body to his hometown of Edna for the funeral. Dixon served as a pallbearer. Afterward he drove to Alice to continue the antitrust investigation.[5]

The "anti-trust investigation in Duval County-to-San Antonio," as Dixon labeled it, was part of a statewide investigation involving alleged price fixing by distilleries and wholesalers. From November 28, 1940, to January 21, 1941, the antitrust case was his primary assignment. Traveling to towns between San Antonio and Houston, he interviewed police officers, constables, sheriffs, wholesalers, beer-joint operators, and others. Eight months after he completed his assignment, the state attorney general filed antitrust suits against seven distilleries and twenty-three wholesalers across the state, charging that they had violated state antitrust laws by establishing fixed territories for wholesalers and fixed wholesale and retail prices for liquor. The attorney general said the firms enforced the agreements by sending agents to retail stores to check on their prices and refusing to sell to those that sold below the agreed-upon price. Within a few months the firms began settling in court, paying fines, and agreeing to cease their illegal practices.[6]

As a state criminal investigator Dixon worked with Federal Bureau of Investigation (FBI) agents during the antitrust case and conferred with them off and on regarding other issues. On December 21, 1940, he drove to San Antonio to take the FBI exam. In his personal papers is a letter from Russell Morton Brown, a U.S. Attorney stationed in Corpus Christi, to J. Edgar Hoover, FBI director, recommending Dixon for appointment as a special agent in the FBI, calling him "an extraordinarily well-qualified applicant." His papers contain no further information on the exam or his application.[7]

On January 22, 1941—the day after Dixon completed his antitrust assignment—he was told to make arrangements to move to Goldthwaite, a small town in Mills County ninety miles west of Waco, and two days later he received written orders from Homer Garrison. A similar order was given to Ranger Earl McWilliams. Although Dixon would continue to carry the payroll title "Senior Criminal Investigator" for two more years, Garrison addressed the letter to "Mr. N. K. Dixon, Texas Ranger." As Dixon understood from the beginning of his service, he was a Texas Ranger, his lower-paying classification title necessitated by the lack of adequate funding for the Ranger force.[8]

On Thursday, January 23, Dixon rode with Ranger McWilliams to Goldthwaite, where they contacted Sheriff Hearn Harris and found places to stay. Dixon rented a house for his family on Highway 183 in Goldthwaite. On Friday, riding with a liquor-control-board inspector, the Rangers apprehended Lonnie H. Rhoades, who was charged with possessing liquor in a dry area with intent to sell. A month later Dixon testified at Rhoades's trial, which resulted in a guilty verdict and a fine of $100 plus costs.

Prohibition ended in 1933, and in 1935 the Texas legislature created the Texas Liquor Control Board (LCB), authorizing it to make rules and to revoke liquor licenses for violations. All peace officers in the state had the duty to enforce liquor laws, including the "open option" law, dating back to 1854, which allowed a county or a political subdivision within a county to vote to legalize or prohibit the sale of any or all alcoholic beverages. An entire county could vote dry, political subdivisions within a wet county could vote dry, but a subdivision in a dry county could not vote to allow the sale of liquor. Of Texas's 254 counties, 123 were dry in 1941.[9]

During the weekend of January 24–26, Dixon wrote reports and conducted office work, including polishing a letter drafted by McWilliams for the twelve sheriffs they would serve in the Goldthwaite substation territory. Dixon loved to write, a rare trait among Rangers, as noted by historian Robert M. Utley. Typical was Ranger Arthur Hill, who "never liked writing in any form or fashion." McWilliams may have fit well into that category. His draft of the first paragraph in the letter to the sheriffs reads, "This will advise you that Col.Garrison Director of the Department of Public Safety.through Sgt. Earnest Best commanding officer of the Texas Rangers of Head Quarters Divission Austin,has made Goldthwaite a Sub.Station and stationed N.K. Dixon and my self here put me in charg,giving us twelve (12) Counties and your Co. is included in our District." Dixon's rewrite reads, "This will advise you that Col. Homer Garrison, Jr., Director of the Department of Public Safety, through Sergeant Ernest Best, Commanding Headquarters Company of the Texas Rangers, has established a sub-station at Goldthwaite, Texas. The Department had placed me in charge of this sub-station and has assigned N. K. Dixon to work with me, our field operations to include twelve counties, of which one is your county."[10]

Dixon's activities during the month of February 1941 included interrogating three Llano prisoners suspected of stealing gas; arresting two drunks; investigating cattle, sheep, and goat thefts; inducing a suspect "to tell the truth re theft of boots by forgery & passing [forged check]"; clearing a suspect who had drunkenly bragged about burning down a rancher's home; seizing a slot machine stored in a storage garage; and arresting a swindler. He also conferred with Sheriff Earl Stewart "re jail conditions & trouble with jailer—& anticipated trouble with prisoners—jailer fired, looked jail over . . . arranged to shake-down jail next a.m."[11]

While he was in Llano on February 3 interrogating three suspected gas thieves, he also examined the scene of a safe burglary at Bruhl's Drugs. On February 11 Joe Bacchus, Llano city marshal, asked Dixon to go to Dallas to interrogate suspects Bennie Lee Lewis and Walter Henry LeMay, who had been arrested for car theft. In Dallas Dixon took LeMay's confession of knobknocking the Bruhl's Drugs safe with Lewis, and two days later he delivered the statements to Llano officers. After Dixon's interrogation regarding the Llano burglaries, Dallas police returned LeMay to Eldorado, West Texas, where he was wanted for car theft and jailbreaking. Two months later in Canyon, south of Lubbock, he was given two twelve-year sentences for burglaries in Randall County. He was also wanted in Albuquerque, New Mexico, for burglary, assault with intent to murder, and auto theft, and in Gallup, New Mexico, for burglary. Records showed that he previously had served in both the Oklahoma and the Texas penitentiaries. On May 15, 1941, Dixon testified in a Llano grand-jury hearing regarding the Bruhl Drug Store burglary. As will be seen in a later chapter, however, this would not be Dixon's last time to tangle with Walter LeMay. On May 26 Dixon returned to Llano for a grand-jury hearing on charges against Bennie Lee Lewis, but at the last minute Lewis jumped bond, disappearing with his mother and sister.[12]

On March 8 in Brownwood Dixon investigated the shooting of Amos Keith, allegedly by Bill White, a "dope head." He examined the crime scene and questioned White. It was the beginning of a valuable relationship: the law and the informant. After Dixon had interrogated White and concluded he was not guilty—he soon had another suspect—the conversation shifted to narcotics trafficking, and soon each had what he wanted. White could stay out of jail and on the good side of the law; Dixon could obtain information he needed to crack down on narcotics trafficking.

Two days later Dixon was conferring with John W. Marsh, U.S. narcotics agent, Sheriff Stewart—and Bill White, prisoner. That night, Dixon, the sheriff, and the prisoner "prowled & discussed plans & info." On April 10 Dixon, White, Marsh, and two other narcotics agents drove to Stamford. There, acting on information provided by White, they set up a purchase of marijuana from drug dealer Teodoro Moreno. After arresting Moreno, Dixon searched him and found his drug money hidden under his right leg. Dixon placed him in the Stamford jail to await the arrival of the U.S. marshal, and drove to the house of his son, Jesse Moreno. After Dixon had searched the house, federal narcotics agents arrived and arrested Jesse. The Morenos pleaded guilty in court, and on April 29 T. E. Middlebrooks, district supervisor of the U.S. Bureau of Narcotics, wrote a letter of appreciation to Homer Garrison commending the work of Dixon and Sgt. Ernest Best in the case of Teodoro Moreno. Dixon, in turn, owed thanks to his informant, Bill White.[13]

Rangers worked mostly in rural areas, serving local peace officers who often were undertrained and whose departments were understaffed. According to Thad Sitton, author of *The Texas Sheriff: Lord of the County Line,* the rural sheriff's power depended upon good information through a "snitch network." One sheriff told Sitton, "It's the thieves . . . that tell you what you need to know." Another sheriff told Sitton that without informers "you're not gonna get no big lot done, far as that goes. . . . A preacher can't give you much information about what's going on out here in the underworld. An old thug can get around and find out more, if he trusts you, and an officer has got to be trusted by his informer." During the rest of his career, Dixon would cultivate informants and use them extensively.[14]

On March 24 Dixon wrote in his diary, "Assisted local & state officers in general police work" in Brownwood. That included searching the Alamo Courts motel and arresting a porter, a maid, three "whores," a housekeeper, and a pimp. The next day Dixon questioned the prisoners and assisted the city judge. The "whores pleaded guilty (one held out till afternoon)." The next day he investigated "procuring" by Douglas Pipes. But going after prostitutes or even "procurers" was far from a high priority with Rangers. A search through Dixon's thirteen Ranger diaries finds very little mention of it. In his memoir, Ranger Lewis Rigler wrote: "Arresting a prostitute is hard enough; convicting one is just about impossible. . . . Live and let live. . . . Most law officers would rather spend their time on serious crimes. Frankly, I've always thought it was a waste of a Ranger's time and talents to go after whores." According to Sitton, the same held true for sheriffs, many of whom believed prostitution was a victimless crime and that "boys will be boys."[15]

Rustling a single red cow was not a victimless crime, however, and on Friday, April 4, Dixon was on such a case. From Goldthwaite he drove about thirty-five miles north to Hamilton, where he picked up Will Henry Short, whose red cow had been stolen. From Hamilton they drove to Dallas, where Dixon contacted Capt. Gonzaullas and picked up Ranger Ernest Daniel. From Dallas they drove north to Howe, about twenty miles from the Oklahoma border, where they checked the records of the A. C. Lupher Commission Company. From Howe they drove west about forty miles to Gainesville, where they reviewed the books of the Gainesville Livestock Commission Company and interrogated A. C. Lupher and Arthur O'Mary. According to O'Mary's records, the cow was at either Morris King's or Lester Embry's place. It was at neither. On Saturday they located her at the ranch of Roy Embry, Lester's brother, and Short got his red cow back.

On Monday Dixon was in Hamilton conferring with Hamilton County Sheriff White and District Attorney Bill Allen regarding filing charges against A. C. Lupher, but they advised him that the case was too weak. That response may have been frustrating for Dixon, but he well understood the difficulties local officials faced when prosecuting their citizens. In *One Ranger Returns,* Joaquin Jackson, author of two books about his own Ranger career, expressed frustration about his many cases of stock theft. "Of all the hundreds of cases that I worked," he wrote, "maybe only half a dozen thieves whom I caught actually went to the pen." In rural counties everyone knew everyone, and victims often declined to file charges—something even Jackson acknowledged was understandable.[16]

The month of May was dominated by antigambling activity, but on Monday, May 26, Dixon traveled to Burnet with Ranger Fred Olson to investigate the theft of six hundred pounds of dynamite from the Uvalde Construction Company, road contractors near Camp Bowie, and the effort by the thieves to sell the dynamite at Burnet, near Buchanan Dam. There were no Miranda rights in the 1940s, and interrogations could be lengthy and harsh. Dixon and Olson interrogated suspect Herschel Prince, and in Dixon's word, "broke" him, leading to the arrest of his three accomplices. The dynamite was recovered, and the four pleaded guilty, receiving prison sentences ranging from two to five years.[17]

At 11:30 p.m. on June 24 Dixon received a call from Colonel Garrison to go immediately to Abilene to investigate an incident involving two stones with notes attached thrown at Governor O'Daniel during a campaign speech. The governor claimed the stones with "scurrilous" notes pelted his sound truck. Traveling with the governor was Capt. R. B. Butler of the highway patrol, who said one of the stones missed the governor by about eighteen inches. Dixon reached Abilene at 2:15 a.m., too early to contact the governor. He conferred first with the Abilene police regarding local criminal activities, then with Captain Butler, and finally with the governor. During the governor's "send-off party," Dixon stayed near him. Then, after O'Daniel had left Abilene, Dixon investigated the case with the chief of police and a juvenile officer. They brought four boys before a county court, where they were judged guilty of throwing the stones and writing the "scurrilous" notes.[18]

Dixon's activities in July included helping local officers police the races, rodeo, and fair at the Brady Jubilee; investigating the dissemination of obscene literature, seizing the material, and arresting Henry Chandler and Fred Hester; apprehending several bootleggers; arresting the operator of a baseball-pitching game of chance, who pleaded guilty and paid an $18 fine; catching two knobknockers and taking their confessions; and conducting a raid in Temple with three other Rangers, seizing twenty-five slot machines from thirteen locations. According to the *Temple Daily Telegram*, viewers of the three-hour raid were "amused" at the "race" as the four Rangers rushed from establishment to establishment grabbing machines while operators tried to remove them from sight before the Rangers showed up. Several owners "nosed the Rangers out by scant minutes." A Ranger told the reporter, "We'll be back if the things show up again."[19]

On July 19 Sergeant Best ordered Dixon to meet Ranger Olson in Fredericksburg at noon the following day for encampment on the highways. Texas cattlemen were suffering heavy losses as rustlers used cattle trucks for quick getaways to far-off markets, where big profits were to be made. On July 20 Dixon and Olson, each in his own state vehicle, drove twenty-five miles south to Comfort, pitching camp two miles south of town. The horse trailer hitched to Olson's car was filled with camping gear. They had a tent, a table, bedrolls, and a kerosene lamp. A chuck box hung on the end gate of the trailer. Near the highway they set up a sign, STOP TEXAS RANGERS, and that evening they stopped all cattle trucks, checking livestock marks and brands, and reviewing paperwork, including a manifest of the shipment with the owner's signature, the driver's name, the source and destination of the shipment, brands, and other relevant information—all required by law but not strictly enforced in recent years.[20]

Norman Dixon, camping out near Comfort, is second from right. *Author's Collection.*

Olson and Dixon maintained the Comfort roadblock for the next four days and nights, breaking camp on July 25, driving ninety-five miles north, and setting up camp outside Brady. Olson left for Austin that night, leaving Dixon in charge of the roadblock until August 5. At times Livestock Sanitary Commission Inspector Dan Westbrook helped him check stockyards and auction sales, drive back roads, and investigate livestock thefts. When Olson returned, he and Dixon moved their camp, setting up at the edge of a prairie dog village near Coleman, about fifty miles north of Brady. On August 8 they moved the camp one last time, to near Comanche, thirty-plus miles north of Goldthwaite. Four days later they broke camp and headed home.[21]

The crackdown on cattle thefts was no secret. The *Brownwood Bulletin* publicized the Comanche blockade, even pinpointing its location. In the midst of the Ranger cattle-theft campaign, Governor O'Daniel resigned to take a U.S. Senate seat and Texas gained a new governor. After being stopped at a Ranger roadblock, the new governor, Coke Stevenson—also a Kimble County rancher—pulled off to the side of the road and for several hours watched the Rangers in action. He was impressed. So was Homer Garrison, who praised the effectiveness of the campaign and promoted Sgt. Ernest Best to captain.[22]

Dixon clearly felt the mission was a success. Among his personal papers is a draft of an essay titled, "The Law, The Cop and You," which probably began as a speech he delivered to a club, church group, or other social organization. He gave many such talks during his career in law enforcement. In this essay he wrote about setting up roadblocks on various highways in 1941 to check livestock haulers for proper forms and such. "However," he wrote, "in the wee hours of the morning, after the commercial traffic had waned, [we] would prowl the back roads for the pickup loads taking routes off the main thoroughfare. Not only did this mere presence of the Rangers and this activity put a stop to the thieving, but in one instance thirty head of sheep were mysteriously restored to the pasture from which they had disappeared the night before." In another story in the essay, Dixon encountered a rancher who told him that the night before he was lying in bed when he heard a vehicle on the road near his home come to a stop. He looked out the window and saw the car parked off the road by his pasture. He was feeling sick at heart at the thought of losing more cattle when he saw a pickup drive by, heard the parked car start up, and watched as it overtook the pickup with its siren wailing. "And boy," he told Dixon, "did I suddenly feel at peace with the world. I knew then that that car was some of you Rangers out there trying to protect us little fellows, and I went back to bed and slept like a baby."[23]

Dixon, who grew up enjoying the outdoors and animals, was in his element during the three weeks out in the open and dealing with livestock. In a letter to Ronald on September 3, about three weeks after returning home, he wrote: "Crazy about livestock and actually want a stock farm some day. Still love all animals. . . . Love camp life and mounted work. . . . Would like to raise cattle and goats." He revealed other things about himself, such as his chain-smoking habit: "I smoke cigarets, roll my own when outside as it is cheaper and I don't smoke so much." He also wrote: "Like to drink a beer occasionally, but can't do it in public and never do get to buy a case and bring it home. Don't give a hoot about whiskey." He told Ronald he was in the habit of "cussing too much." He liked his work, adding, "The rougher the more fun," and he loved "prowling" at night. He hoped someday to be a police chief in a fair-sized city, where he could study and practice some of his "ideas of efficient policing and crime control." As a police chief he might be able to build and own a home. "Your children," he wrote, "would get acquainted with you, your wife would have company, and maybe a little social life."

Commenting on the small town of Goldthwaite, Dixon wrote, "In this town you couldn't find anyone to hire to tend your kids while you even go to a show." He had another negative comment: "Nigirs [Negroes] not allowed here." Though he was using the language of white Texans of the period, he was disturbed by the extent of the bigotry. He had "a vague thought that someday I might write." He liked "the creative, flowers, music, would like to keep my flying up, would like to own a ship." It was a remarkable letter by a Ranger happy with his work but feeling that he was missing out on other things. "Have decided to take more time out for play," he wrote. "Pitching day and night only gets you more work."

He closed his letter to Ronald with an example of "the rougher the more fun." In recent days he had arrested three men: R. E. Bagby, charged with a DWI; L. B. Burns Sr., for assault and battery; and Thelmer Shearer, for desertion from the army and theft. Dixon was with a constable in Brownwood on the night of August 28 when he saw Shearer "and decided he ought to be checked." When Dixon approached him, however, Shearer took off running. In cowboy boots, a big hat, and khakis, and with a half-block handicap, Dixon chased him down. It was, he wrote, "my first foot race in cowboy boots."[24]

On September 19 Sheriff Stewart, who had information that Oklahoma outlaws were planning to rob a Brownwood bank that day, contacted Dixon. Dixon placed officers at the First National Bank and the Citizens National Bank, and he took a stand across the street between the banks. While he was waiting, two officers brought him the letter that had alarmed the sheriff. The writer said he had overheard three thugs talk of robbing a Brownwood bank sometime on a weekend in the fall. Dixon called off the surveillance.

During the next few weeks—his last at the Goldthwaite substation—Dixon continued his investigations into gambling, forgeries, burglaries, and livestock thefts. One report he received was of a car parked in a pasture whose owners were cattle thieves, but in fact they were foxhunters. On October 20 he was in Austin conferring with Captain Best and Colonel Garrison on his new assignment: serving in Austin with Dub Naylor on narcotics. By the end of the month he and Leona had moved to 4202 Avenue D in Austin. Now, instead of hunting down marijuana dealers and checking drugstores for narcotics licenses, he found himself on loan to the state attorney general's office investigating a popular southeast Texas sheriff accused of misconduct, incompetence, and mistreatment of prisoners, and shortly after that assignment he would be sent to investigate a notorious cold case involving the torture and murder of a socialite and her daughter on a lonely stretch of road in far West Texas.[25]

Chapter Six

THE SHERIFF AND THE SOCIALITE

Born on a farm in Nueces County, John B. Harney, who stood 6'3" as a grown man, was elected sheriff in 1938. "No more humane nor kindly man lives in Nueces County," said an old friend of the sheriff in 1939. He was, the Reverend Bill Crook said in the same year, "A man's man . . . a mild-spoken peace officer with a twinkle in his eye that disarms even a child." The preacher stated that when he asked "soured and embittered men . . . ready to spew their hatred at anyone" what they thought of the sheriff, they said, "He's a regular guy," "He's a prince," and, "He's a square shooter."[1]

Nevertheless, just one year later, Harney faced a murder charge. William L. Sammons, a twenty-four-year-old who had been released from the Nueces County jail on May 1, 1940, died in a Corpus Christi hospital on May 24. A Sammons relative filed the charge of murder against Sheriff Harney, but a grand jury exonerated him, stating that the charge was a political attempt to keep him from winning a second term in office. Less than a year later, Harney was again charged with murder, this time in the fatal shooting of thirty-four-year-old William Henry King, a former West Virginia convict who was killed on February 7, 1941. Harney was acquitted in the trial when the judge instructed the jury to return a "not guilty" verdict based on the testimony of a Corpus Christi newspaper reporter who, as a witness for the prosecution, quoted Harney as saying that he shot King in self-defense.[2]

A few months later, on a Saturday night, twenty-eight-year-old Robert L. McDaniel Jr., who worked in the Assembly and Repair Department at Naval Air Station Corpus Christi and was married with two children, took a fifteen-year-old girl skating. In driving her home, he failed to take the correct turn and she jumped out of the car, seriously injuring herself. Two days later McDaniel was arrested for false imprisonment by Sheriff Harney and Deputy Sheriff Herman J. Wendland and taken to the county jail. When he was released two days later, he went to the naval air station, where Lt. Commander H. E. Halland, assembly and repair officer, sent him to the infirmary. McDaniel explained his battered appearance by claiming he had been beaten by the sheriff en route to and in the jail. Roy Scott, an attorney, along with McDaniel's wife and W. W. "Woody" Downs, his roommate, took McDaniel to Austin to meet with Attorney General Gerald C. Mann and Assistant Attorney General Edgar Pfeil.[3]

At the same time that McDaniel was meeting with the attorney general, Dixon was moving his family to Austin from Goldthwaite, and he was still in the process of establishing his new residence when, on October 29, 1941, Attorney General Mann requested and received approval from Colonel Garrison for Dixon to be loaned to his office for an investigation of Sheriff Harney. Dixon left at 8:00 p.m. to join Assistant Attorneys General Edgar Pfeil and Ben Woodall in Corpus Christi. Woodall had assisted in the failed prosecution of Harney for the murder of William Henry King.[4]

Harney was in his third year as sheriff, and this would be the third attempt to prosecute him—an unusual record, although many sheriffs of that era were known for exercising their power in ways that would be unthinkable decades later. Sheriffs commonly solved their cases by obtaining confessions while the suspect was in their custody in jail. They did this, according to Thad Sitton, author of *The Texas Sheriff,* by taking "advantage of the legalities and customs of an earlier day to get a quick admission of guilt." This did not mean that sheriffs routinely beat their prisoners into confessing. Sitton argues that many sheriffs were "low key, friendly and seemingly sympathetic," spending time talking to their prisoners, asking them to repeat their stories, trying to catch them in inconsistencies or slipups. Interrogations could go on for days, and sometimes a sheriff did find himself in trouble by going too far in trying to extract a confession. Dixon, Woodall, and Pfeil were in Corpus Christi to determine if Sheriff Harney had done just that.[5]

At the naval air station on October 30, Dixon, Woodall, and Pfeil met with McDaniel, Lt. Commander Halland, Lt. B. E. Dallas, Ensign W. R. Brooks, and Boatswain's Mate C. W. Campbell, who was McDaniel's superior in the Assembly and Repair Department. Ensign W. R. Brooks was in jail for drunkenness when McDaniel arrived at the jail, and Lt. Dallas was a doctor at the infirmary. That evening Dixon met with city detectives and an informant to learn more, and on the next day he met with the parents of the girl who jumped from McDaniel's car. On the following day, Dixon and Pfeil rode with the girl and her mother to the scene where she had jumped from the car. Through the rest of November and up to Christmas week in December, Dixon continued his investigation of Sheriff Harney, primarily interviewing former prisoners claiming mistreatment and individuals with corroborating information. On occasion during this period he worked on narcotics-related cases, which was the original reason for his transfer to Austin.[6]

The investigation became public knowledge in mid-February when Ben Woodall filed the attorney general's petition seeking Harney's ouster. In part the suit said, "Harney has been guilty of official misconduct, willful[ness] in character, and incompetency in office, and of gross carelessness in the discharge of duties." Fifty-seven charges were alleged, most for the mistreatment of prisoners in the custody of the sheriff or his deputies.[7]

On February 15 Dixon was back in Corpus Christi conducting further interviews and securing relators' signatures. Three days later, Dixon attended a court hearing regarding three additional charges alleging that Harney was intoxicated while performing his duties, including on November 16, 1940, when he tried to draw his pistol on Cyrus L. Heard. During the hearing the defendant startled the spectators when he loudly called for order during a brief disturbance. After the hearing Dixon and Assistant Attorney General Fred Chandler contacted the relators to ease their fears about their safety. That night Dixon and Pfeil tried to calm McDaniel, who thought someone was trying to scare him by parking in his driveway. The next day Dixon called the witnesses (former prisoners alleging mistreatment), assuring them of their safety and encouraging them to contact him immediately if anyone threatened them.[8]

As Dixon watched, the trial began on March 23 with Lt. Commander Halland testifying that four days after his arrest, McDaniel arrived at work with bruises on his face, ears, and head. Next on the stand was McDaniel, who charged that Harney began hitting him en route to the jail, cursed him and hit him again at the entrance to the courthouse, then took him upstairs and put him in the "tank," or "bullpen," an enclosure in which prisoners were allowed to walk around. A couple of hours later, McDaniel testified, he was taken to the first-aid room by Sheriff Harney, Deputy Sheriff Wendland, and two other deputies. "Harney slapped me and asked me 'what my intentions were toward the girl?' and I told him I had none." While the two deputies held him, Harney slapped him and Wendland hit him from behind with a padded instrument. When they finished, McDaniel said, "I couldn't see out of my left eye, and only a little out of the corner of my right eye. I was bleeding from the eyes."

McDaniel testified that Harney "told me not to tell anyone or I'd be found out in the brush and it would be his job to find out who did it and he wouldn't find out." McDaniel said that he refused to sign a statement stating that other prisoners had beaten him but that after he signed a statement that he was driving the car that the girl jumped out of, a trusty named "Smith" typed above his signature a sentence dictated by a member of the sheriff's department stating that he had been beaten by prisoners. When he was released from jail, McDaniel said Harney told him, "If I'd leave the county there would be no trial in the girl's case." The next witness, Ensign Brooks, in jail for drunkenness, testified that McDaniel had no bruises on him when he first entered the bullpen but that later he saw him staggering around as if he had been beaten. Brooks was released after serving two and one-half days in jail and paying a $47 fine.

On Tuesday, March 24, state's witness Jose Lozano testified that he had been jailed in Corpus Christi in October 1941 in connection with the murder of A. B. Evans, a night watchman, and that sheriff's deputies, in trying to get him to talk, put some tin cans filled with spinach or other vegetables on the floor about a foot from the wall, and made him remove his shoes and stand on the cans "from about . . . 7 o'clock in the morning until about 6 or 6:30 that afternoon." Every time he fell off, a deputy hit him with a three-foot hose. The sheriff never hit him, he said, but he was there part of the time. After four days Lozano was released.

Another witness that day was Charles M. Smith, who was serving a five-year sentence at the Retrieve State Farm for burglary in Brazoria County, two hundred miles up the coastline from Corpus Christi. He also had served time in Louisiana for robbery and in Georgia for violation of the Mann Act, and he had been arrested a dozen or more times for other offenses. He was the trusty named "Smith" whom McDaniel had referred to in his testimony. On the day before, the governor had signed a proclamation turning Smith over to the custody of Dixon for five days to serve as a witness in the trial. Dixon left Corpus Christi at 7:00 p.m. and arrived at the state farm at 11:00, where he spent the night. He returned to Corpus Christi with Smith in time for the prisoner to testify the next afternoon.

In his testimony Smith said that while he was in the Nueces County Jail he had typed about fifty statements from suspects for officers. He testified that although he "never saw anybody whipped," he heard sounds like someone "getting cuffed around a little bit" in the questioning room. He also had seen the hose, which he said was kept under a mattress in the room. Smith testified that McDaniel's face was red and that he had a knot or welt on his forehead when he was brought into the identification office, where Smith took his fingerprints. Later, he said, McDaniel's eyes were blue and swollen almost shut. Smith said he typed McDaniel's statement, including the sentence that the bruises were caused by prisoners, not by officers, but that every word was McDaniel's.

On Wednesday Dixon stayed at the hotel with prisoner Smith, who was subject to recall at the trial. In the meantime, at the courthouse the judge dismissed the intoxication charges against Harney on the basis that a removal had to be based on habitual, not occasional, intoxication. The chief witness that day was M. Asher Kennedy, who had faced charges of assaulting young girls in Nueces County. Owing to the nature of his testimony, all women were removed from the courtroom during part of his time on the stand. While in jail in January 1941, Kennedy testified, Harney hit him about twenty-five times: "He slapped the left side of my face until it was swollen, then he slapped me on the other side." He also was struck from behind by Deputy Sheriff Harry Lawrence. Dr. Harry C. Baldwin took the stand to testify that after Kennedy's release from jail, he examined the bruises on his face, cheeks, and ears and his two black eyes.

Micke Charles testified that in October 1941 he had been arrested without a warrant in his house for the murder of Evans, the night watchman. Charles claimed he did not know Evans and had nothing to do with his death. While he was being fingerprinted, officers brought in another prisoner, Severo Reyes, whose face was swollen and whose shirt was partly torn off. Then, Charles testified, he was taken into a room where Harney questioned him. When Charles denied knowing anything about the murder, another man began striking him on the back, legs, and face with a hose. Later, he said, he saw Jose Lozano "with his feet in the air" because they were swollen. Charles then claimed that when he was released, Harney said "to please forgive him, that he had to do that." W. R. Brandt, a labor foreman for a construction company at the naval air station, testified that when Charles returned to work from jail, his eyes and mouth were swollen and that he had "whelps [*sic*] like on a whipped cow" across his back. Clyde Butts, a timekeeper for the construction company, gave essentially the same testimony about Charles's condition after leaving jail.

On Thursday Dixon left Corpus to take Smith back to the Retrieve State Farm, and he returned to Corpus at 1:00 a.m. In the courtroom later that day, Woody Downs, McDaniel's roommate at the time of the arrest, testified that when McDaniel was released from jail, "Both eyes were bruised and swollen, one worse than the other. His eyeballs were red. . . . Both ears were beaten, one, worse than the other, looked like a cauliflower."

On Monday evening, April 6, the jury retired to deliberate. For most of Tuesday the jury remained deadlocked ten-to-two, but after twenty-two hours of deliberation, a verdict was reached: Sheriff John B. Harney was exonerated of all fifty-seven charges. When the verdict was announced, Harney rose from his chair, walked over to the prosecution's table, and congratulated the attorneys. He was pleased, he said, that the "twelve fair men on the jury" had cleared him of "the assertions of law violators."[9]

Two months later Attorney General Mann wrote a six-paragraph, full-page letter to Homer Garrison acknowledging that from the beginning he knew that it would be difficult to remove the sheriff in a court trial. The chances were, he wrote, "remote and doubtful." Convinced that "repeated instances of official misconduct had been conclusively shown," they decided to bring the suit forward. Early in the investigation, he wrote, they asked that "Mr. N. K. Dixon" be assigned to assist in preparing the case. Observing Dixon throughout the course of the trial, Mann "was impressed with his keenness and sincerity of purpose. He worked tirelessly day and night without complaint." Dixon's numerous interviews of witnesses provided "material aid in developing facts," and his ability to convince the witnesses that "they would be protected regardless of threats and intimidations" led to their testimony at the trial.

In his closing paragraph, Mann wrote that Dixon's "integrity and efficiency as a peace officer have won not only my respect and admiration, but that of each member of our staff who worked with him on the Harney case. We think Texas needs more peace officers of his caliber." Dixon was gaining a reputation that would lead to future assignments requested by governors, house and senate investigating committees, and other government leaders.[10]

"Mr. N. K. Dixon" already had the respect of Colonel Garrison, who in the midst of the Harney investigation ordered Dixon to travel to California with Ranger Capt. Royal G. Phillips to bring back suspects in what has been called the most notorious cold case in Texas history. On April 4, 1938, newspapers across Texas carried the Associated Press story of the brutal slaying of Mrs. Hazel Frome, a prominent California socialite, and her pretty daughter, Nancy, a University of California graduate, "their bodies placed face downward in the red earth of the West Texas brush country."[11]

Hazel and Nancy Frome had been en route from their home in Berkeley, California, to visit a daughter and sister in Parris Island, South Carolina. Up to two or three days before the trip, Nancy had planned to go alone by train, but her mother decided they should take a leisurely trip by driving Nancy's new Packard, a gift from her father, Weston G. Frome. An assistant sales manager of a DuPont subsidiary, he had won the car in a charity raffle on the East Coast. The Frome women left Berkeley on March 23, 1938, arriving two days later at El Paso, where, because of car trouble, they stayed for five days, passing the time by making several trips across the border into Juarez. Finally, at noon on March 30, their car was ready and they left the city.

Their original plan was to drive from El Paso through Dallas, but thirty-six hours later their car was found abandoned near Balmorhea, seventy miles east of Van Horn on the highway to San Antonio. The sides of the car had brush marks, indicating it had been driven through mesquite. The key was in the ignition, the engine still worked, and the tank had several gallons of gas. A tire had been changed even though the spare was in the trunk, damaged and without its inner tube. The tire-repair kit was in its original packaging, indicating that another bumper jack and tool had been used to change the tire. Gone was the Fromes' luggage.

A search for the women began immediately. Vehicles traveled the roads; officers, soldiers, and Civilian Conservation Corps workers hiked through the countryside; others rode horseback; and a Coast Guard airplane searched overhead. Weston Frome chartered a plane and flew in from Berkeley. The operator of the service station at the fork in the highway east of Van Horn (left to Dallas, right to Balmorhea and San Antonio) said he saw two men in a car similar to the Packard pass the station at a high speed heading toward Balmorhea. Jim Milam, a truck driver from El Paso, heard about the missing women and contacted the police, telling them that the Frome car and a blue coupe had passed him on the highway east of Van Horn. Milam said two women were in the Packard. The coupe had two sets of license plates and white printing on the door. After passing him, the two cars turned around, the Frome car veering off the highway before getting back on—perhaps indicating a struggle. The Frome car passed him again and, as he watched, turned onto the desert. With Milam's guidance, officers found where the car had been driven into the brush six miles east of Van Horn near an abandoned caliche pit, in which limestone had been mined and crushed to pave the road.

At dusk on the fourth day of the search, in a West Texas county almost the size of Connecticut, Rangers found tracks that matched the Packard tires. Following the tracks, officers and (because kidnapping was suspected) FBI agents discovered the bodies lying next to each other in a clearing about half a mile off the highway. The bodies were stripped of most of their clothing. They had been tortured. Both had been shot in the head. And dirt had been thrown over their bodies. Twenty-two-year-old Nancy, who had dirt, blood, and skin under her fingernails, apparently had fought back and been buried alive. She clutched a man's handkerchief and a small package of matches in one hand and a clump of black hair in the other. Because they had on their undergarments, investigators concluded that they probably had not been sexually molested.[12]

The bodies were taken to a mortuary for an autopsy. Weston Frome, unable to bring himself to look at the bodies, had the caskets sealed and rode the train with them back to California for burial. At his home on the day before the burial, a cigarette in his shaky fingers, he met with the press. Flanking him were his closest friends, including the city manager, and his South Carolina relatives, who Hazel and Nancy had crossed the country to visit. Weston told the press that Texas authorities were doing everything possible. Later he would sell his home and move.

The search for the killers became a crusade for Colonel Garrison. Because no kidnapping had been involved, the FBI was no longer on the case, but many Rangers worked on it along with sheriffs and police officers, not just in Texas but across the nation. Tips and leads poured in from every state. The manhunt quickly spread through Arizona, New Mexico, and Oklahoma. An ex-convict from Atlanta, held in a jail in Bisbee, Arizona, told the undersheriff: "Hurry up and get through with me. I've got to be going because they're lying face down and I've got to bury them." Every lead and tip had to be run down. The changed tire led to an assumption that the Fromes might have been stranded on the highway, looking for help from passersby. Weston Frome thought robbery was the motive. Sheriff Chris Fox of El Paso thought it was someone who knew and hated the Fromes. The Van Horn sheriff thought the murderers had befriended the Fromes while they were in El Paso. The captain of the criminal division of the El Paso County Sheriff's Office thought it was a drug deal gone bad because the Packard was similar to a car suspected as belonging to drug runners. Some suspected German espionage.[13]

On April 9 the investigation focused on sightings from Del Rio of a man and woman in a dark car with a white triangle and printing on the side and with Texas and New Mexico license plates—similar to Jim Milam's description. Farther southeast, along the border, the sheriff of Maverick County reported having seen the car pass through Eagle Pass. Another sighting was at a café in Carrizo Springs, southeast of Eagle Pass. The car seemed to be headed to Laredo. Rangers Pete Crawford and Alfred Allee led a search between Carrizo Springs and Laredo, and by April 11, they and other peace officers had moved into the area around Laredo, casting a tight net to catch the suspects. But the search proved fruitless, and by April 15, attention shifted across the border when Texas authorities passed on all their information about the suspects to Mexican officials.[14]

While Rangers Crawford and Allee were searching highways along the Rio Grande, Dallas police became interested in two ex-convicts as possible slayers of the Fromes. Jack Flippen and Jack Barnes were wanted for robberies in several cities, but of particular interest to Dallas detectives were receipts found in their possession showing they had been in El Paso prior to the killings and had purchased new license plates in Midland the day after the killings. Hairs taken from the heads of Flippen and Barnes were sent to the DPS crime lab to compare to strands taken from Nancy Frome's clenched hand, and a .32-caliber revolver was sent for comparison with bullets removed from the Fromes's heads. No matches could be made. Norman Dixon was not assigned to the lab at the time, but when he reexamined the revolver a few months after the slayings, he also was unable to make a match.[15]

The Frome case made news across the nation. When Mrs. Hester Worcester and her thirty-year-old son Chauncey in Newburyport, Massachusetts, saw pictures of the Fromes in their newspaper, they realized that they were the same women they had seen being pursued across a West Texas highway on March 30, the day of the slayings. In statements forwarded by Newbury port authorities to Albert A. Anderson, sheriff of Culbertson County, the Worcesters wrote that they first saw the Fromes' car parked on the roadside between El Paso and Sierra Blanca with a black car bearing Texas plates behind it. Later the Fromes' car passed them at a high speed with the black car on its tail. They watched as the two cars turned onto the highway toward Balmorhea. The Frome girl was "sitting on the edge of the driver's seat and seemed very excited."[16]

On April 18 Fort Bliss troops on their way to maneuvers near Balmorhea found an abandoned 1937 black Chevrolet with Oklahoma license plates not far from where the Frome bodies were discovered. On that same day Sheriff Fox was on the hunt for Leo Wahler, a fugitive ex-convict wanted for the March 22 murder of a Los Angeles tavern owner during a holdup. His accomplices said that during their flight from California he had separated from them and, with a woman, headed for El Paso when the Fromes were there. On April 26 El Paso officers were en route to Lovington, New Mexico, to grill a couple who became suspects when the "peroxide blonde" became hysterical as she was being quizzed about the Frome murders. On that same day Dixon left his investigation of the East Texas oil-field theft ring and headed to Laird Hill, near Longview, "re Frome case." That night he "wrote reports on Frome case."[17]

A pair of rubber gloves wrapped in a San Francisco newspaper found near Balmorhea led to the theory that the murderer might have medical knowledge. On May 1 a deputy sheriff in San Angelo arrested Dr. Romano Nicholas Trotsky (an alias), a Russian doctor who had registered at a hotel in El Paso when the Fromes were there. Trotsky said he had stayed at the hotel while traveling from South Texas to Las Cruces, where his wife lived, and that he had driven to Van Horn to "look after some practice." His wife had filed desertion charges, he was in the country illegally, and he had been convicted once for practicing without a license, once for transporting a stolen auto in interstate commerce, and twice for performing illegal operations. But state investigators determined he was in Roswell, New Mexico, at the time of the Frome slayings and turned him over to immigration authorities for possible deportation. Two days later the El Paso County Sheriff's Office was seeking an oil-field worker from Marlow, Oklahoma. On April 5 he and a blonde woman had been in El Paso in a black sedan with bloodstains on the backseat, and he had been seen taking women's clothing from a box addressed to the Fromes at a Lubbock tourist camp.[18]

Six weeks after the slayings, as Sheriff Fox was returning from Berkeley, where he had interviewed friends and relatives of the Frome women, DPS director Colonel Carmichael assigned Texas Ranger Frank Mills and Sgt. Guy Smith of the highway patrol to El Paso to work under Fox until the case was solved. The state agency also announced that additional highway-patrol substations would be set up in the area. Only one location, Van Horn, was named.[19]

Potential suspects were available in abundance. When officers in Detroit, searching the apartment of John Deering, found revolvers similar to those used in the Frome slayings and questioned him about the murders, his reply was, "I'll talk about that later." He did confess to a murder, a kidnapping, and the shooting of two policemen in Salt Lake City, but not to the Frome slayings. He had an alibi: on the day the Frome women died, he was committing a holdup in Detroit. When Robert Burgunder drove through Van Horn asking for directions to the murder scene, he was grilled by authorities, who learned that he was wanted in Phoenix for the murder of two auto salesmen and that he had been a student at the University of California when Nancy Frome was attending the school. Although he later received the death penalty for the Phoenix murders, he denied any involvement with the Frome slayings, and authorities were unable to link him to them.[20]

Six months after the Frome murders Homer Garrison told the press, "There is hardly a day goes by but what we painstakingly investigate some rumor or purported clue." He expected to solve the case, saying, "We'll never give up." They had run down more than a thousand leads, and although there had been no recent developments, he said they still received letters from all over the nation and that none would be ignored. At a convention of identification experts in Fort Worth in 1939, Garrison said he had four of the department's ace members assigned to the Frome case and that it would be solved soon. It was, he said, "our number one unsolved murder problem." A year later he still expected it to be solved, saying, "We leave no clue uninvestigated. So far these clues have led us nowhere but eventually one of them is going to cause the finger of guilt to be directed at the killer or killers and then our hard work and persistence will have proven its value." Speaking at the annual convention of the Sheriff's Association of Texas in August 1940, Garrison said that they (including El Paso County's Sheriff Fox) had run down about twenty thousand clues in the past two years and that sooner or later the case would be solved. Then, after another year, a seemingly big break occurred, and Colonel Garrison ordered Dixon to travel to California with Captain Phillips and bring back three suspects who might bring an end to the case.[21]

After reviewing the Frome case files, securing an out-of-state travel order, and receiving extradition papers for Charles and Bonnie Price Hatfield and Jack Reeves, Dixon and Phillips drove westward from Austin, picking up Sheriff J. E. Simco at Rankin and arriving at Van Horn at 11:10 p.m., where they conferred with Sheriff Anderson. Phillips, Dixon, and Simco reached Los Angeles on January 4, and on the following day an FBI agent joined them. The Kerns County sheriff and his deputies met the four officers in Bakersfield and then apprehended Charles and Bonnie Hatfield, turning them over to the Texas officers and the FBI agent, who took them to Los Angeles, placing them in the city jail.

On January 6 the Texas officers drove from Los Angeles to San Diego, where they met another FBI agent and then found and apprehended Jack Reeves. Two days later, Simco and Reeves left Los Angeles by airplane for El Paso. The next morning Phillips and Dixon left with the Hatfields, driving nonstop to Van Horn, where Sheriff Anderson asked them to deliver the prisoners to the Reeves County Jail, which they did at 9:05 a.m.[22]

For the next two weeks Dixon and Phillips stayed at the Brandon Hotel in Pecos, conferring with officers, conducting interviews, questioning informants, interrogating the prisoners, and gathering information from every other possible source to determine if the suspects were guilty of murdering Hazel and Nancy Frome on March 30, 1938, almost four years earlier. The trip to California, the arrests, the return journey with the prisoners, and Dixon's and Phillips's first three days working the case out of Pecos were kept out of the press, but on January 13 the Frome slayings burst into the news once more with announcements that, in Colonel Garrison's words, fingers may actually be pointing at the killers. The *Berkeley Daily Gazette* reported that Texas Governor Coke Stevenson had told the United Press that Texas authorities were on their way to extradite a California couple for questioning. And the *Dallas Morning News* reported that Sheriff Anderson, of Van Horn, said Charles Hatfield and his wife were being held in Los Angeles and would be returned to Texas for questioning. In fact the prisoners had been in Texas jails for three days. Probably the leaks from the governor and the sheriff were deliberately misleading.[23]

On Monday, January 12, Dixon, with Phillips and Anderson, took a statement from Lois Van Court Hatfield, a relative of Charles Hatfield; on Tuesday they obtained a statement from Bonnie Hatfield; on Wednesday they took a statement from Jack Reeves; and on Thursday Charles Hatfield gave them a statement. On Friday they obtained a statement from Naomi Jean Butler, a forty-five-year-old farm wife near Mexia, arrested under the name Naomi Reeves, who previously had been married to Jack Reeves in California.[24]

On Sunday, January 18, the district attorney in El Paso admitted that unless more evidence was forthcoming there would be no trial of these suspects. According to former sheriff Chris Fox, the Hatfields had been checked repeatedly through the years as possible suspects. A month after the murders, Charles Hatfield was arrested on a charge of forging checks to buy women's clothing in El Paso, but he was released for lack of evidence. Bonnie Hatfield, in her early thirties and the mother of two children who lived in Ft. Worth, formerly operated a tavern in Odessa.[25]

On Friday evening Dixon and Phillips met with other officials at Van Horn to discuss the case and their findings. The alleged link among the suspects may have been, in the widely reported words of one unnamed officer, "a narcotic ring." But the findings were insufficient, and on Saturday, January 24, 1942, the suspects were released. Dixon, his investigation finished, returned to Austin, where he spent Sunday sleeping. The cold case was not, however, put to bed. In the summer of 1945 Colonel Garrison repeated that every clue, no matter how minor, still was being checked. The prevailing belief was that the Frome women had been mistaken for two other women transporting narcotics and that they had been killed when they would not reveal where the narcotics were hidden. State authorities were clear: the killers eventually would be caught.[26]

Norman Dixon was back on the case for a few days in August and September 1950, contacting informants and conducting interviews in East Texas. Two decades later Capt. Alfred Allee, who had searched for the suspects along the border with Mexico soon after the murders, briefed Ranger Joaquin Jackson on the case and sent him to Dallas to interview two brothers, G. W. and

Leroy Garner. The Garner brothers told Jackson that their father, Howley Garner, had been told by his brother-in-law, Leslie Daniels, that he tortured and killed the two women whose bodies were found in the desert near Van Horn. The brothers' father had been killed in 1940, and they believed Daniels had done it to keep him from talking. Jackson went to Los Angeles, where Daniels was living, and subjected him to four polygraph tests. All were inconclusive. By then Daniels was elderly, drank heavily, abused drugs, and took various medications for a bad heart.

Jackson also interviewed M. R. Gill and a Mr. Coyne in Dilley, in South Texas, regarding another suspect, Roy "Monk" Thurmond. The interviewees said that a couple of days after the Frome murders, Thurmond and his blonde wife had been in Dilley driving a black car and that Mrs. Thurmond had tried to sell three rings for five dollars each to Mr. Coyne, who turned her down. Thurmond told Coyne he had followed the Fromes from California to El Paso but had car trouble and lost sight of them. Jackson was unable to locate Thurmond. As Jackson wrote in *One Ranger Returns* in 2008, seventy years after the slayings, the Frome case was still open.[27]

Chapter Seven

HOME FRONT

WORLD WAR II BEGAN IN SEPTEMBER 1939. ON MAY 20, 1940, GOV. W. Lee O'Daniel dramatically announced that he had confidential reports of un-American activities in Texas. "I shall appreciate," he said, "any and all information that any of our citizens can give me concerning any specific cases of un-American activities they know about or surmise. I will ask that all reports be submitted in writing and signed, but the names of senders will be confidential if so requested." The governor said he was launching a program to use highway patrolmen and Texas Rangers "to make sure that all un-American activities within the borders of our state be properly investigated and handled." William H. Richardson, chairman of the commission overseeing the DPS said that its officials had no reports of un-American activities and that the governor, whose announcement had provided no details about his knowledge of suspicious activities, had given them none.[1]

Response to the governor from Texans was immediate and overwhelming. On May 22 T. O. Walton, president of Texas A&M, told Governor O'Daniel he had received a copy of an unsigned letter addressed to the governor claiming that teachers at the university were making pro-German statements and that the university "is honeycombed with German sympathizers." Watson pleaded with the governor to investigate the charges. Another unsigned letter charged that the University of Texas was rampant with Communism, socialism, and "Hitlerism" and expressed the wish that "there was a way to get at these Un-Americans in the University of Texas." The wife of a faculty member in East Texas State College wrote that "town gossipers" were branding her husband and a dozen other faculty members of German descent as "Fifth Columnists." James E. Taylor, a state representative, wrote to the governor recommending "commissioning . . . the Texas National Guard and the American Legion to combat 'Fifth Column' un-American activities in Texas."

A "red blooded American" complained about a German couple who could never be Americanized, "talking incessantly in German, rather joyously, always raving about their wonderful country and their grand leader Hitler." The husband was a professor at Southern Methodist University, and his job "should be given to one of our own people, as I am positive he [is] a

German spy." A San Antonio writer was worried about "subjects of Germany working in our court house here. . . . Do you think these men not loyal to Hitler—I refuse to think different and I think we will live to regret all this." A North Gulch writer was suspicious of a man who "doesn't believe in saluting the flag." A woman in Carthage claimed that a German spy was running the town hospital. She made this discovery when she saw a foreign-looking woman talking in a foreign language to the doctor.

As Governor O'Daniel pledged in his May 20 announcement, information acquired by Texas officials regarding subversive activities was turned over to appropriate federal authorities. On June 11, Gus T. Jones, FBI special agent, wrote to Colonel Garrison regarding five DPS reports, fifteen governor's office reports, and excerpts from twenty-five letters on file at the governor's office that had been forwarded to his office. He asked that the state furnish the names of the informants. Three days later he wrote again: "It is noted that those [statements] furnished you from the Governor's office continue to be unsigned. It would be greatly appreciated by this office if these communications bore the signatures of the senders in order that if it became necessary to contact the informants for more information, it would be possible to do so without having to consult the governor's file in each instance." When Garrison forwarded the request to William J. Lawson, secretary to the governor, Lawson replied that the governor's office was withholding the names to protect everyone but that the FBI was welcome to come by and review the files.[2]

Dixon received his first assignment on alleged un-American activities on May 31 when Colonel Garrison ordered him to interview T. E. Darcy, supervisor of correspondence in the state welfare department, who suspected "5th column" activity in and around the Terlingua mining district. Dixon investigated and wrote a report for Colonel Garrison. Another suspected subversive-activity case assigned to Dixon involved large purchases of 8mm Mauser ammunition. He identified the buyer and tailed him, searched his room, interrogated him, and wrote a report. On June 13 Colonel Garrison assigned Dixon to work with Captain Phillips on a subversive case involving residents of San Marcos (many of whom were of German descent) and the Lower Colorado River Authority (LCRA), which delivered electricity to area residents and managed the water supply in the lower Colorado River basin. For three weeks Dixon interviewed people of non-German ancestry, with names such as "Dickens" and "McGee," regarding their attitude toward people of German descent, with names such as "Dideke," "Ficke," and "Moeller." He interviewed a University of Texas professor, Dr. W. E. Gidley, regarding a "pro-Nazi" former student identified by a Mrs. G. W. Luckey. He interviewed an F. M. Ivy, regarding a Eugene Schrobenhauser, and a person named Clayton, regarding a Mrs. Koch. He conferred with sheriffs and other peace officers and met with LCRA officials.[3]

San Marcos was only one of many Texas towns with substantial numbers of citizens of German descent. Large numbers of Germans migrated to Texas in the 1840s and 1850s, settling south of Austin, in San Marcos and New Braunfels; to the west, in such towns as Fredericksburg, Comfort, and Boerne; and in numerous other towns to the east and southeast. The vast majority of German Americans in Texas had been loyal to the United States during World War I, serving in the military, buying Liberty Bonds, and supporting U.S. policies. Nevertheless, anti-German attitudes were apparent during that war. The State of Texas prohibited the teaching of the German language in public schools and discouraged its use in public conversation. Texas school districts banned German music, books, and plays. Switchboard operators listened in on telephone calls between German Americans to catch any seditious talk.

After the Nazis took power in the 1930s, few German Americans supported Hitler, but those who did were very vocal and attracted attention. Fritz Kuhn, a naturalized U.S. citizen and founder of the German-American Bund in 1936, proclaimed loyalty to Hitler and Germany, but his Bund never had more than a few thousand members across the nation, and only one fairly quiet branch in Texas, located in the Central Texas town of Taylor. Still, the Bund worried many Americans. It also worried many Texans of German descent, who feared that pride in their German heritage would be misconstrued as support for Hitler.[4]

Attacks on the Bund by veterans' groups, Congressional hearings on pro-German activities, federal legislation and Roosevelt administration actions against German aliens, an FBI list of "potential sympathizers with the Nazi cause," Governor O'Daniel's announcement, and the resulting torrent of letters from Anglo-Texans against German Americans and German immigrants—all these led German communities to protect themselves by deemphasizing their ties to the homeland. In 1940, for example, Fredericksburg's annual "Schutzenfest" became the "48th Annual Shooting Festival." And Gillespie County's annual "Saengerfest" became the "Annual Gillespie County Singing Festival."[5]

During the nine months in 1941 when Dixon was stationed in Goldthwaite, he investigated seven people of German descent suspected of participating in un-American activities. From February through July 1942, while stationed in Austin, he investigated eighteen individuals with German surnames, most from towns with high concentrations of German Americans, including New Braunfels, Taylor, and Coupland. Each such investigation was unique, based as it was on the circumstances of the alleged activity and the characteristics of the suspect. Dixon's investigations included conferring with local peace officers and FBI agents, interviewing complainants, observing suspects, and checking postal records, draft-board information, telephone directories, poll-tax and property records, credit reports, military records, marriage records, driver's license records, personnel records, and naturalization records. His Ranger diaries do not indicate that he found anything incriminating in any of these investigations. The FBI did not maintain the reports it received from DPS, and DPS destroyed all its Ranger records for these years. No records found in newspaper archives report that action was taken against any of the individuals Dixon investigated.[6]

The Federal Bureau of Investigation complained about the un-American activities reports it was receiving from DPS and the governor's office, but it praised the reports of "Senior Criminal Investigator N. K. Dixon." On June 15, 1942, the same day Dixon had an ear lanced, M. W. Acers, FBI agent in charge of the San Antonio office, wrote to Colonel Garrison expressing his appreciation for Dixon's "excellent reports." Acers wrote, "Mr. Dixon's reports have been thorough and exhaustive and have greatly facilitated decisions by this office as to the proper dispositions to be made of these cases."[7]

On July 27, 1942, Colonel Garrison called Dixon into his office to inform him that, at the request of Captain Gonzaullas, he was being transferred to Company B in Dallas. After devoting the next six days to cleaning up his final reports and preparing for his transfer, Dixon drove to Company B headquarters for a two-day orientation with the captain. On August 20 Dwight Whitwell, assistant criminal district attorney for Collin County, wrote to Captain Gonzaullas recommending McKinney as a place to headquarter the new member of his company. Whitwell, scheduled to become district attorney on January 1, 1943, said he had conferred with the sheriff, who agreed to provide facilities at his office. Not all county officials in Texas appreciated having Rangers "interfering" in their affairs, but Gonzaullas had excellent relations with local officials. The McKinney *Daily Courier Gazette* welcomed the Dixons, reporting that "N.K. Dixon, Texas Ranger, wife and two children, Kenneth Ray and Frederick, have recently moved to McKinney from Austin to make their future home. . . . Mr. Dixon . . . is a friendly, courteous, efficient and well liked law enforcement officer."[8]

As was the practice in all Ranger companies, each Ranger in Company B served a subdistrict containing several counties and lived in one of its towns, which became subdistrict headquarters. Subdistrict Number 7, Dixon's assignment, contained eight counties between Dallas and the Oklahoma border: Montague, Wise, Cooke, Denton, Hunt, Fannin, Grayson, and Collin (with McKinney as county seat).

Although Dixon began reporting to Captain Gonzaullas as a member of Company B in early August, the official transfer date was October 1. In a letter to Colonel Garrison dated September 26, the captain formally requested the transfer. The original plan was that Dixon would work out of Sherman, but as Gonzaullas explained in his letter, "It is practically impossible to secure housing facilities at that place at the present time and also the living expenses have greatly increased. These conditions are due to the construction of Military

Company B in 1944. From left: Tully Seay, Kelley Rush, Stewart Stanley, Dick Oldham, Capt. Gonzaullas, Bob Crowder, Ernest Daniel, Joe Thompson, Bob Badgett, Norman Dixon. *Courtesy Texas Department of Public Safety.*

Encampments and Defense Projects, etc." Gonzaullas attached the letter from Whitwell and explained the virtues of McKinney as Dixon's headquarters. Three days later, in a letter addressed to 703 South Parker Street in McKinney, where the Dixons already were residing, Colonel Garrison told Dixon of his official transfer to McKinney, effective October 1.[9]

Investigations of alleged un-American activities continued to be a major part of Dixon's assignments during his first half-year in Company B. From September 1, 1942, to February 28, 1943, he devoted parts of thirty-eight days to investigating suspected subversive activities. For the remainder of the European war—more than two years—the total number of partial days he spent on such assignments was a mere twelve. Texans of German descent had become more sensitive to activities that made Anglo-Texans suspicious, and the Allies had begun to win the war in Europe.

Not all un-American charges were directed at German Americans and aliens. On May 20, 1940, a mass meeting was held in San Benito, a few miles from the Mexican border, to discuss "fifth column and Trojan horse" activities in response to an incident that had occurred two days earlier. A man, a woman, and fifteen girls between the ages of thirteen and seventeen who called themselves Jehovah's Witnesses were caught by members of the American Legion distributing materials that, the members claimed, were designed to interfere with the war effort. They rounded up the group and took them to city hall, where they were asked to leave the city.[10]

Jehovah's Witnesses believed in house-to-house preaching, as they were doing in San Benito, but they also believed that saluting national flags and singing the national anthem were forms of idolatry, and they refused to fight in wars. This seeming lack of patriotism angered Americans, whose feelings of loyalty to country were heightened in times of military conflict. Governor O'Daniel's announcement about un-American activities in Texas came two days after the San Benito incident and on the same day as the mass meeting against "fifth column and Trojan horse" activities that resulted in a number of letters to the governor about Jehovah's Witnesses. For example, "A Loyal American" wrote that when Jehovah's Witnesses "reference Jehovah and Christ King in their literature . . . they mean Hitler."

Jehovah's Witnesses wrote to the governor complaining of mistreatment. A woman distributing material in Henrietta, in North Texas, claimed that a mob of fifty people chased her and several others and burned some of their materials, and that when they asked the sheriff to take action, he said, "We don't want you Jehovah's Witnesses in this town, and we are going to do something to get rid of you." In Atascosa County, in South Texas, Witnesses claimed they were distributing literature when a deputy sheriff told them to get out of town. In Port Arthur, on the Gulf of Mexico, Witnesses claimed two plainclothes policemen beat some of the men severely in the face and body and pushed and shoved some of the women "shamefully."[11]

On November 19, 1942, Sheriff W. C. Button called Dixon in Dallas, asking him to come to McKinney to help him respond to some Jehovah's Witnesses who charged that he was threatening mob violence unless they left town. Dixon drove to McKinney, where he met with the sheriff and FBI agent Lawrence Donahue. Then he "interrogated Phillip Alfred Myres, Frances Wallace & Wm. Alfred Wallace, Jehovah's Witnesses. Myres made statement retracting threat by sheriff to mob violence or leave town."[12]

Soothing confrontations between Witnesses and local peace officers was only a small part of Ranger work during the war. Surveillance of the large German-American population was far more time-consuming and was, in the words of historian Robert M. Utley, "rightly viewed as a waste of time." As noted, Ranger reports were turned over to the FBI, and between December 1941 and May 1945 its agents apprehended 299 German Americans in Texas for questioning. Whether they interned any is unknown, but of seven million persons of German descent nationwide, almost eleven thousand were interned. Most prisoners held at the three internment camps in Texas—Seagoville, Kenedy, and Crystal City—were Japanese, German, and Italian nationals deported from Latin America.[13]

World War II was a tremendous burden on the Texas Rangers, on DPS, on the state corrections system, and on local sheriff and police departments because so many of their employees left to serve in the military. DPS, for example, lost 264 employees, many from the highway patrol, by August 1944. Dixon tried to join. On June 8, 1942, he wrote to Maj. George D. Thomas of the Texas Adjutant General's Department asking "as to what specific capacity the writer may best serve the Government of the United States in the war effort." In his two-page letter, he mentioned every bit of relevant experience he could conjure up, from his premedical coursework at the University of Florida to his eleven months as a flying cadet; from his athletic training in football, track, swimming, water polo, boxing, and wrestling to his ability to handle horses, mules, trucks, trailers, and motorcycles. He added that he would have no difficulty learning to handle snowshoes and parachutes. Major Thomas enclosed the letter in a memorandum to a Captain Taft, stating, "Mr. Dixon has a reputation with the State Department here of being the best investigator on their staff. It is thought that even though he desires 'Commando Service,' he would serve excellently as a civilian intelligence police [*sic*] or in combat intelligence." But nothing came of it, perhaps because Dixon, being thirty-four years old and married with two children, was in the III-A draft classification. Dixon's letter states that although he had to support a family, "arrangements can be made." There was that farm near Smiley where Leona's parents had extra bedrooms.[14]

In the summer of 1942 Dixon's draft board was Local Board No. 1, Travis County, Texas. Across the United States there were 6,443 draft boards and thirty million men under twenty-six years of age—the military's targeted age group. When it was announced that married men would be exempted, many quick weddings took place prior to the first draft. Four million young men in essential occupations, including two million farm laborers, received occupational deferments. Sixteen million men and women, including almost 750,000 Texans, served in uniform during the war, most for the duration, averaging three years of service. By the end of the war, Texas had more military training camps, airfields, and naval stations than any other state, with twelve major army training camps, thirty-five major army airfields, and five naval air stations, including the world's largest naval air-training station at Corpus Christi. Better than 1.5 million Americans received their military training in Texas. The Eighth Service Command, which supervised combat training in nine states, was headquartered in Dallas.[15]

During 1943 and 1944 Dixon spent parts of twenty-eight days searching for Selective Service violators who had neglected to register or were evading draft orders. The violators were from towns all over his subdistrict, including

Denison, Denton, Sherman, Bonham, Mineral Wells, McKinney, Greenville, Ravenna, and Nevada. One was turned in by his father-in-law, who declared him a "general no-count." If the individual had not registered, Dixon apprehended him and took him to the draft board, as he did with James Gordon Collum, whom he located at a dairy farm west of Fort Worth on March 29, 1943. If the violator was evading draft orders, Dixon turned him over to the FBI, as he did with Willie Oscar Walker on June 28, 1943.[16]

Deserters from the military and escapees from military prisons—262 military prisoners in the United States escaped during the war—could be considered a more serious threat than Selective Service violators because they were more likely to commit crimes. On Wednesday, September 17, 1941, when Dixon was stationed in Goldthwaite, he received a call from Captain Gonzaullas. Two days earlier four army deserters who had fled the guard house at Camp Wolter, an army camp near Mineral Wells west of Fort Worth, had abandoned a stolen car at Cross Plains, about sixty miles north of Goldthwaite. Dixon drove to Gorman, east of Cross Plains. There, with Sheriff Woods, Deputy Steel Hill, and Patrolman Pat Ross, he checked out a farmhouse reported to be a possible hideout. From there he traveled to Cross Plains and, with Gonzaullas, several other Rangers, and numerous local peace officers, searched the area through the night.

Following their escape from Camp Wolter, the four deserters had robbed a service-station operator of his car and thirty dollars, a café cash register of ten dollars, and a café customer, Mrs. E. E. Neal, of the twenty-one cents she had in her purse. A farmer who was salting his cattle had found the car in a clump of brush in a pasture four miles north of Cross Plains. According to the *Cross Plains Review*: "Wednesday night Cross Plains resembled a convention city for peace officers. Broad brimmed hats were on almost every head and six-shooters adorned more than a hundred hips." Throughout Thursday morning two government search planes and dogs helped the multitude of peace officers scour the countryside while other officers halted all traffic on the roads and warned drivers not to pick up hitchhikers. One driver said he had been stopped at gunpoint three times. At 1:00 p.m. planes spotted two of the deserters, who, seeing the aircraft overhead and hearing dogs approaching, surrendered. The other two were picked up later on a country road. The four deserters were still carrying the four riot guns they used in the robberies. After the capture, Dixon returned to Goldthwaite.[17]

Dixon tracked down several deserters during a ten-week period in 1943. On July 30 near Corsicana he arrested Pvt. John C. Lowrey for desertion from Camp Maxey, and took him to the military police in Dallas. A month later, at the request of the commanding officer of the 101st Airborne Division, Fort Bragg, North Carolina, Dixon conducted a search for Pvt. Oleander A. Winchester, wanted for desertion and swindling. Gathering information from city records and relatives in Durant, Oklahoma, and tracing Oleander to a residence in Denison, he arrested him there and took him to the military police in Dallas. Two weeks later Dixon and a Collin County deputy sheriff apprehended Pvt. Luizye Hendrix, a deserter from the 369th Infantry, 93rd Division, Ft. Huachuca, Arizona. And a month later, after several days of searching, Dixon and two Dallas detectives captured Larken Dudley Beaty, deserter and car thief, turning him in to the Provost Marshal at Perrin Field, in Grayson County.[18]

The Ranger force of forty-five men had enough to do without the additional responsibilities placed on them because of the war. Along with close surveillance of thousands of German Americans and chasing down Selective Service violators, deserters, and escaped military prisoners, Ranger duties included training air-raid wardens, taking statewide inventories of the armament and munitions of all law-enforcement agencies in the state, and instructing civilians and peace officers in the latest techniques for protecting factories, refineries, power plants, dams, and vital industries from sabotage. They also rounded up enemy aliens and tracked down escaped prisoners of war.[19]

Ranger Dub Naylor had the primary responsibility for traveling the state teaching local officials how to recognize enemy aircraft, how to cope with a gas attack, and so on. Dixon and other Rangers helped counties organize aircraft-warning programs. At 8:30 a.m. on Wednesday, February 4, 1942, Dixon picked up C. C. Cook at the governor's office and drove to San Marcos, where they conferred with the county judge and the organizer for the county aircraft-warning system. By 10:25 a.m. they were in New Braunfels meeting with the county judge, county aircraft-warning-system organizers, and an official of the U.S. Employment Service. They held similar meetings in Seguin, at 11:35 a.m., Floresville, at 2:10 p.m., Karnes City, at 3:15 p.m., and Beeville, at 4:45 p.m. They covered six more South Texas counties on Thursday and four on Friday before returning to Austin. The next week they held aircraft-warning-system meetings throughout southeast Texas, including Houston and Corpus Christi.[20]

Americans were worried enough about sabotage that in a Gallup poll in February 1942 two-thirds of the respondents supported requiring all Americans to carry an identification card that contained a picture and fingerprints. In March FBI chief J. Edgar Hoover warned the American people that foreign agents "bored like termites deep into our social structure with a brazenness that was as daring as the blitzes of Hitler's blood-crazed forces." But a month later the *Dallas Morning News* carried this headline: "Sabotage Damage Light in This War." Late in the war, the FBI reported that there had been "no successful foreign-directed act of sabotage to date," and that most acts labeled sabotage "were due to spite, carelessness, juvenile mischief and similar reasons." Nevertheless, the FBI investigated almost twenty thousand cases of reported sabotage. Many, perhaps most, might hardly have been noticed in peacetime but looked suspicious in wartime.[21]

Dixon rarely mentions incidents of possible sabotage in his diaries. In July 1941, while stationed in Goldthwaite, he investigated the "subversive egging of army convoy." In September 1942 he met with Lt. Harold V. Johnson in Sherman regarding information the lieutenant had received that subversive elements might be using prostitutes to incapacitate troops. He passed the information on to two FBI agents in Sherman. In November 1943 he investigated a report of an attempted sabotage of the Frisco Bridge a few miles above Dallas, interviewing the farmer who called in the complaint, examining the bridge, and searching for the "hobo" sighted at the bridge. On April 28, 1944, Dixon flew to Marshall, where he joined the other Rangers of Company B on a confidential assignment to keep pump stations, storage tanks, and petroleum pipelines from the East Texas oil fields under surveillance to prevent reported "contemplated" sabotage.[22]

During the war Texans worried about escapees not just from military guardhouses but also from state prisons and prisoner-of-war (POW) camps. Owing at least partly to a shortage of correctional guards, 255 prisoners escaped from the Texas State Penitentiary during the war. A far smaller number of POWs held in camps within the United States escaped during the war—142 out of nearly 500,000 Axis prisoners, mostly Germans. Only about two dozen of these escapes occurred in Texas. Of the approximately five hundred POW camps in the United States, seventy were in Texas, and these held up to fifty thousand prisoners at any given time. Many of the large camps, known as base camps, were built on existing military bases and could hold up to several thousand prisoners. Base camps were responsible for several smaller branch camps, which were set up for specific work projects, such as agriculture, mining, and logging.

POWs were surprised that they were fed beef, tomatoes, green vegetables, milk, and coffee—items some had not tasted in years. The reasoning was that treating them well would result in fewer discipline problems and efforts to escape and would improve the likelihood that U.S. POWs overseas were treated well. The strategy worked: only a tiny percentage of prisoners escaped, some doing so simply out of boredom, wandering away from their work party and being recaptured quickly in nearby towns. None remained at large longer than three weeks, and no civilians were hurt during any of the escapes.[23]

From 1:30 to 3:00 a.m. on February 19, 1944, Dixon patrolled North Texas highways for German POWs who had escaped from McAlester, Oklahoma, and allegedly were heading for Mexico. At 3:00 a.m. he contacted officials at Durant, Oklahoma, and learned that the escapees had been recaptured. On April 24 he was in Gainesville responding to the escape of five German POWs two days earlier from nearby Camp Howze, which held up to three thousand prisoners. Three had been recaptured earlier, and the remaining two were apprehended that day. On May 24 Dixon joined other Rangers in the vicinity of Bastrop, east of Austin, searching for Hans Jung and Heinz Daberko, POW escapees from Camp Swift. Well past midnight, the officers briefly sighted the escapees near railroad tracks. Bloodhounds picked up the trail and led the officers to a hideout in the brush, where Dixon, four other Rangers, and three highway patrolmen caught the escapees at 3:20 a.m. In a letter to Colonel Garrison, R. C. Suran, the FBI special agent in charge of the San Antonio office, wrote regarding Dixon and the other Rangers, "The cooperation and assistance that they rendered in this matter was invaluable." At 8:00 p.m. on February 5, 1945, Dixon joined state, county, federal, and military officials in search of four German POWs who, earlier that day, had escaped from Camp Swift. Dixon was posted at a railroad trestle crossing the Colorado River south of Bastrop. The escapees were caught and returned to military authorities where they were interrogated. Dixon participated in the interrogation or witnessed it. He returned to Austin at 4:45 a.m.[24]

Dixon had major military bases in his eight-county subdistrict. Perrin Field, near Denison and Sherman, in Grayson County and close to the Oklahoma border, was the first basic flight-training school to open in Texas after the Pearl Harbor attack in December 1941. Its 2,500 enlisted men and 300 officers trained about ten thousand student pilots during the war. Camp Howze, situated on almost sixty thousand acres near Gainesville in Cooke County, was established in August 1942 as an infantry training camp with a capacity of almost forty thousand men. Several hundred thousand received their training at the camp during the war. POW facilities also were on the site. As a result, troops endured grueling training while nearby POWs played soccer.[25]

Near Greenville, in Hunt County, was Majors Army Airfield, situated on two thousand acres with as many as five thousand pilots, support personnel, and civilian employees. One day during the war Dixon picked up three British pilots who were in training at Majors Field and hitching a ride into Dallas for the weekend. One of them told Dixon that he "wanted to be one of the famous Texas Rangers," that in England "we read more about the Rangers than we do about the Royal Canadian Mounted Police." On March 4, 1943, a heavily overcast day, two pilots from Majors Field were killed in crashes, one near Kaufman, more than forty miles south of Greenville, and the other about twenty-five miles southwest of Kaufman. Around midnight two other cadets, named Kelley and Heinrich, having lost their way on a cross-country flight from Majors Field, landed their planes in a field near McKinney. Dixon had spent the day in Denison and Sherman searching for a deserter and had apprehended Mildred Fay Howard, charging her with harboring the deserter. Heading home to McKinney when he learned of the crash landing, Dixon drove to the site and helped them for three or four hours. In his diary he wrote, "4:00 a.m. retired."[26]

A few months later Dixon had another opportunity to assist troops needing help. One mile north of McKinney was the 1,520-bed Ashburn General Hospital, 110 buildings spread over 266 acres, which the U.S. Army had opened in the summer of 1943 to receive sick and wounded soldiers from all overseas battlefronts as well as ill and injured soldiers from Texas training camps. The hospital was staffed with about eighty officers, 165 nurses, and approximately six hundred enlisted men in the medical department. On Sunday, September 19, 1943, two troop trains with Pullman cars especially equipped to carry war casualties, pulled into McKinney. Dixon spent several hours helping unload more than five hundred military casualties destined for the hospital.[27]

Sacrificing part of a Sunday was a small price for Dixon to pay to help in the war effort, but this was a war in which all Americans were called upon to do their part to ensure that the troops were well fed and equipped. The U.S. War Production Board halted the production of new automobiles for civilian use (the last automobile chassis rolled off the assembly line on February 10, 1942) and the manufacture of radios, refrigerators, vacuum cleaners, washing machines, and similar products. The board even banned men's double-breasted suits, vests, trouser cuffs, and patch pockets. Some commodities, such as gasoline, automobile tires, coffee, sugar, meat, cheese, fats, butter, and canned foods, were rationed. When Dixon, living in McKinney, ordered a pair of boots from the Nocona Boot Company, an iconic boot maker in Nocona, Texas, he had to mail them a shoe-ration stamp. When the war (and rationing) ended, Leona and Norman Dixon's last ration books still contained all the coffee stamps but only one sugar stamp. The Dixons were not coffee drinkers, but they each had a sweet tooth.

Some items not rationed—including brand-name cigarettes (Dixon, a chain-smoker, sometimes rolled his own), soft drinks (Coca-Cola in particular), candy bars (Hershey's), toilet paper, diapers, and nylon hose—suffered from severe shortages, which could cause a spike in prices. In 1944, when Dixon and other Company B Rangers ran into a shortage of rope and twine, he wrote to a deputy U.S. marshal on the border in Del Rio asking if he could "pick up a couple of Mexican grass (maguey) ropes at a near normal price" the next time he went across the river. Shortages of workers also caused problems. When Dixon shipped a hat to a hat-renovating company in Houston, the company returned it, explaining that because they were "so short of experienced help" they were unable to service his hat. After the war a Texas magazine reported that a Dallas department store advertised one thousand pair of "genuine nylon hose" for sale to ladies "with sufficient bravery and reckless abandon to venture to enter the contest for the stocking. It is not recorded how many casualties occurred during the resulting scramble, but suffice it to say, there were many bruises, some skinned knuckles and a lot of blasted hopes."[28]

Texans did not seem particularly perturbed that they could not find nylon hose or buy wartime Fords or Chevys. The one item whose rationing garnered opposition from the start, including from Gov. Coke Stevenson, was gasoline. The fact that Texans, in the largest state in the Union, drove greater distances than drivers in most other states, together with the fact that the state produced massive amounts of oil and gas, made the restrictions seem punitive, particularly given that gasoline was rationed not to save oil and gas but to save rubber. In a radio address to Texans, Governor Stevenson said, "Gasoline is the 1943 counterpart of the rifle, the ax, and the saddle which our fathers used a century ago." He said he had voiced objection to imposing gasoline rationing on Texans "by persons who had no understanding of our conditions and made no investigation." However, despite resistance from Texans and other Americans, Pres. Franklin D. Roosevelt announced that full gas rationing would begin December 1, 1942, "to support our fighting forces." William M. Jeffers, the rubber director of the War Production Board, stated that civilians "must conserve our tires" because the military "must have rubber." The nation's cars and trucks, he said, "are going to have to run from now until mid-1944 on the tires now in use. . . . That's the reason for the thirty-five-mile speed limit and for periodic tire inspection."[29]

There were several categories of gasoline ration books, depending on motorists' needs. Most motorists received "A" ration books, but as a peace officer, Dixon was eligible for "C" ration books, allowing greater amounts of gasoline, which could be purchased only by handing the service-station operator the ration book for him to tear out the perforated coupons. Lewis W. Bailey, involved in setting up the tire-conservation program in Texas, told peace officers that they should "not take advantage of their privilege." He acknowledged that sometimes they would need to drive above the thirty-five mile speed limit but cautioned, "Don't abuse it because it wears out tires." At 4:30 p.m. on November 30, 1942, the day prior to the lowered speed limit, Dixon noted in his diary that he exceeded thirty-five miles per hour in running down a car that he thought contained a fugitive. Instead the passengers were federal officers.[30]

Dixon's state cars did not fare well during the war years. Based on entries in his diaries, his car, Unit HQ 64, was in the repair shop six times between March 20, 1943, and April 7, 1944, when it broke down for the last time. Three days later he and Rangers Bob Crowder and R. L. Badgett drove their cars, Units 64, 71, and 72, in a caravan from Dallas to Austin. There they turned in their vehicles, and the next morning Dixon left Austin in his new vehicle, HQ 25-B. On the following day in McKinney, he cleaned, washed, and polished it to remove stains that had collected during a long period of standing exposed to the weather before being assigned to him. Unfortunately, polishing HQ 25-B did not make it reliable. It was in the car repair shop thirty-two times between April 11, 1944, and November 29, 1946. After driving the car for only three months, he personally "tightened the body, etc." He had to replace three sets of tires—in June 1945 and in January and November 1946. He had to have tires repaired, usually as the result of a puncture, in November 1944 and in March, April, and August 1945. Among other things, he had the brakes and valves worked on; replaced the shock absorbers, generator, distributor (twice), fuel pump (twice), and battery (twice); and repaired the front end, tailpipe, windshield, rotors, and radiator (twice).[31]

Because of war restrictions, thieves found a stolen-goods market eager for automobiles, tires, and gas coupons. On Tuesday, August 25, 1942, James "Raggedy Pappa" Stark and George Ford were arrested in Gainesville on suspicion of car and tire theft and brought to the jail in Sherman. At 4:00 p.m. Dixon joined Sherman Police Chief Les Tribble, Denison Police Chief Paul Borum, and a highway patrolman in interrogating Stark and Ford, who confessed to stealing four cars and thirty-four tires and committing two burglaries. On Wednesday Dixon took the confession of Johnny "Boy" Thomas, who admitted to tire theft, and interrogated Paul Nelson on the same charge. When O. H. Woodrow, a lawyer, entered the room during the interrogation, Nelson accused Dixon of hitting him. Dr. W. I. Southerland examined Nelson, but found no evidence of abuse. Dixon reported the accusation to Captain Gonzaullas and, with Tribble, filed thirty-one complaints with the district attorney against the prisoners, all of whom had served time in prison for other crimes.[32]

Robert Bruce Wyers was a soldier and, as it turned out, a tire thief. When Dixon was investigating the burglaries of motor companies in Denton and Gainesville in April 1945, he interrogated Private Wyers in Oklahoma City, Oklahoma, where he had been caught with goods from the Denton burglary. Wyers confessed to stealing tires from the two motor companies, transporting the tires across state lines, and selling them to a "fence," James Edward Vancuren, in Oklahoma City. Taking Wyers with him, Dixon located and arrested Vancuren, recovered twelve tires, and took a statement from Vancuren, who was charged with receiving stolen property. In a court-martial Wyers was sentenced to ten years in a federal penitentiary.[33]

Gas-coupon thieves grabbed Dixon's attention during the last year of the war. In February 1945, the *Dallas Morning News* ran an article with the headline, "Gas Scarcity Ups Thefts of Coupons." An April headline read, "Gas Coupon Burglaries Hit New High." In his diary on March 26, Dixon wrote, "Spot checking & contacting informers re series of burglaries throughout North Texas for gas ration coupons." He continued his investigation through April and into May, with the case taking him to Oklahoma and New Mexico. By early May he was focusing on Loron "Country" Seay, Alton Fields, and Ruby Whitlock, alias Ruby Harris. In March, Seay, a federal fugitive with a long criminal record, and Whitlock, whose record included narcotics, robbery with firearms, and kidnapping, had been arrested in Dallas with fifteen thousand gallons worth of coupons stolen from wholesale warehouses in Bonham and Honey Grove, towns in Dixon's subdistrict. Dixon interrogated Whitlock and Fields, but apparently they did not confess to other thefts of gas coupons. Regardless, they were headed to jail, and their specialty, gas-coupon theft, soon would be a thing of the past.[34]

On the morning of August 14, 1945, Dixon was in Decatur with Sheriff Malcolm Branch investigating forgeries committed by prisoner T. A. Davis. In the afternoon he continued the investigation in Lewisville and Denton and returned to Lewisville. Then he drove home, arriving in McKinney at 8:45 p.m. For Dixon this had been a normal workday. But it was not a normal day for Texas or the nation. Beginning at 1:52 a.m. radio networks and stations broadcast news continuously to the largest listening audience in radio history. It was the fifth day, according to the *New York Times,* "of waiting, of rumor, intimation, fact, distortion—five agonizing days." Finally, at 6:00 p.m. CST, the White House issued the highly anticipated announcement. At that, two million people jammed into Times Square in New York City, and by 6:30, according to the *Dallas Morning News,* thousands had flooded into downtown Dallas, producing "the most blaring, howling mob in recent Dallas history." When the sirens wailed in McKinney, the Dixons' two young sons, nearing their fifth and seventh birthdays, ran to their mother and asked what was happening. Given the news, they excitedly ran to every house in the block, pounding on the doors, yelling to everyone, "The war is over! The war is over!"

The next day was a Wednesday, but not even Dixon went to work. He stayed home on alert for any emergencies growing out of the peace celebrations, which went on throughout the day all over his subdistrict. For the first time in its history, the sheriff's office in Denton was closed, with a deputy standing ready at home to receive any emergencies. Federal workers across the nation were given Wednesday *and* Thursday off with pay. In Dallas and in cities across the country, nearly everything was shut down except the post office and some movie theaters. It was V-J Day, and at long last, it was time to rejoice.[35]

Chapter Eight

RAPE AND RACE

FOUR A.M. MONDAY, NOVEMBER 29, 1943. ON THE OTHER END OF THE line was Sheriff Roy Moore of Denton, who told Norman Dixon that a couple of hours earlier a seventeen-year-old white girl had been raped and her seventeen-year-old boyfriend beaten and robbed by an "unknown negro." Within twenty minutes, Dixon was on the road to Denton. There was no time to waste. A posse of white farmers was already on the manhunt, and Dixon fully understood that he had a clear obligation as a Texas Ranger to take possession of the suspect while he was still alive.[1]

In a book on the social and cultural history of Texas in the twentieth century, John W. Storey and Mary L. Kelley write: "Blacks faced a deep-seated ideology of racism that colored the way most white Texans viewed and reacted to them. Such racism was so endemic to life in Texas that few white Texans consciously analyzed it." According to historian Robert M. Utley, "Racial subordination, segregation, discrimination, and deference—Jim Crow—were simply unquestioned features of Texan culture, and any perceived violation of the social order could instantly transform white Texans into savages." The system of white supremacy was enforced in Texas through laws, customs, and practices. Blacks had separate libraries, restrooms, drinking fountains, health facilities, and schools. Hospitals and prisons were segregated. There were no medical schools and only one state-supported college for blacks. They could not eat in most restaurants, stay in hotels, or go to the movie theater, although in some cities they could sit in the balcony. They could buy clothes in a department store but could not try them on. Blacks could not serve on juries, and the vast majority was denied the right to vote. Few of the 924,391 blacks living in Texas in 1940 (15 percent of the population) graduated from high school. Most worked in menial jobs and lived in poverty.

Perceived violations of the laws, customs, and practices of white supremacy could quickly lead to race riots and lynchings, which were common throughout the South late in the nineteenth century and during the first decades of the twentieth century. Only Georgia and Mississippi lynched more blacks than Texas over the years. In Texas, almost 200 blacks were lynched between 1883 and 1903 and another 171 from 1904 to 1930.[2]

On May 9, 1930, a black man named George Hughes was on trial in Sherman for raping a white woman in Grayson County. Four Rangers, including Capt. Frank Hamer, National Guardsmen from Denison, and the local sheriff and his deputies were present to protect the prisoner from the mob that filled the courtroom, the courthouse, and the streets. When the rape victim was brought to the courthouse by ambulance and into the courtroom by stretcher, the white mob went wild and demanded that the prisoner be handed over to them. The judge, realizing that the officers were unable to control the mob despite the use of tear gas, had the prisoner removed to a steel and concrete vault in the district clerk's office. That proved to be his death sentence: the mob set fire to the courthouse, burning through the fifty-year-old dry wood interior. When the mob slashed the fire hoses, efforts to put out the fire proved fruitless. As Hughes was suffocating and roasting to death inside the vault, additional guardsmen and peace officers from nearby counties were called in. Realizing the officers were only firing into the air, the mob cut their way into the vault, where they found Hughes's body. The corpse was taken ten blocks to a black section of Sherman and hung from a tree. A large pile of wood was constructed below the swinging corpse and set on fire as two thousand white men, women, and children watched. Other mob members started nine more fires in the black section of town.

More military units and Rangers, including Lone Wolf Gonzaullas, arrived to maintain order and apprehend the mob leaders. The mayor of Sherman claimed that the mob was not from Sherman but from nearby rural communities "and from Oklahoma!" Twenty-nine members of the mob were jailed, fourteen were indicted, and one was convicted—only because his trial was held in Austin, far from Sherman, where no white man could have been found guilty.

At Honey Grove, in Fannin County, nine days after the burning of the Sherman courthouse, George Johnson, a black farmhand, killed his white overseer in a dispute over debt. As a crowd watched, officers killed Johnson by firing up to two thousand bullets into the cabin where he was barricaded. When the officers removed the dead Johnson from the cabin, the crowd grabbed him and dragged him facedown across a muddy field. He was chained to the back of a car and dragged to the black section of Honey Grove, where he was hung head down from a tree limb, doused with gasoline, and set on fire.[3]

In 1930, white supremacists in Grayson and Fannin Counties were not interested in law and order when it came to Jim Crow violations, nor did they particularly care if the black violator was dead or alive when they strung him up and set him on fire. The question was not whether the accused would die, but who would carry out the sentence. Sometimes lawmen won; sometimes the mob was victorious. When Dixon, whose subdistrict included Grayson and Fannin Counties, received his 4:00 a.m. phone call on November 29, he was well aware of the ugly history of white mob violence against blacks in Texas and in his subdistrict, and whatever he might not have understood when he transferred to Company B he certainly would have learned from Captain Gonzaullas.

The efforts of Texas white supremacists in Congress to block antilynching bills required their constant vigilance. In 1940 the *Sheriff's Association of Texas Magazine* credited U.S. Senator Tom Connally of Texas with leading the fight year after year. The argument against these bills was that in recent years Texas officers had succeeded in preventing lynchings. But the argument was undermined two years later when a white woman accused Willie Vinson, a black man, of having raped her. Shot while being captured, Vinson was hospitalized in Texarkana. A white mob yanked him out of his hospital bed, dragged him behind an automobile to a cotton gin, and there lynched him. Governor Stevenson took no action on the basis that outrageous crimes by blacks could result in mob violence.[4]

At 1:00 p.m. on June 16, 1943, a year after the lynching of Vinson and several months before Dixon's 4:00 a.m. phone call, Dixon climbed into state vehicle HQ 47 with Captain Gonzaullas and other Company B Rangers to assist in riot duty in Beaumont, where racial tensions had exploded and a huge white mob was on the rampage. Beaumont was a wartime boomtown. With people moving in to take jobs in the shipyards, oil refineries, and war plants, in three short years the city had grown from a population of 59,000 to about 80,000, one-third black. The largest employer, Pennsylvania Shipyards, employed 8,500 men building and repairing cargo and Liberty ships. The fast growth led to forced integration, with the races living close together because of housing shortages, working together in skilled as well as unskilled jobs, and riding together in crowded buses and transport trucks back and forth between the city and the shipyard or plant. Several incidents occurred on buses because whites insisted that blacks stay in the overcrowded black sections to prevent contact between black men and white women. In one incident a black military policeman's knees protruded into the white section, a violation of Jim Crow. When he refused to move, the resultant confrontation led to his being shot four times by Beaumont policemen. Somehow he recovered, and the federal district attorney in Beaumont conducted an investigation, but a grand jury of local citizens exonerated the Beaumont officers.

Racial tensions in Beaumont worsened on June 4, 1943, when Curtis Thomas, a young black man, beat and raped an eighteen-year-old white telephone operator. Police captured him after shooting him several times. A mob gathered outside the hospital calling for Thomas, but when Police Chief Ross Dickey convinced them that he was dying, they dispersed. Thomas did die four days later, but on Tuesday, June 15, another white woman claimed a black man had raped her and a manhunt began. With rumors flying around the Pennsylvania Shipyards, about two thousand white workers marched from the plant to downtown Beaumont, joined by perhaps another thousand along the way. They reached the police station prepared to lynch the alleged perpetrator, but he was not there. When some went to the county jail, the sheriff escorted them through the facilities to prove the accused rapist was not there either. By midnight the mob, now numbering nearly five thousand, began rioting in the black sections of town, beating every black encountered, burning stores and cars, looting goods, and breaking into two hundred homes. Several hundred of the mob, discovering fifty-two black draftees waiting at the depot for a bus to take them home, attacked them with iron pipes and other weapons, injuring many, one of whom later died. Another black getting off work was shot and died.[5]

One hundred and fifty Beaumont National Guardsmen were called up during the rampage. On Wednesday morning, as scattered white mobs continued to attack blacks wherever they could be found, city and county officials asked the state for more help. Eight cars loaded with highway patrolmen headed for Beaumont from various Texas cities. At the same time, Ranger Capt. Hardy B. Purvis with his Company A Rangers drove up from Houston and Captain Gonzaullas, Dixon, and other Company B Rangers came from Dallas. Additional Rangers arrived from the headquarters company. Because few employees showed up for work, the Pennsylvania Shipyards shut down for the day. The city closed its swimming pools and playgrounds. Movie theaters, restaurants, and many businesses did not open their doors. Liquor stores and beer parlors were shut down. The jail and police headquarters were barricaded with barbed wire and protected by Army National Guardsmen with fixed bayonets and submachine guns. And roadblocks were set up to prevent mobs from coming in from nearby towns.[6]

At 5:55 p.m. on Wednesday, in the absence of Governor Stevenson, who was on a train headed to Washington, D.C., Acting Gov. A. M. Aiken declared martial law in Beaumont. At 7:00 p.m., when Gonzaullas, Dixon, and the other Company B Rangers arrived, a total of twenty-four hundred Guardsmen, highway patrolmen, Rangers, and police and sheriff's deputies were protecting the city. Dixon spent the evening answering alarm calls and enforcing the 8:30 p.m. curfew. Gonzaullas's tactic, which other officers copied, was to walk up to a cluster of men and ask, "What are you doing here on the street?" When told they were there to protect their families, he would look around and say, "I don't see your families. Aren't they with you?" Learning they were at their homes, he would tell them quietly but firmly that they had five minutes to head home. They obeyed.[7]

The ferocity of the white mobs led blacks to flee the city, about a thousand on foot and another fifteen hundred in automobiles. Other blacks hid in vacant lots or clustered together in homes, some in the homes of white families, where they worked as servants. Although fifty to sixty injured blacks were in hospitals, many others were afraid to go to a hospital. By Thursday the city was peaceful and close to normal activity, although it had the appearance of a military zone. Three hundred mob members were in jail, and authorities had confiscated 156 pistols, 36 shotguns, 44 rifles, 43 clubs, 11 brass knuckles, a large quantity of ammunition, and other items, such as hammers and pipes.[8]

Continuing his riot duty and enforcement of the curfew, Dixon spent Friday and Saturday watching shipyard workers as they went on and off shift duty and guarding black employees as they stood in line to receive their paychecks. On Sunday he was back in Beaumont, and even though martial law was lifted that day, he remained on riot duty until Tuesday, June 22, when he and Captain Gonzaullas returned to Dallas. In Beaumont twenty-nine rioters were charged with loitering, drunkenness, or carrying firearms and fined $30.20 each. The rest were released for lack of evidence. No one was punished for the blacks who died. On Wednesday, June 16, the day after the rioting, a leading Beaumont physician had examined the woman who had charged that a black man raped her. She had not had sexual relations within twenty-four hours of the alleged assault.[9]

A little more than five months later, on the afternoon of Sunday, November 28, a seventeen-year-old boy and his seventeen-year-old girlfriend, a student at Texas State College for Women in Denton, stopped on a country road five miles northeast of Denton to listen to the car radio. A black man approached the car and asked for money. When the boy began to get out of the car, the man pulled a gun and knife and forced the couple to walk to a ravine, where he stabbed the boy in the arm and shoulder, causing him to pass out. The assailant grabbed the girl and carried her a short distance, struck her with the pistol, and raped her. Returning to the car, he took the boy's tan coat from the car and tried to burn his own coat. He held the couple captive until past dark, when the girl ran to a farmhouse for help.[10]

When Dixon received his 4:00 a.m. phone call from Sheriff Roy Moore that an "unknown negro" had raped a seventeen-year-old white girl and assaulted and robbed her male companion, he grabbed his khakis, boots, and hat and dressed quickly. He was on the road by 4:20 and in Denton by 5:00. He joined the manhunt, scouring Denton, Collin, and Grayson Counties for the next eleven and one-half hours. He had two goals: apprehend the assailant and protect him from mob violence. Receiving word that the suspect had been seen near Aubrey, he drove north, through Aubrey to Tioga, Pilot Point, and Whitesboro, checking with railway section crews and agents along the way. Driving back, he was called to Celina, where he joined Sheriffs Button and Moore to follow up on information that the assailant had been seen at Mobley's Place. He started to stake out the area when he received a further tip that took him to some woods that he searched for tracks.

In midafternoon, receiving word that the attacker had been identified, Dixon rushed to Denton to search for records on "Allen Murray." In the meantime, City Marshal C. P. Nicholson and two farmers found Murray, wearing the boy's tan coat, near Pilot Point, north of Denton. Murray fired four wild shots at them and threatened them with a knife. While the marshal pointed his gun at Murray, Adolph Jurecka, one of the farmers, took Murray's gun and knife, and then they transported him to the Tioga Jail. As soon as Dixon was notified, he rushed to Tioga, took Murray into his custody, and called Sheriff Moore. With Moore, Dixon took the offender to the Dallas County Jail for safekeeping. His two goals had been accomplished. In the meantime, the two victims were taken to the Denton Hospital, where they would recover from their wounds. Over the next several days, Dixon worked with Sheriff Moore and District Attorney Earl Coleman gathering evidence for the case. On December 3 he drove to Austin, taking Murray's clothing, pistol, and knife to the state crime lab.[11]

On December 8, nine days after the alleged crimes, Murray was indicted by a Denton County grand jury on two charges. The first, robbery with firearms, was that he violently assaulted the male, used a pistol against him, and took from him twelve dollars and his billfold, valued at one dollar. The second charge, rape, was that he "did then and there by force, threats and fraud, and without the consent of the said [girlfriend], ravish and have carnal knowledge of her." The names of both victims were used throughout court documents, but in keeping with journalistic practice, only the boy's name appeared in the numerous newspaper accounts. The rape victim's name would have been known by reporters and countless other people, including county officials and peace officers such as Dixon, but it was kept out of the press.

On December 11 Murray was brought into district court for arraignment. Deeming the defendant too poor to afford an attorney, the court appointed T. B. Davis as his counsel. The arraignment document, signed by Judge B. W. Boyd, states that Murray "had been duly served with a copy of the indictment herein at least two entire days prior to the present day." The indictment was read aloud to the defendant, and, "He was asked whether he was guilty or not." Murray pleaded guilty.

Late on December 13 Dixon returned Murray to the Denton County Jail to allow his court-appointed attorney to talk to him prior to the December 16 trial. Attorney Davis was not pleased; the justice system was moving too swiftly. According to sworn depositions, Davis said he was able to meet with the defendant twice on December 14, two days prior to the trial. The first meeting lasted two minutes, the second about five minutes. Murray told Davis he had escaped from a penitentiary in Oklahoma about sixty days earlier, spending the past thirty days in Dallas and Denton Counties, and he gave Davis the address of an aunt who lived in Oklahoma City. Davis wrote to the aunt that day, informing her of the charges.[12]

Allan Murray (Murry Allen), still wearing the tan coat he took from the boy he stabbed, being held in Denton by Sheriff Roy Moore, rear left, and other authorities. *Author's Collection.*

On December 16 the jury was selected and the trial began on the rape indictment. In his diary Dixon wrote, "With Capt. M. T. G. & Rangers Crowder, Daniel, Rusk, Badgett & Tully Seay assisting Roy Moore, sheriff, in guarding Allen Murray against bodily harm & prevention of mob violence at his trial for the rape of. . . ." Among those testifying that day were the two victims, farmer Adolph Jurecka, Sheriff Roy Moore, Ranger Norman Dixon, and Glen McLaughlin from the state crime lab. Once again the defendant pleaded guilty. At about 11:00 p.m. Davis received a phone call from a Reverend Thompson, a black pastor in Oklahoma City, who told him Murray had escaped from the insane asylum for Negroes at Taft, Oklahoma, not the state penitentiary. Shortly after midnight Davis learned from the superintendent of the asylum that the institution did have an "Allen Murray" who in his opinion was permanently insane and had been so for many years, and who had escaped from the asylum about sixty days earlier. The superintendent said neither he nor one of his doctors could appear at the trial that day.[13]

When the trial resumed a few hours later, Davis explained what he had learned overnight and asked both that Murray's plea be changed to "not guilty" and that he be granted a continuance of the trial to give him time to gather information on Murray's mental condition and to locate pertinent witnesses either to appear in court or to give depositions. He wanted to find a psychiatrist—there were none in Denton County—who could examine the defendant, and he wanted the testimony of doctors involved in the lunacy hearing in Oklahoma City. Judge Boyd accepted the change of plea to "not guilty" but overruled the request for a continuance. Dr. M. L. Hutcheson, the county health officer, who had talked to Murray on the day of his arrest, testified that he believed the defendant was of sound mind. Murray did not testify.

In his instructions to the jury, Judge Boyd explained that if the jury found the defendant guilty of the charge of rape, the penalty assessed could be death, life in prison, or for a term of not less than five years. He also explained that since the court of Oklahoma County had adjudged the defendant to be insane, the jury must find not only that he did commit the crime but that "he had sufficient reason and mental capacity to know the nature and consequences of his act and to know that he was doing wrong and to know the right and the wrong of the particular transaction." At 3:30 p.m. the jury retired to deliberate. At 3:38 it returned with the verdict that Murray was guilty of rape and gave him the death penalty.[14]

Attorney Davis petitioned the court to set aside the verdict of the jury and grant a new trial on grounds that the court erred in not granting a continuance and that the jury's verdict was not supported by the evidence. On December 24 the judge overruled the motion for a new trial. Davis petitioned the Court of Criminal Appeals to revise or reverse the district-court judgment, but on May 10, 1944, the appeals court determined that there had been no error in judgment, which it affirmed in writing to the Denton County district court on October 13. On October 19 Judge Boyd brought Allen Murray back into the courtroom, explained to him that the motion for a new trial had been overruled and that the appeals court had affirmed the district court's judgment, and he asked if Murray had anything to say why the sentence should not be carried out. He replied that he had nothing to say. The judge turned custody of Murray back to the sheriff "to be by him safely kept" and ordered the district-court clerk to issue a warrant to the warden of the state penitentiary at Huntsville to execute the sentence on December 1, 1944. The sheriff was ordered to transport the prisoner to Huntsville prior to the execution date. On that date, "anytime before the hour of sunrise," ruled the judge, "the said warden shall execute such warrant, by causing to pass through the body of the said defendant, Allen Murray, a current of electricity of sufficient intensity to cause death and the application and continuance of said current of electricity through the body of such defendant, Allen Murray, so convicted, until such defendant, Allen Murray, is dead."

Attorney Davis petitioned the governor's office for a reprieve, resulting in a thirty-day stay of execution, and to the State Board of Pardons and

Paroles for a commutation of the sentence to life imprisonment, which was denied. On December 31, 1944, H. E. Moore, warden at the Huntsville prison, signed a document stating he had received the death warrant and Allen Murray from the Denton County sheriff on October 19—the day of the judge's order—and had "duly executed" Allen Murray at 12:20 a.m. on December 31 "by causing to pass through his body a current of electricity of sufficient intensity to cause his death." His body, the document stated, was buried in the prison cemetery on December 31, 1944.[15]

Murray was buried at Huntsville because his Oklahoma family could not afford to bury him. Denton County was responsible for paying $25.00 for the costs of feeding Murray while he was on death row, $10.00 dollars for the casket, $8.92 for clothing, and $1.00 for a tombstone, which would have read "Allen Murray," as did all Denton County and State of Texas records regarding the case—but not Oklahoma records obtained by Attorney Davis and placed in Denton County records. According to the order admitting Murray to the Oklahoma state hospital for the Negro insane and the physician's certification that he was insane, both signed on July 15, 1943, his name was "Murry Allen."[16]

A little more than two years later, on February 7, 1946, Dixon, with Captain Gonzaullas and Rangers Crowder, Daniel, and Dick Oldham, joined with the Henderson County sheriff and two of his deputies to transport Clyde Moore, a twenty-one-year-old black man, from the Dallas County Jail, where he was being held for safekeeping to Athens in Henderson County, where a grand jury indicted him for raping a fourteen-year-old white girl on February 4. After the grand jury completed its action, they brought Moore back to the Dallas County Jail. In his diary, Dixon wrote, "Mob violence feared."

On February 25 the defendant requested a change of venue, stating he could not receive a fair trial in Henderson County, as shown by the need for Texas Rangers and other officers to protect him from mob violence when he appeared before the grand jury, and in addition that the special venire (jury pool) of two hundred and fifty men "has been summoned and no man on the venire is his color." The district attorney responded by stating there was no threat of mob violence and no prejudice against the defendant in the county. The motion was denied, and the trial was held in Athens, the county seat. Moore had signed a confession, and the jury convicted him, giving him the death penalty for raping the white girl. Moore's attorney, E. A. Landman, asked for a new trial based on the fact that no blacks were on the special venire, the prejudice against him was prevalent, and the trial should have been moved. The motion was denied. The governor did issue a thirty-day stay, stating that such reprieves had become standard practice, but the Board of Pardons and Paroles refused to commute his sentence to life imprisonment, and Clyde Moore was executed at 12:13 a.m. on May 8, 1946, three months after the crime had been committed.[17]

Walter Crowder Young, a twenty-seven-year-old mechanic, was scheduled to be executed later the same month for a similar crime—raping a fourteen-year-old white girl. Young, Billy Joe Riddle, and James Jett forced a car carrying three white schoolgirls home from a baseball game onto a country road in Dallas County, and each defendant took a turn standing guard while the others each raped a girl. By prearrangement they called each other by numbers rather than their names and left the scene of the crime at a prearranged time. Riddle received a life sentence, and Jett was given a five-year suspended sentence. A campaign was launched to commute Young's death sentence to life in prison on the basis that the other offenders received lighter sentences. The State Board of Pardons and Paroles recommended commutation, and Governor Beauford H. Jester accepted the recommendation, commuting Young's sentence to life in prison. Rangers did not spirit the youths to hidden jails after they were first arrested, nor did they pack the courtroom during the trials to protect them from mob violence. Nor did citizens protest the commutation of Young's death sentence. Young, Riddle, and Jett were white.[18]

More than a quarter-century after Clyde Moore had been executed for raping a fourteen-year-old girl and Young's death sentence for raping a fourteen-year-old girl was commuted, rape would no longer be an offense subject to the death penalty. HB 200 became Texas law in 1973 after the U.S. Supreme Court ruled in *Furman v. Georgia* that capital punishment was being applied in an arbitrary and capricious manner. By then, white supremacy in Texas (and throughout the South) had been largely broken down by a series of court decisions, legislative actions, and societal changes. The history of white supremacy in Texas was brutal and ugly, but it could have been even worse, perhaps much worse, except for Lone Wolf Gonzaullas, Norman Dixon, and other Texas Rangers—all white men in a racist society—who upheld the law and faced down large, threatening mobs while protecting black men accused of heinous crimes.[19]

RED RIVER RANGER

One of Norman Dixon's role models was his chief in the Bureau of Intelligence and his captain in Company B, Lone Wolf Gonzaullas. If Dixon's birth in Vermont was unusual for a future Texas Ranger, Gonzaullas's birth in Cadiz, Spain, was even more so. Born on July 4, 1891, to naturalized U.S. citizens—his father from Spain, his mother, of German descent, from Canada—Gonzaullas was orphaned at age eight when his parents died in the 1900 hurricane that destroyed Galveston. In 1920 he married Laura Isabel Scherer, a petite and lovely woman from New York. They never had children, which led Gonzaullas to take a deep interest in the Boy Scouts, as did Dixon, though he had two sons.

A few months after his marriage, at the age of twenty-nine, and standing only five feet ten and one-half inches in height, Gonzaullas joined the Texas Rangers. Dixon, two inches shorter, also joined the Rangers at the age of twenty-nine. Always well groomed, Gonzaullas customarily wore well-polished custom-made boots and diamonds on his rings, a style Dixon did not emulate. Gonzaullas earned the sobriquet "Lone Wolf" in the North Texas oil fields in the early 1920s, where he became so effective and well-known that wherever he made an appearance, hustlers and gamblers told him they were leaving town immediately, before he had a chance to tell them to leave. His own label for himself during those early Ranger years was "eager beaver."

Gonzaullas left the Rangers three times, in the 1920s and in the 1930s, only to return each time, and in 1935, when the Texas Department of Public Safety was established, Gonzaullas was selected to head up the newly created Bureau of Intelligence. By 1938 the bureau's crime lab ranked second in the United States. The FBI crime lab ranked first—but only, according to Gonzaullas, because it received more funding. Effective February 26, 1940, Gonzaullas moved to Dallas to take over Texas Ranger Company B, serving as its captain until his retirement on July 31, 1951, by which time he had a collection of 580 guns plus assorted knives, daggers, clubs, and such, taken from criminals he had captured, and a tall stack of scrapbooks filled with newspaper clippings of his exploits through the years—a practice Dixon would follow.

Capt. M. T. "Lone Wolf" Gonzaullas in a classic pose. *Author's Collection.*

He also had high words of praise from his boss, Col. Homer Garrison: "He's the finest, most fearless and efficient gentleman I ever served with."[1]

Gonzaullas and Dixon were opposites in some ways. Gonzaullas was vain in his appearance—to the extent of trying to look taller with high-heeled boots and a tall hat—and possessed a strong outgoing personality that could dominate a room. Dixon was modest to an extreme, never seeking attention and often blending into the background. Gonzaullas courted attention; Dixon avoided it. But Dixon was one of "his boys," as the childless Gonzaullas called his Company B Rangers, and the captain gave his boys a great amount of independence, expecting them to handle their counties without his help. He told Ranger Lewis Rigler not to call with little problems, but to call if he shoots someone, and to be available in case of emergency. Otherwise, "Good-bye."[2]

Norman Dixon, as a new member of Company B, likely received the same message from Gonzaullas at the end of their two-day meeting on August 4–5, 1942. On August 6 he was on his own. In the 1940s his subdistrict counties were all rural. With a population barely topping nine thousand, McKinney, thirty-four miles northeast of Dallas, was the largest town in Collin County. Frisco, about twelve miles west of McKinney, had a population of about seven hundred. Twelve miles north of Frisco was Celina, with around one thousand residents, and fifteen miles to the east of McKinney was Farmersville, with fewer than two thousand citizens. Plano's two thousand lived a dozen miles south of McKinney.[3]

The most populous county in Dixon's subdistrict was Grayson County, which bordered on the Red River, across from Oklahoma, with a population of seventy thousand, almost half living in two cities, Denison and Sherman (the county seat). Montague and Wise Counties, on the western edge of Dixon's subdistrict, had the smallest populations, around twenty thousand each. Six of the eight counties lost population between 1940 and 1950, but in the same decade the population in Dallas County increased dramatically, from under four hundred thousand to more than six hundred thousand. Texas was on its way to becoming an urban state.[4]

A month after Dixon became responsible for the eight North Texas counties, Captain Gonzaullas gave a talk to the Lions Club in Texarkana. The Ranger of 1942, he explained, had to be well versed in modern crime-detection methods. He had to write up all his criminal investigations in great detail, including findings on ballistics, fingerprinting, and plaster casts. He had to cope with murderers, gangs of thieves, and cattle rustlers. He had to be well equipped, able to pursue criminals who had high-powered vehicles with modern radio systems and who carried sawed-off shotguns and machine guns. He had to step in not caring whose toes he steped on when a sheriff is hampered by local politics.[5]

Although he continued to carry the title senior criminal investigator for eleven months after transferring to Company B, Dixon was in every other respect a full-fledged Texas Ranger—a title he officially earned with a promotion on July 1, 1943. His experience in the crime lab provided him all the modern crime-detection methods. He had broken up a gang of oil-field thieves in East Texas, sought cattle rustlers in West Texas, gathered evidence on prisoner abuse by a powerful sheriff on the Gulf coast, and investigated murders in South Texas and the desert near Van Horn. His state vehicle

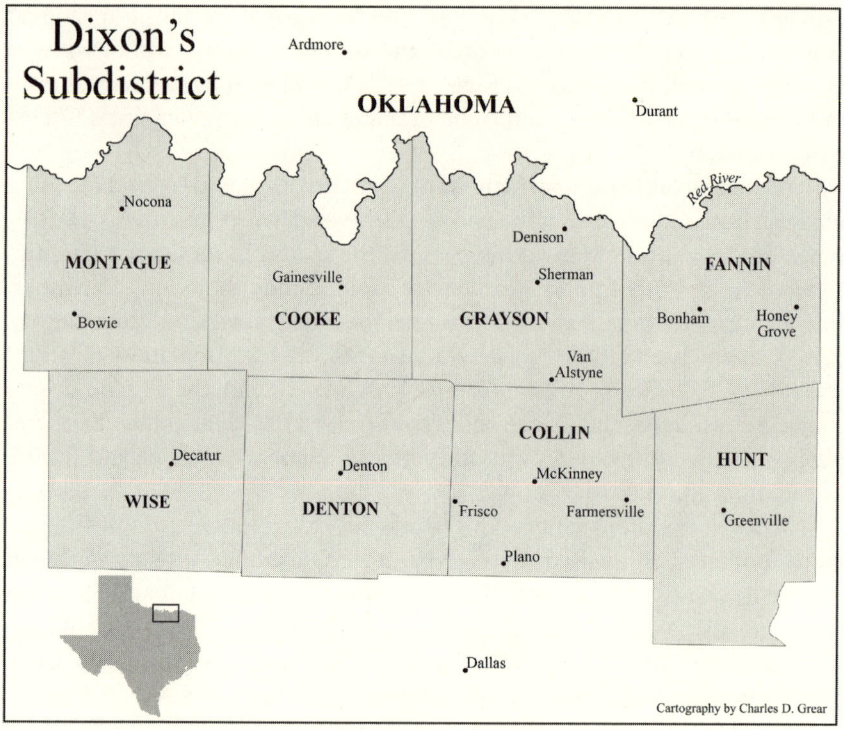

The eight counties in Norman Dixon's subdistrict. *Map courtesy Charles D. Grear.*

contained an assortment of lethal weapons mounted on the inside of each front door. But it was not equipped with a radio system.[6]

The first radio systems were capable of no more than transmitting a message from a headquarters transmitter to a patrol car. In the 1920s, police departments in Detroit and then in Chicago had the nation's first law-enforcement radio systems, but these sent out signals only a few miles from headquarters. Texas relied on the telegraph, telephone, and mail well into the 1930s, but in 1940 the Dallas Police Department began replacing its cumbersome, unreliable shortwave sets with a two-way radio system by installing transmitters in the cars that allowed policemen to send messages to headquarters as well as to receive them. Denison, in Dixon's subdistrict, did the same.[7]

When the Texas Department of Public Safety was created in 1935, the legislature considered but did not fund a comprehensive radio-broadcasting system. In 1939, using volunteers, gifts, and loans, DPS constructed a 500-watt radio transmitter in front of the Ranger horse stables at Camp Mabry, allowing Rangers within Travis County to hear (but not send) messages, and by 1940 DPS had established working agreements with the Gregg and Smith County radio stations. The DPS biennial report for fiscal years 1938–39 and 1939–40 presented a vivid example of the need for two-way communication. "In the conduct of a blockade . . . an officer seeing the fugitives who are being hunted has two alternatives: He may rush in foolishly without assistance in an attempt to make the capture, with the probable result that he will be killed, or he may take a chance on allowing them to escape by letting them out of his sight to scurry to the nearest telephone and flash the recent location of the fugitives to headquarters." Change continued to be slow. In 1941, at its log-cabin headquarters in Fair Park, Company B installed a small transmitter that could broadcast to a car not more than fifteen miles away.[8]

Lewis Rigler, a Ranger who had served as a highway patrolman in Dallas, wrote in his memoir that when a patrolman did not respond to a call in 1941, service stations along the roads he traveled were asked to hang a white cloth to catch his attention. A year later he was equipped with his first two-way radio. "The transmitter," he writes, "required about an eight-foot cane pole wrapped tightly with copper wire." He had to weave his way down streets with low-hanging tree limbs to avoid breaking the pole. "You'd think a drunk was driving," he writes.[9]

On Friday, April 6, 1945, Dixon studied for and took the examination for a "restricted radio telephone operator permit" at the Federal Communications Commission (FCC) office in Dallas. On Saturday Dixon had his picture taken and a Photostat made of his birth certificate; on Monday he gave the photograph and Photostat to the FCC and received his temporary permit. On May 7 he was issued a five-year FCC permit "to operate the classes of radio stations for which this permit is valid under the rules and regulations of the Commission." Dixon's method of communicating with headquarters had been mostly by long-distance telephone or by driving to Dallas. On June 19, 1946, a year after Dixon had received his permit, a transmitter was installed in his car, and the next day it was fitted with a waterproof cover.[10]

As a two-way radio operator, he could communicate with Company B headquarters from his car. In doing so, he used codes, or "signals," standardized by DPS for Rangers and highway patrolmen. For example, "10–1" meant "receiving poorly," and "10–2" meant "receiving well." The quality of reception depended on distance and on interference caused by buildings and terrain between the two transmitters. A "10–1" from Dixon might result in a "10–21" response from headquarters, meaning, "Call this station by telephone." "Acknowledged" was "10–4." "We have prisoner in custody" was "10–15." If he wanted to notify headquarters he had arrived at the scene, he would call in a "10–97." By September 1, 1948, with fifty-one Rangers and four hundred highway patrolmen, DPS had equipped 290 automobiles with radio transmitters and receivers and was operating nine radio-broadcasting stations, ranging from KTXA in Austin with 1,000 watts to Uvalde with 100 watts.[11]

For most of Dixon's service in McKinney he was without two-way radio communications, and certainly without three-way radio, which would have allowed him to communicate with other officers as well as with headquarters. At times, however, he was able to send messages via the McKinney Police Department radio station, KTWP, to the Camp Mabry station, KTXA, as he did on November 27, 1942, requesting a check on license numbers (Code 10–52), and on December 10, checking numbers on stolen tires. Gainesville police, needing Dixon's help at 4:30 a.m. on December 4, radioed the McKinney Police Department, and Officer Alex Burks relayed the message by telephone.

Long-distance telephone calls were an option, particularly in emergencies, but they were expensive and had to be held to a minimum, leaving face-to-face contact as the most common means of communications. Day after day, often seven days a week, Dixon was on the road, making the rounds of his subdistrict. Ranger Joaquin Jackson's lament that he slept little, drove a lot, and spent many days away from home describes Dixon's years in North Texas, as does Ranger historian Mike Cox's statement in *Time of the Rangers*: "Rangers willingly accepted the hard work, long hours, and low pay. Existing in a workaholic culture, they got by on nicotine, caffeine, adrenaline, and the calories from an occasional quick meal."[12]

As an example, on Saturday, January 9, 1943, Dixon left McKinney at 9:00 a.m., driving eastward to Greenville and a meeting with Hunt County Sheriff Frank Wolf and Deputy Duke Harrison regarding burglary cases. Next he investigated un-American activities and Selective Service violation cases in Commerce, Klondike, and Cooper—in Hunt County and adjacent Delta County. In the evening he was back in Commerce and Greenville before returning to McKinney at 10:00 p.m. On Monday he conducted office work in McKinney before leaving at 10:00 a.m., driving west to Denton, Denton County, where he served a burglary warrant on a prisoner. In Decatur he met with Wise County Sheriff Malcolm Branch on several crime issues. In Montague he discussed pending burglary cases with the new sheriff for Montague County, W. B. Henley. By 6:30 p.m. he was in Gainesville meeting with Cooke County Sheriff Carl Wilson and Chief of Police Henry Kirchenbauer regarding burglaries, gambling issues, and other criminal activities. At 9:15 p.m. he met with FBI agent F. W. Doerner in Sherman, Grayson County, regarding an investigation. He returned to McKinney at midnight. On Tuesday he left McKinney at 8:00 a.m. and drove northeast to testify to a Fannin County grand jury in Bonham regarding some burglary cases. By noon he was in Honey Grove, where, with Fannin County Deputies Claude Phillips and George Biggerstaff, he arrested Elbert M. Martin at the request of Collin

County Sheriff W. E. Button. After taking Martin to the Collin County Jail, in McKinney, Dixon headed to Sherman, exceeding the thirty-five-mile speed limit in the hope that a tip he had just received would lead him to Pete Norris, a fugitive. From Sherman he searched for Norris, without success, in Van Alstyne, Blue Ridge, Desert, Trenton, Bells, and points in between. He was back in McKinney at 11:00 p.m.[13]

During those three days Dixon spent time in each of his eight counties, listing in his diary face-to-face contacts with the sheriffs in five counties and deputy sheriffs in a sixth. Sheriffs, the leading local law-enforcement officials in Dixon's subdistrict, were responsible for keeping order, protecting the citizens and their property, preventing crime, arresting lawbreakers, maintaining the county jail, and serving county- and district-court writs, subpoenas, and summonses in civil and criminal matters. For a newly elected sheriff who had never worn a badge or carried a pistol, the responsibilities could be daunting—and salaries were low. As a result, in many counties the sheriff's family lived in an apartment at the jail, and some wives prepared meals for inmates as well as their own family. Dixon, whose long working hours frequently kept him away from home overnight—often noting in his diary "at no expense"—likely stayed in jails many of those nights. Low salaries also meant high turnover among deputy sheriffs—if the sheriff could afford a deputy. Few could afford a receptionist to answer the phone, nor could many afford two-way radios until the 1950s.

When Captain Gonzaullas told Lions Club members in Texarkana that Rangers had to step in when politics prevented sheriffs from acting, he was referring to the sheriffs' vulnerability as elected officials. Every action a sheriff took against a county resident could cost him votes, but a Ranger was not elected, had statewide authority, and was available to provide assistance at any time. At the same time a Ranger could monitor a sheriff's actions and intervene in his affairs. Case in point: Dixon's investigation of Sheriff Harney in Nueces County.

Each of Dixon's eight rural counties had a judge who presided over the district court, which tried felony criminal cases in the county. The district judge, working with the sheriff, would choose five grand-jury commissioners, who in turn selected secret members of the grand jury, which usually had a six-month term. The sheriff and the district attorney—an attorney for the state in district court—would present secret information regarding potential felony cases, and the grand jury would either indict or no bill the individuals charged. Those indicted faced a district-court trial. Dixon testified many times to grand juries and at district-court trials.[14]

Norman Dixon also worked frequently with police chiefs and their officers in his subdistrict. In 1940, Denison, one of his larger towns, with a population of fifteen thousand, had a thirteen-man police force led by Chief of Police Paul Borum. With the town bordering on the Red River, Borum had to deal not only with Texas lawbreakers but also with burglars, robbers and gangsters from Oklahoma. In the twelve months preceding the summer of 1940, the police force jailed more than fifteen hundred individuals and convicted upward of thirteen hundred, including almost seven hundred for drunkenness and two hundred for vagrancy. The two murders, two bank robberies, and one rape were all solved. The police also dealt with 766 dog calls and killed 494 dogs.[15]

As previously noted in this chapter, Dixon met with Henry Kirchenbauer, the Gainesville police chief, on January 11, 1943. Before he became chief, Kirchenbauer had been serving as a constable in Cooke County. Constables served in precincts within a county, and although they had the same powers as a sheriff, they mostly served papers. They had no jails, and most were inexperienced in dealing with violent lawbreakers, which may help explain why more constables—at least twenty-five out of one hundred and thirty nationwide—were killed in Texas than in any other state during the twentieth century. Some constables also served as deputy sheriffs, town marshals, or private security officers, and their precincts, which might cover a town or a rural section of a county, could be confusing. Sometimes these factors led to resentment or jealousy. On December 7, 1946, for example, Dixon received a call from Grayson County Deputy Sheriff Harold Tanner for assistance in handling the Whitesboro constable, Harold Self, who was drunk and had pulled his gun on the town marshal. Dixon drove to Whitesboro and settled the row. Three days later he returned to Whitesboro and was relieved to find that Self was no longer carrying a gun.[16]

Dixon's eight-county jurisdiction gave him wide flexibility in gathering information during investigations and when pursuing lawbreakers. Local officers, by contrast, were limited to a precinct, city limits, or county lines. He worked frequently with FBI agents and sometimes with federal narcotics agents, who could operate across county and state lines, and with state liquor-control officers, who could work statewide. Another peace officer who also had a wide jurisdiction became, in some ways, a partner with Dixon, working with him on many investigations. D. C. Robnett was stationed at Sherman as a special agent for the St. Louis–San Francisco Railway, commonly known as the Frisco. His territory extended from Ft. Worth and Dallas to Sherman and on up to Ardmore and Durant, Oklahoma. An Oklahoma native, Robnett began his law-enforcement career in 1927 with the Okmulgee, Oklahoma, police force as its first fingerprint expert. Two years later he gained some fame by handcuffing "Pretty Boy" Floyd. By 1933, when he went to work for the Frisco, he had risen to assistant police chief.

With its independently operated subsidiaries, the Frisco system contained almost six thousand miles of track, most in Oklahoma and Missouri but more than six hundred miles in Texas. Each railroad in Texas had its own police department whose inspectors, special agents, and special officers were authorized to conduct investigations connected to the operation of the railroad. The State of Texas commissioned Robnett and other railway police officers to operate as peace officers within their territories in the state, and few territories were more important to Robnett than Dixon's subdistrict. In the 1920s Denison, a few miles from Sherman, had the largest freight yards in the country south of Chicago. In 1939 a superintendent with a railroad company based in Galveston wrote, "The Railway Police Officer is in a position to frequently render valuable assistance to other officers and this is becoming better realized." An article on Robnett in 1945 stated, "He lends whatever aid he can to local officers, especially in tracking down persons suspected of operating on both sides of the Texas-Oklahoma border."[17]

Although Dixon had consulted with Robnett on earlier occasions, they partnered for the first time on November 25, 1942, when they traveled undercover to Van Alstyne and Denison to investigate a widespread car-theft and burglary ring. On the evening of November 30, after driving from Sherman with FBI agent F. W. Doerner Jr., they checked all the "honky-tonks" in and around Denison and into Oklahoma. On the evening of December 2 the three officers worked together again, joining with two Denison police officers.

A break in the case occurred early on the morning of Friday, December 4, when burglars were discovered at work in Gainesville and given chase by police in a northeasterly direction. Dixon was notified at 4:30 a.m. (This is the occasion, previously noted, on which Gainesville police radioed McKinney police, who telephoned the information to Dixon.) By 5:00 Dixon was on the road, exceeding the thirty-five-miles-per-hour speed limit while checking traffic en route. Finding that the burglars had abandoned their Ford during the pursuit, Dixon spent the morning patrolling county roads and checking pastures and barns. The search paid off. At 1:00 p.m. Dixon, with four officers from his subdistrict, raided a country home, arresting M. L. Rainey and Ruth Grabowski and recovering stolen property including several hundred gallons of gasoline, dry goods, groceries, guns and ammunition—all of which later that day was inventoried and identified by the victims.[18]

At 2:00 a.m. Dixon, with two deputy sheriffs and two policemen, arrested George Lambert at his home in Sherman and seized stolen property in his possession. All together, stolen property was seized through a coordinated effort in six Texas counties and one Oklahoma county. Dixon had worked nonstop thirty-seven hours, from 4:30 a.m. on Friday to 8:00 p.m. on Saturday. On Sunday he and Denton County Sheriff Roy Moore interrogated prisoners Rainey and Grabowski and worked with victims to identify their stolen property. For the next ten days Dixon, often with Robnett and other officers, continued working on the burglary/car-theft investigation in Texas and Oklahoma.[19]

On December 17 Dixon and Sheriff Moore drove to the Panhandle, where Ranger Raymond Waters and several local officers joined them in arresting

Jess Lewis and recovering stolen property from him. On December 21 Dixon attended the Denton grand-jury hearings on Lambert, Rainey, and Lewis, in which each was indicted on three charges of burglary. Over the next several days Dixon restored the stolen property to its owners at several locations and testified at a Bonham trial on Rainey. One month later Dixon testified at a second Denton County grand jury on Lambert, Rainey, and Lewis. Almost a month after that, at a Denton trial, he testified against Lambert, who pleaded guilty and was sentenced to five years in prison, and Rainey, who also pleaded guilty and was given a ten-year sentence. Two weeks later Dixon testified at the Spearman trial, in which each of the three was sentenced to seven years in prison. Nor was that the end of it. Five months later, on September 30, 1943, Jess Lewis, serving as a trustee at a prison farm, escaped, and during the following week, Dixon and Robnett searched for him in North Texas and Oklahoma, providing information to sheriffs and police chiefs. More than a year later, with Lewis remaining a fugitive, Dixon resumed his search, but to no avail.[20]

On Monday, September 14, 1942, Ethel Bridgefarmer was found dead of a gunshot wound in her car on her farm a few miles north of McKinney. Dixon, who was writing reports at Company B headquarters in Dallas when the death was reported, drove to the scene with Captain Gonzaullas. There they interviewed Bridgefarmer's sister and several others and took possession of a suicide note, and Dixon made paraffin casts of Bridgefarmer's hands, which he took with other evidence to Camp Mabry on Tuesday. By Wednesday the investigation indicated that, although the death seemed to be a suicide, Bridgefarmer apparently had been swindled out of fifteen hundred dollars. Evidence soon pointed to Fred L. Powell as the swindler, but when Dixon tried to track him down, Powell had disappeared. Then, on October 1, Collin County Sheriff Button informed the Ranger that Powell had been arrested in Shreveport, Louisiana.

While awaiting Powell's extradition from Louisiana, Dixon continued his investigation into the apparent swindle, gathering evidence that Powell had signed a contract with Bridgefarmer in Dallas County on or about June 19, 1942, promising to transfer to her some oil and gas leases. On that date, at her bank in McKinney, Bridgefarmer purchased a cashier's check in the sum of fifteen hundred dollars payable to Powell, who, on the same day, deposited it in a Dallas bank and promptly withdrew seven hundred dollars. That withdrawal led Dixon to Houston, where he took a statement from Lelia LaFollette, who had filed a lawsuit against Powell charging that he had swindled her but had dropped it after he paid her the seven hundred dollars he had taken out of the Dallas bank.

On October 19, 1942, Dixon testified before the Collin County grand jury regarding *State of Texas v. Fred L. Powell.* When the trial began, on May 24, 1943, Dixon was present as a witness, but on the next day Powell did not appear. His bond was forfeited, and he was arrested, but then, by error, he was freed again on a new bond for the same amount. Several months later, on October 11, Dixon was back in court for Powell's trial, in which Powell was sentenced to five years in prison for swindling Ethel Bridgefarmer out of fifteen hundred dollars.[21]

Four of the eight counties in Dixon's subdistrict abutted the Red River border with Oklahoma, stretching approximately one hundred miles westward from Fannin County to Grayson, Cooke, and Montague Counties. On March 17, 1943, Dixon, with Robnett and another Frisco special agent, C. D. Cochran, met with police chiefs in Madill and Ardmore, Oklahoma, to encourage cooperative enforcement along the Red River border country. The next day they attended a conference of Oklahoma peace officers who served near the border. The close cooperation of Oklahoma sheriffs and police chiefs, together with Robnett's intimate knowledge of his southern Oklahoma territory as a special agent for the Frisco, was of immeasurable help to Dixon in chasing down cross-border lawbreakers.[22]

During the first two weeks of August, Dixon worked with Robnett, Dallas detectives, Cooke County Sheriff Carl Wilson, and Ardmore officers on an alleged July 27 swindling of Mrs. Jose Shilling of Ardmore out of five thousand dollars "by unknown parties" at Gainesville. On August 14 Captain Gonzaullas made a long-distance telephone call to Dixon in McKinney relaying information from the Dallas Police Department that a suspect in the Shilling swindle was being held in the Dallas County Jail. At Dixon's request, Mrs. Shilling drove to Dallas from Mineral Wells to view the suspect. He was not the swindler, she said, but as she worked her way through photographs that Dixon had compiled of other possible suspects, she stopped at Eddie and Dewey Freeman and identified them, without doubt, as the villains. Dixon and Robnett, joined by Sheriff Wilson, took the swindle investigation across the border to Ardmore, Ada, Seminole, Tecumseh, Shawnee, and Oklahoma City. Dixon continued working on the swindle case with Robnett throughout September, conferring from time to time with various Rangers, detectives, FBI agents, and other officers on leads and any other information that might help them apprehend the Freeman brothers. But few leads developed, the Freemans remained free, and Dixon's attention shifted to other cases.[23]

The Freemans, however, were not forgotten. By January 1945 the FBI had listed them as two of the nineteen worst criminals in the United States. Finally, on Wednesday, April 25, 1945, the FBI notified Dixon that Eddie Freeman was in the custody of federal marshals in Oklahoma City. There, on the following day, with Cooke County Deputy Sheriff Emory Horn, Dixon interrogated Eddie Freeman from early in the morning until 4:00 p.m. On Saturday morning Dixon received a long-distance call from another FBI agent, who reported that Dewey Freeman had been apprehended in

Handley, his hometown in Tarrant County, and was being held in Dallas. Dixon quickly called Robnett in Sherman, and by early afternoon they were in Dallas interrogating Dewey Freeman.[24]

On September 17, 1945, five months after being captured, the Freeman brothers sawed through two steel window bars in the basement of the federal prison in Muskogee, Oklahoma, and escaped. The FBI broadcast a nine-state alarm, but their freedom lasted ten months. Ft. Worth officers caught Dewey Freeman on July 20, 1946, and ten days later, Eddie Freeman was apprehended in Marlin, southeast of Waco. Now, on top of being indicted for violating the National Stolen Property Act, they faced charges that they had violated the Federal Escape Act. Dixon, who had spent considerable time investigating the Freemans' swindling activities, spent part of only one day—February 24, 1946—searching for the escaped brothers. But he and Robnett were singled out by the Sheriffs' Association of Texas after the Freemans were first arrested: "It was through the good work of Robnett and Texas Ranger N. K. Dixon that the arrest of Dewey and Eddie Freeman was brought about."[25]

BAD MEN

By the time Norman Dixon had transferred to Company B, in August 1942, he was well experienced in going undercover in taverns, nightclubs, drugstores, service stations, and cafés in search of illicit gambling; in arresting and filing charges against the operators; and in seizing and destroying slot machines and other gambling devices. From August 17 to August 20 he canvassed the business establishments in Sherman and Denison, and on Monday, August 24, he, Captain Gonzaullas, and Rangers Ernest Daniel, Bob Crowder, and R. L. Badgett took three cars and one horse trailer to Denison from Dallas, arriving at noon. Their first target was Eagle Lodge, on West Main Street, but when a search turned up no gaming in operation and no gambling paraphernalia, no arrests were made. They searched forty-one businesses and in thirty-six seized a total of forty-nine slot machines. While Gonzaullas and his Rangers loaded the confiscated machines into two cars and the horse trailer and drove back to Dallas, Dixon filed complaints against the operators, all of whom pleaded guilty. Thirty-four paid fines of $28.45 each, and two paid $42.50 each.

In Dallas later in the week, Dixon helped Gonzaullas, Crowder, and Badgett destroy the machines, the scraps to be converted into war goods. But he did not forget about Eagle Lodge. Two months later, Dixon and Deputy Constable Pearl Townsend burst through the front doors of the lodge, arresting twenty-six individuals and seizing $202.20 from a slot machine and the dice and poker games that were under way. The officers confiscated the slot machine, destroyed it for salvage, and turned the money over to the Red Cross. According to the *Denison Herald* they warned the operators, "Next time we'll break up the furniture." Dixon filed the twenty-six charges. Twenty-five individuals paid fines of $67.50, and one paid $18.50.[1]

Two years later, Dixon's undercover work in a gambling crusade would result in a vicious attack on him in the courtroom. On October 18, 1944, at the request of Colonel Garrison he was in San Antonio working under cover at the Turf Club. He spent the evening at the bar on the first floor and returned the next day making inquiries about where he could get into a game. After hearing Dixon express his interest in gambling, Red Pipkin, the

In front of Company B headquarters in Dallas. From left: Norman Dixon, Capt. Gonzaullas, Bob Crowder, and Ernest Daniel. *Author's Collection.*

elevator operator, brought V. E. "Red" Berry down to meet him. Presenting Berry a card, Dixon identified himself as "George Herbert," a research agent from Chicago. When Berry asked if he was from Chicago, Dixon said his home was Asbury Park, New Jersey. After chatting for a minute, Berry gave him access to the gaming room on the third floor, and during the next hour and a half, Dixon gambled away twenty dollars at the dice table.

At 7:00 the next morning Dixon was in Austin conferring with Colonel Garrison and Ranger Capt. Fred Olson on plans to raid the club, and at 10:00 p.m. he was back in the club gaming room. Purchasing twenty dollars' worth of chips, he began shooting craps with Martin Whitten, who was operating the game, and about eleven other players. At 10:35 Dixon heard a faint buzzer go off, and Whitten called for everyone to put their chips in their pockets. Lifting his badge for all to see, Dixon announced that he was a Texas Ranger and that everyone was under arrest. At that moment Captain Olson and Rangers Dub Naylor and Trueman Stone rushed into the room. Berry walked over to Dixon and asked if he really was from Chicago. Dixon said, "I never told you I was from Chicago." Berry replied, "You're a whiz of a con." Thirty-three guests were arrested. Berry, Whitten, and a Slim Lambert were accused of operating a gambling house but were all allowed to go home after the Rangers took their names and addresses. The Rangers spent most of the night searching and seizing more than a thousand dollars in cash, two large dice tables, one roulette table and wheel, one blackjack table, furniture, books, dice, chips, cards, and so on. When the dice tables would not fit into the elevator, Berry sawed the legs off, and the Rangers hauled the confiscated goods to a storage house in San Antonio.[2]

On Monday, February 5, 1945, Dixon was in San Antonio with Captain Olson, subpoenaed for the trial of Red Berry. When the trial was deferred until Wednesday, Dixon joined the search for four German POWs who had escaped from Camp Swift. Described by the *San Antonio Light* as "the undercover man and the star state witness," Dixon testified for several hours on Friday and Saturday, describing his role and the events in great detail. Under cross-examination, he was asked if he had used an assumed name for the purpose of deception. Dixon replied, "Yes." The defense attorney asked, "You're a ranger and supposed to uphold the law? When you gambled did you know you were violating the law?" Dixon answered, "Yes. But I considered it a part of my investigation." Asked whose money he used, Dixon said, "The money was furnished to me by the State Department of Public Safety." "In other words," said the defense attorney, "you were gambling with taxpayers' money." The courtroom broke into laughter.

On Monday Judge W. W. McCrory told the jury that the state must prove Berry had control of the third floor and that he used the floor for wagering and gaming with dice. Benton Davies, closing for the state, reminded the jury that Red Pipkin, the elevator operator, had testified that he worked for Berry and that he took people to the third floor, where he had seen dice games in progress. Referring to the defense attorney's charges that Dixon entered illegally, Davies stated, "The only way Dixon could have gotten in was by a ruse."

State Sen. Franklin Spear, speaking for the defense, said of the Rangers, "Their conduct in this case is so reprehensible that it stenches in the nostrils. . . . If you place your stamp of approval on these rangers' high handed conduct, then nobody can feel secure in their home." Gesticulating and walking back and forth in front of the jury, he zeroed in on Dixon: "I don't think much of a man who lies in any kind of a case. I am of that old fashioned school that believes a lie is justified at only one time and that is when the honor of a woman is at stake. . . . But this here Ranger fellow, alias George Herbert, I excoriate him and condemn him for lying. . . . The raid on the Tarp [*sic*] club was both immoral and illegal." It worked. Berry was acquitted.

In an editorial on its front page titled "Your Verdict," the *San Antonio Light* said the issue was whether state laws were to be enforced in Bexar County. "That jury has answered the question in the negative. . . . That jury heard a complete and convincing case made against a known law violator, and yet it voted NOT GUILTY. . . . The Texas Rangers DID THEIR DUTY, honestly and efficiently." But for Dixon, his assignment was complete when he finished his testimony on Saturday; by Monday, the day of the verdict, he was in Dallas conferring with Captain Gonzaullas on his reports and current assignments. Red Berry would go on to serve three terms as a Texas state representative and one as a state senator.[3]

If Berry had been convicted, he likely would have joined the several hundred prisoners serving time on the 7,424-acre Retrieve Prison Farm in Brazoria County, raising livestock and growing cotton, corn, sugarcane, and other crops. A year earlier Dixon had driven to the farm to pick up a prisoner to serve as a witness in the Harney trial. Another prisoner at the farm was Walter Henry LeMay, whom Dixon had helped put behind bars in 1941 when stationed at Goldthwaite. LeMay had a long criminal record, dating back to 1928 when he was arrested for burglary at the age of nineteen. Between 1928 and 1943 he served one term in an Oklahoma reformatory and four prison terms in Texas. Serving with LeMay at Retrieve was C. M. Mershon, who was first arrested in 1931 for auto theft in Dallas, when he was nineteen, in 1934, and again in 1938, when he was sentenced for robbery and burglary in four counties.

On April 4, 1943, seven men escaped from the prison farm. They were soon recaptured. On April 18 fifteen men escaped, sawing their way to freedom. Six were recaptured quickly with the use of bloodhounds, and seven more were caught over the next several weeks. The two remaining at large were LeMay and Mershon. When a rash of burglaries and car thefts in Gladewater, Tyler, and other towns were attributed to them, Captain Gonzaullas, Bob Crowder, and Dixon worked with police departments around the state to track their whereabouts. On the evening of June 4, with reports indicating the convicts were in the Ft. Worth area, Gonzaullas, Dixon, Crowder, and Tully Seay drove there and spent several hours patrolling, checking beer taverns, and the like.

On the following day the four Rangers, Dallas police inspector J. W. Fritz, and detectives Leon Mash and J. T. Luther, working on tips that the escapees were in Dallas and would be found at a residence on Michigan Street, staked out the house and area. At 11:30 a.m. the police officers spotted LeMay and Mershon pulling up to the house in a 1941 Mercury. Seeing the officers, the convicts sped off. The officers gave chase, hitting ninety-five miles per hour on Dallas streets and firing at the Mercury as they drew closer. Trying to turn a corner, Mershon lost control of the car and landed in a field of tall Johnson grass. Mershon and Steve Roberts, a third person in the car, came out with their hands up, but LeMay leaped from the car and ran into nearby woods.

Within minutes Gonzaullas, Crowder, Dixon, and Seay arrived. Twenty squad cars sped to the scene. Three airplanes from nearby Curry Field soon were circling the area. And ten men on horseback along with armed volunteers on foot were tramping through the tall grass. But, as Gonzaullas quickly surmised, LeMay was not in the grass. He had slipped into the garage of a nearby home, climbed onto the top shelf of a large storage closet, shoved paint cans and boxes in front of him, and closed the closet door. After searching the residential area for three hours, the Lone Wolf walked into the garage with gun in hand, opened the closet door and ordered LeMay to come out. As LeMay climbed down, Gonzaullas fired two shots into the air, and Dixon, Crowder, Seay, and other officers rushed to the garage to secure the prisoner.[4]

In his diary Dixon estimated that they recovered almost four thousand dollars' worth of "money, car, bonds & merchandise." Dixon interrogated Mershon, who, along with LeMay, confessed to committing between twenty and twenty-five robberies and burglaries during their seven weeks of freedom. Their routine, they explained, was to enter a town late at night, capture and bind the night watchman, and break into stores along the main street, taking merchandise and breaking knobs off safes for money.

On June 10, only five days after their capture, LeMay and Mershon were tried, convicted of six cases of burglary, and sentenced to 24 years in prison in Canton, Van Zandt County, between Dallas and Tyler. On the same day a grand jury at Groesbeck, Limestone County, east of Waco, indicted them in sixteen other cases. Five days later LeMay and Mershon were tried on the Groesbeck indictments and received sentences totaling 249 years each. A month later LeMay received a life sentence in a trial in Hillsboro, Hill County, between Dallas and Waco.

Fritz, Mash, and Luther—the Dallas officers involved in the high-speed car chase—traveled from county to county testifying in the LeMay and Mershon trials, and several more counties lined up to have a crack at the burglars. When the officers went to West Texas to testify, Mershon told them about the catfish in the Brazos River in Parker County. "I don't intend to serve all that 300 years even if I live that long. . . . I'm going to go right back to that spot in Parker County and catch me a big cat." At that Fritz replied, "Well, we'll know where to catch you next time."[5]

Dixon had another fish to fry a few days later when a neatly dressed man entered the State National Bank at Denison, walked to the back of the lobby, and sat down beside the desk of the cashier. Holding a pistol under the cashier's desk, he demanded five thousand dollars in twenty-dollar bills. A teller brought the money and began to count it out, but the robber scooped it up, saying, "That won't be necessary," fled through a side door, climbed into an automobile, and drove off. His license number was reported, and only twenty-five minutes later a man wearing an army uniform was stopped and arrested by two Grayson County deputy sheriffs as he drove over a bridge on the outskirts of Sherman. He was Cpl. Emmett C. "Pete" Gary, a clerk in X Corps headquarters and a former candidate for sheriff in Henderson County. Notified of the arrest, Dixon drove to the county jail and took his confession. Joining Dixon were FBI agents who were trying to determine whether Gary's crime was a civil or a military matter. Four days later, the decision made, Gary was transferred to Camp Howze, at Gainesville. There, in a court-martial, he was found guilty of robbery with firearms and sentenced to ten years at hard labor in a federal prison.[6]

Gamblers and fugitives were natural targets for Texas Ranger Norman Dixon, and when a gaming establishment was raided and shut down, or when a fugitive was apprehended, Dixon felt a sense of accomplishment, knowing that justice was served, and moved on to the next case. But some incidents entailed more than simply enforcing the law. On November 1, 1943, twenty-one-year-old John Edmond Parks, recently honorably discharged from the Marine Corps owing to a severe respiratory condition, sat in the living room of his widowed mother's house, at 6263 Belmont Street in Dallas, cleaning a .22-caliber rifle he had hunted with the day before. He did not realize, he said later, that there was a cartridge in the rifle. His forty-six-year-old mother, Tommie Lee Parks, was in the hall walking toward a bedroom when his rifle went off, striking her in the head, splitting the bridge of her nose. John Parks ran frantically to a neighbor's house calling for help, but by the time an ambulance arrived, his mother was dead. In the Dallas Police Department conferring with Will Fritz when the call came in, Dixon rode to the scene with Fritz and other police officers. They found Mrs. Parks lying in a wide pool of blood, and her son inconsolable with grief. Longtime neighbors told the officers that the son, an only child, was deeply devoted to his mother and that only a year ago his father had died of a heart attack.[7]

On Tuesday, November 20, 1945, sixteen-year-old Bill Purcell, his twin brother, Joe Purcell Jr., and a companion, Howard Stevens, were hunting along a creek bank four miles northeast of Gainesville when they heard a shot fired and a bullet whistled over their heads. They yelled out a warning and crouched down. A second shot hit Bill in the neck as he tried to hide behind a tree. After trying to stop the bleeding, Joe and Stevens carried Bill to the car, but he collapsed and died on the way. The only evidence Cooke County Sheriff Carl Wilson found at the scene that afternoon was a knee print in the soil, indicating that someone might have kneeled to take aim before shooting. Wilson learned that the creek was on a farm leased by Travis Deaton. When he returned to his office in Gainesville, he tracked down Dixon in Sherman, where, with D. C. Robnett and Grayson County Deputy Sheriff Sam York, the Ranger had just apprehended, fingerprinted, and jailed C. D. Moss, a fugitive wanted by the Lea County sheriff's office in New Mexico. Sheriff Wilson asked Dixon for his assistance "in murder of Bill Purcell."

On Wednesday Dixon, with Sheriff Wilson, Deputy Horn, and Gainesville Police Chief Kirchenbauer, examined the scene, conducted several interviews, test-fired guns owned by those interviewed, and examined the bullet that killed young Purcell. Two days later, the Ranger and Sheriff Wilson conducted another series of interviews. At noon, Sheriff Wilson, who had been feeling ill for several days while working long hours on the Purcell case, became too ill even to drive his car. He was persuaded to go to his

From left: Cooke County Constable Bill Fletcher, Sheriff Carl Wilson, Jailer E. "Hoss" Cogburn, and Deputy Sheriff Emory Horn. Photograph taken August 1945, three months prior to Wilson's death. *Author's Collection.*

doctor's office, where, at 4:05 p.m., the forty-nine-year-old sheriff suffered a heart attack and died, leaving a widow and seven children.[8]

Carl Wilson's sudden death was a shock to everyone. Dixon, who had worked regularly with Wilson for almost three years, put aside the Purcell case and worked on a death message to Wilson's relatives. For the next eight hours he helped the sheriff's staff handle details regarding his death, and at

2:00 a.m. he left Gainesville. Four days later he attended Wilson's funeral and then renewed the investigation of Bill Purcell's death. His investigation determined that seventeen-year-old Bobbie Deaton, Travis Deaton's son, had fired the gun that killed Purcell. On Tuesday, December 4, Dixon testified before the Cooke County grand jury that Deaton's killing of Purcell was negligent homicide. That afternoon, according to Dixon's diary, he was "with Sheriff Emory Horn at 1:00 p.m. escorting and guiding Grand Jury to the scene of said shooting, showing them the blood, tree, tracks, etc.—At request of Grand Jury & County Attorney remained in attendance in event Grand Jury had further questions, etc."

On Thursday, the Cooke County grand jury indicted Bobbie Deaton, charging him with negligent homicide, a misdemeanor, in the fatal shooting of Bill Purcell. Based on Dixon's testimony, the indictment said Deaton had been searching for persons he believed were hunting on his father's land, and "without any apparent intention to kill anyone . . . negligently and carelessly, discharged a rifle toward Billy Purcell." On Friday, armed with a warrant, Dixon and Deputy Sheriff A. E. Cogburn arrested Bobbie Deaton, fingerprinted him, and took him before the county judge, who set the bond. Dixon's diary does not mention attending or testifying at a trial on Deaton, although he did meet with Sheriff Horn and District Attorney Ray Winder on January 8, 1946, regarding a "pending trial." Possibly the negligent homicide charge, a misdemeanor, was settled without a trial.[9]

Meanwhile, back on December 13, 1945, two thousand miles away, in Seattle, Washington, a man walked into a Florsheim Shoe Store and was measured for a pair of shoes by the sales clerk. Another man entered the store armed with a shotgun. One of them—they were working together—yelled, "It is a stickup. I want your money." Standing at a back desk, the store manager, Clayton Stockberger, began raising his hands, but the first robber, apparently concerned that people outside the store might see his hands up, ordered him to put them down. As he did so, the man with the shotgun, perhaps confused about Stockberger's movements, shot him. At that the two men fled without any money, leaving forty-seven-year-old Stockberger, husband and father of a three-year-old daughter, dead on the floor.

Seattle police searched the area, discovered a hat and a jacket hanging on a parking meter nearby, and interviewed six people who saw the two men at the scene of the crime. The hat was soon identified as belonging to Richard Britton, the jacket to his brother Homer. Four of the six witnesses identified Richard Britton in a lineup as one of the two robbers but not the one who fired the shot. On the night of the holdup and murder, the brothers had left Seattle, driving southeast about one hundred miles to Ellensburg, where they spent three days with a friend. From there they drove several hundred miles to Hagerman, Idaho, where they stopped on December 17 for three days for car repairs.[10]

As the Seattle police tracked the Brittons' movements from Seattle to Ellensburg to Hagerman, they learned that the men had at one time lived in Van Alstyne, Texas, in southern Grayson County. Shortly after they notified the Van Alstyne police to be on the lookout for the Brittons, Dixon received the notice, and from 7:00 p.m. to 1:30 a.m. on Wednesday, December 26, he was in Grayson County with Sheriff G. P. Gafford "investigating whereabouts" of Richard and Homer Britton, and coordinating information with Company C Capt. Manny Gault, Ranger Waters, the Denison Police Department, and the sheriff's office in Durant, Oklahoma. The next afternoon, Deputy Sheriffs Fred Prestage and Clarence Faeke encountered the Brittons in Denison and arrested them. Dixon, who had been checking records on the fugitives at the U.S. Post Office and other federal agencies, was in Denison when the arrests were made. After he searched their car and interrogated the two men separately, he sent a teletype to the Seattle police notifying them of the arrests and interrogations.[11]

Articles on the Britton case appeared later in two popular crime magazines. An article in the December 1946 issue of *Timely Detective Cases* states: "Ranger N. K. Dixon questioned the pair. Both said they had come to Texas at the invitation of an oil man—an old friend—to take jobs. Somehow the jobs hadn't materialized." A January 1948 article in *Inside Detective* states: "On the evening of December 27, two weeks exactly after the murder, Mahoney rushed into Lawrence's office excitedly waving a teletype report. 'This is it!' Mahoney exclaimed, handing the sheet to Lawrence. The message stated that N. K. Dixon had just reported the arrest of Richard Britton and Steve Collins [the article used a pseudonym for Homer Britton] at Dennison [*sic*], Tex. . . . Ranger Dixon had questioned the men separately, the message stated, and learned from Britton that he had left Seattle about the first of December with Collins, but that he could not remember much about the trip because he was doing considerable drinking along the way."[12]

At 10:30 p.m., after receiving a telegram from the prosecuting attorney for King County, Washington, Dixon and Harry Smith, Deputy U.S. Marshal, transferred the prisoners to the Grayson County Jail in Sherman, and drove to Van Alstyne, where they contacted Constable Ira McNeely. The three officers drove to the residence of H. M. Britton, the father of the fugitives, interviewing him at 1:30 a.m. On Friday, December 28, Dixon worked with Smith, Robnett, and FBI agent Tim Aterberry on aspects of the Britton case and on another fugitive case, returning home at 2:00 a.m. Saturday. Thirty minutes later he received a phone call from the Denison Police Department relaying information that Seattle Detective V. L. Webb would arrive at the Dallas airport in a couple of hours. At 5:15 a.m., as Detective Webb disembarked from Braniff Flight 39, Dixon met him and took him to Company B headquarters, where they conferred with Captain Gonzaullas. Robnett joined them in Sherman, where they worked together on the investigation until midnight.

On Sunday Dixon took Detective Webb to the Grayson County Jail, where they interviewed the Britton brothers, received extradition waivers to Seattle, and escorted the prisoners to the Bryan County Jail in Durant, Oklahoma, where they would be held until they were transferred to Seattle. On Monday, December 31, Dixon received warrants for the Brittons from Seattle, collected documentary evidence from their father, transcribed his notes on the investigation, and wrote statements for the Seattle Police Department. He remained overnight in Sherman Tuesday and Wednesday, January 1 and 2, 1946, as the investigation continued. On Thursday, when two Seattle detectives joined Dixon, Smith, and Robnett, the five officers conferred and then drove to Durant, where they interrogated the Brittons. In his diary Dixon wrote that he then decided to "start them rolling" by escorting the detectives and prisoners "out of Durant" and sending them on their way to Seattle.[13]

Six months later, at 4:22 p.m. on Saturday, June 1, 1946, Dixon boarded an American Airlines flight from Dallas to Los Angeles; he arrived at 12:45 a.m., Pacific Time. At 7:00 a.m. he left Los Angeles on Western Airlines; at 8:45 a.m. he landed in San Francisco. Until that evening he was unable to book a flight to Seattle. At 2:30 a.m. on Monday, he boarded a United Airlines flight to Portland, Oregon, where he was bumped but reseated. At 9:30 a.m., fifty-three hours after leaving Dallas, he arrived in Seattle.

The trial against Richard Britton, in which he was charged, not with murdering Stockberger but with being an accomplice, lasted four days. Dixon testified early in the trial and again during rebuttal arguments near the end. Homer Britton, originally charged along with his brother, had his charges dropped and was called as a witness, but he refused to answer questions on grounds of self-incrimination. The dramatic moment in the trial came when a surprise witness, Albert Ritchie, who had broken his back, was wheeled into the courtroom on a stretcher. In such pain that he could barely raise his hand to be sworn in, he told the court, in a voice so low that the jury had to stand and lean forward to hear him, that he had loaned his automobile to Homer Britton at 2:00 p.m. on the afternoon of the murder. This shattered Richard Britton's alibi that he and his brother had spent that afternoon drinking at a beer parlor. The jury found him guilty of first-degree murder, giving him the death penalty, and the next morning the judge sentenced him to hang on November 10. After the sentencing Dixon met with the county auditor in the prosecuting attorney's office to settle his expense account, and on the following day began his flight home.[14]

Seattle police were not yet satisfied. The actual killer was still on the loose and unknown. In late January 1947, at the request of Seattle detectives, Dixon interviewed the Brittons' father again and investigated leads on possible suspects. The Seattle detectives also turned to Richard Britton, who received stays of execution in return for his commitment to help bring the murderer to justice. Britton pointed his finger at Orbin Basil Smith, who had served

Richard Britton being led to the courtroom. *Inside Detective 95,* no. 1 (January 1948), Dell Publishing Company.

time in a Texas prison with him. Smith was located, arrested, and put on trial in January 1948, two years after Britton's conviction as an accomplice to murder. In the trial Britton testified that he and Smith had planned the robbery and that Smith, standing behind Britton, had fired his sawed-off shotgun at Stockberger, killing him. But Smith, who was on the stand for most of a day, testified that he was in the store simply to buy a pair of shoes and that Britton fired the shotgun, killing Stockberger. Smith was acquitted, and because Britton had fulfilled his commitment to testify, the governor commuted his sentence to life imprisonment.[15]

The long hours of intensive work, often seven days a week, fueled by smoking one cigarette after another day and night, together with poor eating habits—eating on the run or skipping meals—and lack of sleep and exercise, took their toll on the thirty-eight-year-old Ranger. In November 1945 he witnessed forty-nine-year-old Sheriff Carl Wilson die of a heart attack while working with him. The long hours Dixon worked on the Britton brothers' case in late December 1945 and early January 1946 were routine and exhausting. Six weeks later, on February 18, 1946, he was diagnosed with pneumonia. To cope with the illness, he slowed down, which for him meant working a normal eight-hour day, returning home to McKinney by 5:00 p.m. on most days. But he did not recover, and on Saturday, March 2, he wrote in his diary, "Changed Doctor—worst relapse & lowest ebb." He convalesced at home on Sunday, subject to call, and stayed home Monday, writing reports and contacting local officers. On Tuesday through Thursday he worked on cases in the McKinney area and visited the doctor twice. Twelve days later, on March 19, he suffered another relapse.

This was a wake-up call for Dixon, and worrisome for Captain Gonzaullas. However a solution was at hand: for the next two weeks Dixon took over the secretarial duties at Company B headquarters while Muriel, the office secretary, took her vacation. On March 20, his first day at Muriel's desk, Dixon might have typed a memo from Captain Gonzaullas to all Company B Rangers, including himself. Attached to the memo was a special bulletin announcing death benefits for DPS commissioned officers and their spouses and families, amounting to as much as four thousand dollars. Dixon, suffering as he was through a serious illness, undoubtedly welcomed this news. (A few months later, in another memo, the captain said he had paid the first death-benefit installment for all his Rangers, whom he considered his family, and that they could reimburse him at their convenience.) Dixon's deskwork would help him recover in time to go after the Phantom Killer, who had already claimed his first victims.[16]

THE PHANTOM AND THE WAR HERO

On the night of February 22, 1946, nineteen-year-old Mary Jeanne Larey and twenty-three-year-old Jimmy Hollis parked fifty feet off a country road half a mile northwest of Texarkana. A man wearing a white mask with holes cut out for his eyes and mouth walked up to the car and ordered them out. As the masked man struck Hollis, he told Larey, who was wearing high heels, to run down the road. After beating and stomping on Hollis, he caught up to her and beat her, but when a car's headlights came into view, he fled, leaving her lying in the middle of the road. Both victims were hospitalized. When they were questioned, they could provide very little information about their assailant. Larey thought he was black; Hollis thought he was white. Neither knew how tall he was. Two months later, still reliving the horrifying experience, Larey moved to Frederick, Oklahoma, to live with her aunt and uncle. Hollis, still suffering three months after the attack, was considering a move to Shreveport to get away from the area.[1]

A month after the first attack, on the morning of March 24, seventeen-year-old Polly Ann Moore, who had graduated from Atlanta High School, south of Texarkana, the previous May, and twenty-nine-year-old Richard L. Griffin, who had been discharged from the Seabees a few months earlier, were found dead in the backseat of an automobile on a gravel road near Highway 67 west of Texarkana, not far from the attack on Larey and Hollis. Each had been shot in the head. Blood was found splattered inside the car, on the bodies, and on the ground twenty feet away. But any other evidence that might have been useful—fingerprints, footprints, and tire tracks—had been wiped out by the hundreds of people who flocked to the scene.

Three weeks later, on Sunday, April 14, two teenagers were found shot to death near Spring Lake Park. Fifteen-year-old Betty Jo Booker, of Texarkana, and seventeen-year-old Paul Martin, of Kilgore, had been to a dance at the Veterans of Foreign Wars Hall, where Booker had played the saxophone as a member of the high school orchestra. Martin's body was found on the road two miles from his car. He had been shot in the face and, apparently having tried to escape, in the back of the head. Booker was found in a field a distance up a dirt road, a mile from where Martin's body was found. She had been shot in the heart and head and raped. Again, large crowds visiting the crime scene had obliterated any clues.[2]

At 9:30 a.m. on that Sunday, after Paul Martin's body had been found but before the discovery of Betty Jo Booker's body, Captain Gonzaullas telephoned Dixon, instructing him to proceed to Texarkana. By midafternoon, Captain Gonzaullas and seven of the Company B Rangers were in Texarkana working on the investigation, with Dixon at the funeral home examining the bodies for evidence. He would remain in Texarkana from April 14 to May 30, searching for evidence, reviewing records, interrogating suspects, interviewing individuals, reporting suspicious persons or activities, patrolling country roads, and more.

For Leona Dixon, this was one more long, unexpected absence to endure. The phone call from Captain Gonzaullas had come on a Sunday morning less than two weeks after Norman's recovery from his devastating case of pneumonia. Apparently back to full strength, he had resumed working long hours and weekends. From the day of the call to May 30, Leona saw her husband only briefly on Sunday, May 19, and then only because an investigation took him to Dallas for a few hours, giving him a chance to swing by McKinney. He came home at 5:00 p.m. on Thursday, May 30, primarily to prepare for his Saturday flight to Seattle for the Britton trial. On Sunday, June 9, he returned from Seattle at about midnight, but he left again for Texarkana at 3:00 p.m. the next day. Captain Gonzaullas and most of his Rangers had pulled out, but for the rest of June and all of July, Dixon was assigned to Texarkana every other week, partnering with Ranger Stewart Stanley; on alternate weeks Rangers Joe Thompson and Tully Seay continued the investigation.[3]

For the Dixon boys, seven-year-old Kemp and five-year-old Kenneth, a frequently absent father was part of their life. But the older son always remembered the day when a policeman came to the front door and spoke to his mother and when, after the officer had left, she went to her bedroom, lay on the bed, and cried. Most likely Norman had radioed the McKinney Police Department a message for Leona: he would not be home anytime soon.

The April 13 slayings—the third attack and the second double-murder within two months—put fear into the hearts of the citizens of Texarkana. Men armed themselves and sent their wives and children out of town. Lights stayed on through the nights in house after house. Few wandered out after dark, not just because they feared the "Phantom," as he was now called, but also because they feared trigger-happy neighbors. To help bring an end to the reign of terror, DPS sent four crime-lab technicians and a force of highway patrolmen in patrol cars with new two-way radios to join the Company B Rangers. The Rangers and local police set up decoy teams made up of an officer in civilian clothes and another dressed as a woman to trap the killer. But they were up against a psychopathic killer who not only was a sexual pervert but also was intelligent enough to avoid the trap.[4]

Dixon's diary contains sporadic details of his daily activities in Texarkana. On April 17 he received a long-distance call from Ranger Badgett regarding the possible location in Texarkana of Luther Bone, one of four men who burglarized a liquor store in Big Spring, West Texas, on February 27. Dixon, with Bowie County Sheriff W. D. Presley, FBI agents, and Ranger Oldham, apprehended Bone, and on April 18, at the request of Badgett, Dixon searched Bone's car and seized burglary tools from it. On April 27 he investigated the suicide of sixty-nine-year-old Sue Murray of Fort Worth, who leaped to her death from the fire escape of a downtown Texarkana hotel. On May 2 he investigated and cleared a Phantom suspect in Shreveport.[5]

Ten miles northeast of Texarkana on the night of Friday, May 3, the Phantom stood with a .22 rifle outside the rural Miller County, Arkansas, home of thirty-six-year-old Virgil Starks. He watched through the windows—the shades were raised, the lights on—as Starks sat in an easy chair in the living room listening to the radio and Katy Starks, his attractive thirty-year-old wife, was in the bedroom undressing and putting on a nightgown. When she heard the sound of glass shattering, she rushed into the living room, where she found her husband standing with blood dripping from his head. When he sank back into the easy chair, she ran to him and then to the telephone, ringing it twice but unable to get the operator. Next the killer shot her twice in the face and she fell to the floor, but when he ran to the back door and tore at the screen, she ran out the front door to a neighbor for help.

Gonzaullas, Dixon, and other officers rushed to the scene. The killer had walked through pools of the Starks's blood, enabling the officers to trace his steps in the house, and because of recent rains, they could follow his footsteps in the mud outside as he retreated to the road and, apparently, his car. The officers also found a .22-caliber shell and a red metal flashlight that he had dropped. Dixon noted in his diary that he was at the Starks farmhouse all night and through Saturday morning. But there was no evidence—tests on the flashlight, for example, revealed no fingerprints—that helped find the Phantom Killer. Nor did the questioning of more than four hundred possible suspects.[6]

DPS sent more reinforcements, several squad cars, and a mobile three-way radio transmitter. The city's liquor dealers issued a joint statement declaring that they were voluntarily closing their stores at 9:30 p.m. "Any person who drinks whisky at this time to get drunk and wander about the streets of Texarkana," the statement said, "is further complicating the work of the police and is placing himself in grave danger of being shot by people whose nerves are on edge from the recent murders." When young people began tailing possible suspects or setting themselves up as decoys, parking on dark country roads, Gonzaullas warned that "amateur sleuthing" was "a good way to get killed."

The Phantom Killer was now an international story. According to Michael Newton, author of *The Texarkana Moonlight Murders*, "No other manhunt since the search for London's 'Jack the Ripper,' back in 1888, had generated such publicity around the world." As more officers poured into Texarkana from other parts of the state, the fear spread to other cities. In Kilgore a man said he had picked up a hitchhiker who robbed him and claimed to be the Phantom. Citizens in Lufkin worried that a red-haired peeping Tom might be the Phantom. A man in Houston confessed to killing a man and woman in Texarkana, but an hour later he denied it, saying he had been drinking. Oklahoma Highway Patrol and FBI agents searched for an escaped German prisoner of war who, they said, was a Phantom suspect. Commenting on the widespread reports, Gonzaullas said, "It's a cinch this man can't be in Kilgore, Lufkin, Corsicana, Oklahoma, and Texarkana at the same time."

On May 8 the mutilated body of Earl Cliff McSpadden, an itinerant oil-storage-tank builder, was found on a railroad track near Texarkana. The coroner ruled he had been killed before being hit by a train. For a time he was thought to be the sixth victim of the Phantom. On May 30 Aleene Peavy, a divorcee, was found in a parked car dead of bullet wounds to her head and body. In a car parked by Peavy's but facing the opposite direction, Mrs. J. C. Johnston was found in critical condition, shot in the head, a pistol by her side. The cars were on a gravel road north of De Kalb. Officers denied it was the work of the Phantom.[7]

In his diary for Saturday, May 4, Dixon writes, "Plant—Prowl—All night." The word "Plant" suggests he served as a decoy, either with another officer, one of them wearing a wig, or alone with a borrowed mannequin in the car beside him. At 4:45 a.m. on May 7, working with Ed Marshall of the Texarkana Police Department, he investigated a complaint by a woman that she had been raped. He closed the investigation after determining she was "on dope" and unreliable. On Monday, June 24, he arrested a man who, a woman claimed, had threatened her with a pistol and intended to rape her. Dixon considered the man a suspect in the Phantom killings but on Thursday cleared him as a suspect, and at her husband's request, the woman dropped her complaint.

On July 22, local officers asked that Dixon, Ranger Stanley, and Deputy Sheriff Frank Riley drive to DeKalb, thirty miles west of Texarkana, to apprehend a café operator who had fired a shot from his café and barricaded himself inside. When the Rangers threatened to throw tear-gas bombs through the windows, he gave himself up. On July 23, during Dixon's last week in Texarkana, he and Stanley traveled to Lewisville, Arkansas, to help Lafayette County Sheriff Ocie Griffin investigate a Phantom suspect who had been arrested for assault with intent to rape. On July 25 Dixon and a railway special agent fingerprinted and identified the bodies of Lugean "Shade" Bead and

Henry "Trotting Horse" Graves, which had been found on railroad tracks near Texarkana. The officers determined that a train, not the Phantom, had killed the men.

On July 27, two days before his last departure from Texarkana, Dixon had been in the city long enough to be mentioned in the society section of the *Texarkana Daily News:* "Sheriff Bill Presley and Texas Ranger N. K. Dixon forsaking their usual felt hats for 'ranch style straws.'" He also had been mentioned earlier in an International News Service article laudatory of the Texas Rangers in Texarkana that referred to Dixon as a "slight, tightly-knit Ranger whose rugged history includes Olympic boxing not to mention numerous gun battles."[8]

Dixon did not forget the Phantom during his alternate weeks in McKinney. He continued investigating suspects by making long-distance telephone calls, collecting information within his subdistrict, and conferring with Captain Gonzaullas at Company B headquarters. But on Sunday, August 4, he forgot it all, storing HQ 25-B in Dallas and taking a vacation, not retrieving his state vehicle until Saturday, August 17. On Monday, August 19, he was back at work, plunging into an investigation of the murder of eighty-year-old Mrs. N. O. Kreager, an event that, at the end of the year, the Associated Press would vote the number-eleven top story in Texas for 1946. (The Phantom was the number-one story.)

Kreager, who had lived frugally in a modest house and made many contributions to Grayson County churches, was known by her nine adult children to have carried thousands of dollars in a money belt wrapped around her waist. On June 17, the day she disappeared, she had cashed a check for $8,344, saying she was going to buy a house. Almost two months later, when two farmers looked into a dry well on a farm five miles north of Sherman trying to find a missing cow, they found Kreager's decomposed body covered with lime. Because Dixon was on vacation, Gonzaullas sent Ranger Badgett to aid in the investigation of Kreager's death.

A Denison man, interested in collecting the thousand-dollar reward, had asked a fortune teller for the location of the body. She described the location, said that Kreager was being held in a shack, that she would be poisoned, and that her body would be tossed into a nearby well. The man never collected the reward, but he was arrested and questioned. The fortune teller also was questioned. Beginning on August 19, working closely with Ranger Badgett and Sheriff Gafford, Dixon threw himself into the investigation during his last five months in Company B, conducting innumerable interviews, interrogating a number of possible suspects, and checking records at banks, county government offices, and the like. He interviewed all Kreager's adult children and their spouses, and on two occasions he interviewed Ernest Millsap, one of Kreager's sons-in-law. On November 3, 1948, long after Dixon had left Company B and after Grayson County had changed sheriffs, Ernest Millsap was arrested at his home in Sherman for the murder of his mother-in-law, but the Sherman grand jury no billed him, leaving unsolved the murder of the money-belt-wearing eighty-year-old grandmother.[9]

While working on the number-eleven story in Texas for 1946, Dixon continued thinking of the unresolved top story. On October 30 Martin Stover Tuley, a thirty-two-year-old Van Alstyne farmer and ex-convict, was charged with rape, kidnapping, and armed robbery in an attack on a sixteen-year-old girl. Collin County District Attorney Dwight Whitsell told the press that Tuley's tactics were similar to those of the Phantom, and Sheriff W. L. Brown said he was taking extra precautions by moving Tuley to an unnamed jail. Captain Gonzaullas told the press he was investigating the possibility that Tuley might be the Phantom but that the similarity between his case and that of the Phantom "was not as marked as some believed." The following morning, at Gonzaullas' request, Dixon interrogated Tuley. Later he told the press that Tuley was not a "good suspect" in the Phantom slayings. A few weeks later, Tuley was convicted of rape and sentenced to fifty years in prison. The Phantom killer remained unknown and uncaught, although years later Gonzaullas would claim that officers thought they knew who he was but lacked sufficient evidence.[10]

Three days prior to interrogating Tuley, when Dixon was in Montague County investigating Robert and J. B. Posey, brothers accused of stealing cattle, he was contacted by Sheriff "Buck" Jameson, who relayed a message from Captain Gonzaullas: "Dick, I talked with Mrs. Dixon at noon today October 28, 1946. She tried to reach you by telephone to tell you that your son Kenneth broke his arm yesterday, and wants you to call her at home as soon as you possibly can. I tried to reach you at Ft. Worth, but could not do so. We called the Sheriff at Montague, and asked him to deliver this message to you." Always solicitous of "his boys," the captain continued, "In the Guest Room, you will find some blankets folded up on the settee. Two of these are for you, so pick them up and take them home with you, and let me know how your boy is getting along." He closed with "Your Friend" and his signature. In his diary Dixon does not note when he received the "emergency call" from the sheriff, nor does he mention if he called Leona long distance. He did not arrive at home until midnight.

Dixon continued the Posey cattle-theft investigation, working with the other Rangers and sheriffs. With Ranger Norvell Redwine he interrogated the brothers, and with Cooke County Sheriff Horn he recovered property stolen by the Poseys. Two days later, Howard County Sheriff Bob Wolf announced that a major cattle-theft case had been broken, the Posey brothers were in jail, and some of the stolen cattle and other goods had been recovered, including fifty cakes of cottonseed meal, farm wrenches, and plow tools. Over the next several weeks, the brothers received five-year prison terms in a Dawson County trial and eight-year sentences in a Howard County trial.[11]

On December 11, 1946, Dixon encountered a rare situation—a victim who turned the tables and made his attacker the victim. The aggressor, six feet two inches in height, weighing one hundred ninety pounds, was walking in heavy rain along Highway 75 about 2:00 p.m. when a small man, five feet seven inches and one hundred thirty pounds, stopped his car to give the large man a ride. "It was raining like the devil and I thought I would do the fellow a favor," the small man said later. "I picked him up and we drove about a mile. I didn't say much. Suddenly this guy jammed something in my ribs, slapped me across the mouth, and said: 'I'm the boss now. If you won't talk, this .45 will. I can use this car.'" After four more miles, the passenger said to pull over at the service station they were approaching. The driver did as instructed, and as the large man took the keys, with his left hand still jammed into the driver's ribs, he told him to move across the seat and get out on the passenger side of the car. Instead the driver grabbed the large man's hand, discovered there was no gun, and hit him so hard that the man fell out of the car. The "victim" jumped on top of him and began swinging away, and for the next ten minutes, they fought all over the service-station lot until the large man lay still.

During the fight the station owner ordered the two to leave, and the owner's wife, holding a baby, stood watching along with others who had stopped at the station because of the heavy rain. With the large man lying still, the small one rushed to another station about a mile away to telephone his old friend Brandon Everett, a highway patrolman. The two were often seen drinking coffee together in McKinney cafés. Brandon, his partner S. H. Denton, and Ranger N. K. Dixon (who that morning had attended the trial of Martin Stover Tuley) jumped into Brandon's patrol car and sped to the scene. Dixon and Brandon, both stationed in McKinney, had worked together on a number of cases. By the time they arrived at the station, the large man had fled toward a house several hundred yards down the road. The officers and the small man rushed to the house, which was the home of Mrs. Park Grissom. Inside they found the offender trying to force Mrs. Grissom to give him clothes to replace his bloodied and torn shirt and pants. The officers and the little man quickly subdued him. Grinning, the slightly built man said, "This home-coming wasn't like the last one."

He was referring to his return to Texas the year before as the most decorated American soldier of World War II, recipient of the Medal of Honor and thirty-six other medals. His name was Audie Murphy. Just that morning he had returned from Hollywood, where he was being made into a movie star, and he was driving to his sister's house in Farmersville, a few miles east of McKinney, when he gave the man a ride. The next morning, newspapers all over Texas carried a *Dallas Morning News* photograph of the war hero, his tie loose and his clothes ruffled, standing in front of his car with the door open, smiling broadly as he described his encounter to Brandon, Denton, and Dixon.[12]

Audie Murphy gives his account of the incident to two highway patrolmen and Norman Dixon, who is on the right. *Courtesy Dallas Morning News.*

The Dixons had lived at 703 S. Parker St. in McKinney since Norman's transfer to Company B four years earlier. Leona and Norman had a circle of friends in the town, and the boys, turning six and eight in 1946, were within walking distance of school and enjoyed playing with young friends in the neighborhood. But the landlord sold their rental house, and in June 1946 Norman had to start searching for a new place to live. Finding nothing available in McKinney, he had to consider moving to another town in his subdistrict. He wanted another rental house, but he could find nothing in Denton, which seemed to be his first choice. Nor was a house available in Sherman or Gainesville. By December 14, with time running out, he gave up the search for a house and wrote a letter responding to a classified ad in the Sherman newspaper for an unfurnished five-room upstairs apartment, explaining that he had been a Texas Ranger for nine years. Would they, he asked, be willing to rent to him?[13]

If Dixon received a response, he did not keep it. Nor did he move his family to Sherman—or any other town in his subdistrict. On January 31,

1947, Captain Gonzaullas told him he was being placed on a leave of absence. Effective February 2 he would be on the payroll of the state senate, assigned to the Senate General Investigating Committee to conduct an investigation of a scandal involving the Board of Pardons and Paroles. The two-month investigation would leave him homesick for Leona and the boys, who were allowed to continue living on S. Parker St. in McKinney. But after completing his work for the senate committee, instead of returning home, he was loaned to a joint legislative committee to conduct an investigation at Texas A&M College. That would take another two months.

Norman Dixon never returned to McKinney, to his subdistrict, or to work for Lone Wolf Gonzaullas. In June 1947 Colonel Garrison transferred him to the Office of the Director, DPS, where he would report directly to Garrison as a special investigator. Instead of Dixon returning home to his family, his family would come to him and a new home.

Chapter Twelve

AGGIES REVOLT!

On the morning of December 23, 1946, Norman Dixon, Denton County Sheriff Roy Moore, and Deputy Sam Gentry investigated the December 1 theft of fifty-one tires from the Huffines Motor Company in Lewisville, Denton County, and its connection to a December 17 theft of fifty-three tires from the Co-op store in Frisco, only a few miles from Lewisville. That afternoon Dixon was in Gainesville with Cooke County Sheriff Emory Horn investigating a bank-robbery. It was a fairly typical day for a Texas Ranger, but unbeknown to Dixon, his "typical" Ranger duties were coming to an end. Because of trouble brewing two hundred miles away, in Palestine, East Texas, his career soon would take a new direction.

The day before, more than a thousand people had gathered at the First Baptist Church in Palestine, Anderson County, to protest a clemency ruling. The Pardons and Paroles Board had recommended, and Gov. Coke Stevenson had approved, setting aside a one-year prison sentence and reducing a fine of five hundred dollars to one hundred dollars for Marshall Morris, who had been convicted of beating a twenty-three-year-old nurse so badly that she was hospitalized for a week. Telegrams protesting the clemency ruling poured into the governor's office, and a delegation of Anderson County officials made plans to drive to Austin to meet with the governor in person. Stevenson's image was that of a calm, pipe-smoking, low-key politician whose idea of a curse was "goldang." During the uproar over Marshall Morris, Stevenson calmly puffed on his pipe as he listened to both sides and mulled his options.[1]

A decade earlier, in response to charges of corruption and leniency in the clemency process under the previous governor, Miriam "Ma" Ferguson, and the lack of supervision of parolees, newly elected Gov. James Allred set up a new clemency system with voluntary parole boards and a reorganized Board of Pardons and Paroles. Not all agreed with Governor Allred, and by 1945 the pardons and paroles system was becoming mired in controversy. Wharton County Sheriff Buck Lane, one of the more influential peace officers in the state, said, "I have been told that some convicts and trustees in the penitentiary system are working a 'shake down' racket on applicants for clemency." Houston Police Department Inspector C. V. "Buster" Kern estimated that parolees and former convicts were responsible for about 80 percent of major crimes in Texas. The president of the Sheriffs' Association of Texas asked why convicts sentenced to two or three years in prison were being released after having served only a few months. Abner Lewis, a member of the Board of Pardons and Paroles, responding at an annual sheriffs' convention, said board members face heavy pressure from mothers, wives, and leading citizens to give clemency to prisoners who are eligible for parole. They were eligible if they had served one-third of their term with good conduct.[2]

In Palestine the heavy pressure came from citizens demanding that the governor rescind the clemency he had extended to Marshall Morris. On December 30, 1946, following a meeting with a delegation of officials from Palestine, Governor Stevenson announced his decision to rescind the clemency: Morris would go to prison and pay the full fine. The governor explained that clemency recommendations came to his office from the Board of Pardons and Paroles in batches of thirty to forty. He looked carefully at those involving a major crime, he said, but usually followed the board's recommendations on others.[3]

The citizens of Palestine calmed down, but as the clemency process continued to be an issue, the Pardons and Paroles Board asked for an investigation of charges that convicts thought one thousand dollars could buy them freedom. In January 1947, Lt. Gov. Allan Shivers, who presided over the Senate, appointed a general investigating committee to look into the system. A. M. Aikin Jr., of Paris, chairman of the committee, asked Colonel Garrison to provide an investigator who could ferret out the information needed for the committee. Garrison contacted Captain Gonzaullas, who called Dixon to his office on Friday, January 31, and told him to be in Austin Monday morning to meet with Garrison and Senator Aikin to begin his new assignment. He would be put on a leave of absence from the Ranger force and placed on the senate payroll. He had about forty-eight hours to get everything in order, notifying county officials in his subdistrict that he was leaving for several weeks, tying up loose ends on pending cases, packing, and saying good-bye to Leona and the boys.[4]

In Austin on Monday morning Dixon and Colonel Garrison met with Senator Aikin, and that afternoon Dixon met with the full committee and the state auditor. Settling into his new assignment, Dixon alternated between attending closed sessions of the committee and investigating leads. In the latter role, he identified subjects in suspected parole cases at the identification bureau in Camp Mabry, researched Texas prison records in Huntsville, checked the files of the Board of Pardons and Paroles, making photocopies of key documents, and gathered information on ex-convict Fred P. Kohut of Houston. On February 24 he met with committee members regarding suspected cases, and on February 26 the committee held its first open hearing. That same day Leona called Norman long distance. She had the mumps.[5]

Abner Lewis, chairman of the parole board, was grilled for four hours as the sole witness in the committee's first public hearing. Making extensive use of photocopied documents and records prepared by Dixon for the hearing, the committee members questioned Lewis about specific cases pulled from board files, showing clemency given to convicts with multiple convictions, records of escapes and attempted escapes, and violations of prison rules and clemency conditions. Lewis, described by the *Austin American* as "a chunky, square-faced, whitehaired man," chain-smoked cigarettes as the committee members "hammered away at the tall stack of records before them." He admitted that it looked bad but complained that only the bad ones had been picked out.

The questioning became especially intense when the subject turned to Fred P. Kohut, whom Dixon investigated for two days in Houston. Lewis said he had known Kohut, an investigator for a Houston law firm, for twenty-five years but learned only recently that in 1926–1927 Kohut had served fourteen months in a federal penitentiary in Georgia. Lewis said Kohut had visited his office and phoned him on numerous occasions regarding clemency requests. Senator Harris produced a lengthy list of telephone calls Lewis had made to Kohut and a photocopy of a letter dated January 2, 1946, from Lewis asking Kohut for "instructions" on what to do about Earl Gaddis Woolley, a deserter and jail escapee who had been sentenced to seven years for a series of burglaries but had turned down an "out-of-state" conditional pardon to face burglary charges in the state of Washington. He did not want to face the charges. Later that month Kohut won a six-month reprieve for Woolley. Lewis, stating at the beginning and again at the end of his testimony that the parole board had no law to follow in making clemency decisions, suggested that a law providing the board some guidance would be helpful.[6]

The next morning Dixon notified the committee members that he had to go home to take care of Leona. After a few days he returned, and through the month of March he continued his work for the committee, which included drafting their report to the legislature and the governor. On the morning of April 3, Senator Aikin asked Dixon to contact Sen. Fred Harris, who was on Aikin's committee but also had been made chairman of a Joint Legislative Investigating Committee to look into charges against Texas A&M College. By 10:30 a.m. Dixon had been made the investigator for the joint committee and was on the road to College Station, carrying with him subpoenas for eight students to appear at a committee hearing. But it was Easter weekend; none of the students were on campus.[7]

Issued on May 5, the official report of the Senate General Investigating Committee on the Board of Pardons and Paroles called for the immediate resignation of Abner Lewis, the board chairman, charging that he was more responsible than other board members for abuses of the system. The report alleged that Lewis had "numerous direct contacts with regular and frequent clemency seekers, some of whom went to his office 'up the back stairs.'" Lewis responded quickly, saying, "I positively refuse to resign." He thought it odd that the only specific complaint made against him was that "I talked to convicts and people dealing in clemency matters, which is a principal function of this board." The committee also found that the board frequently had not considered convicts' current prison records, that there had been a lack of uniformity in the board's clemency recommendations, and that the governor's office was too lax in handling clemency requests. The committee recommended a constitutional amendment to eliminate the parole board and return the issuance of clemencies to the governor, where it had been before Governor Allred reformed the system. But the governor said he had no intention of abolishing the parole board.[8]

The legislature passed a compromise bill that the governor did sign into law. Under the new act, courts had the authority to place on probation persons convicted of crimes other than murder, rape, and morals if their sentence was under ten years and they had no prior convictions. The act also provided for paid parole and probation supervisors, but because no money was allocated for salaries, the use of county volunteer boards continued. The act also established a five-man commission to investigate the eligibility of persons proposed for appointment to the Board of Pardons and Paroles. The next vacancy was expected to occur on February 1, 1949. The incumbent: Abner Lewis.[9]

When Dixon arrived at College Station on April 3, he set foot on the oldest public institution of higher education in the state: Texas Agricultural and Mechanical College. Texas A&M opened its doors in 1876 as an all-male military institution in which every student was required to be a member of the Corps of Cadets—a requirement that would be relaxed through later generations, as would the "male-only" rule. Its students had served honorably and with distinction in every war since the Spanish-American War. In World War II approximately twenty thousand members of the armed forces, including fourteen thousand officers (of whom twenty-nine were generals), had attended the college. More officers had gone to Texas A&M than to both military academies combined.[10]

During the 1944–45 school year—1945 being the last year of World War II—enrollment dropped below two thousand, but in June 1944, Congress passed unanimously and President Franklin D. Roosevelt signed the G.I. Bill of Rights, which offered vocational training and higher education to military personnel who had served during the war. Consequently, during the postwar years better than a million returning veterans would use the G.I. Bill to go to college. The 1946–1947 school year saw Texas A&M overflowing with 7,750 students, of whom 5,500 were war veterans. Because these students were older and had been through war, they were more mature, ambitious, and dedicated than typical college students.[11]

But the trouble did not begin with the veterans on campus. On January 28, 1947, an article in *The Battalion,* the student newspaper, announced that, at the recommendation of Texas A&M President Gibb Gilchrist and with the approval of the A&M board of directors, discipline of the cadet corps had been transferred from John W. Rollins, the dean of men, to Col. Guy S. Meloy Jr., corps commandant, and that new antihazing rules had been adopted. Senior officers could no longer require freshmen to clean their rooms, run their errands, or perform other personal service for them, nor could they require extra drills for freshmen except as authorized by college authorities. Use of the paddle or any other form of physical hazing was prohibited.

Anger shot through the cadet ranks. At midnight, accompanied by the corps band playing the "Aggie War Hymn," many of the 2,100 members of the cadet corps marched from their dormitory to the home of President Gilchrist, where fifteen cadet officers handed him the resignations of about two hundred commissioned and noncommissioned corps officers. They were resigning, they told the president, because the new rules for discipline of the corps took away their basic responsibilities and because hazing was as old as A&M. Gilchrist accepted the resignations "with regret." But in a meeting the next night, the senior officers voted to rescind their resignations and ask for them to be restored. They had the responsibility, they said in a statement, to carry out their duties as representatives of the U.S. Army and to carry out the orders of the A&M military authorities. However they also voted overwhelmingly to ask for President Gilchrist's resignation, and they drafted twelve proposals that would give them more voice in student government.

George R. White, head of the A&M board, said that hazing had become so bad that the board felt it had to be stopped. He also said the board was pleased with the work of Gilchrist. According to Gilchrist, hazing led 48 percent of freshmen to leave A&M after the first year. A majority of those who had left in the previous semester had no time to study, he said, because they were too busy cleaning rooms, running errands, and undergoing extra drill by order of senior officers. Commandant Meloy, who was also professor of military science and tactics, blamed three or four "senior irreconcilables" for stirring up the cadets. He said those who wanted their commissions restored must make their request in writing.[12]

Two teams of corpsmen took their campaign on the road to force Gilchrist's resignation. One team met with ex-students in Amarillo. The other team was in Dallas, where Cadet William Gilbert told members of the local A&M Club that the president's statement about hazing was an insult to cadets. What the cadets wanted, he said, was not hazing but class distinctions. "We want," he said, "to see A&M put back on the basis of what it was when you older men were in school—when the senior's word was law." According to the Associated Press, "Gilbert's talk aroused a storm of debate and table pounding among the Aggie alumni present, but the club took no formal action." Back on campus, the cadets held a series of meetings. In response Colonel Meloy warned them to quit "fiddling around." The demands of the cadets were unanswered. They continued to insist on no compromises, but most submitted written requests for new commissions.[13]

At a Texas A&M board meeting on February 21, Bill McCormick, president of the senior class and one of seven senior cadets who spoke at the meeting, told the board that Gilchrist should be removed because he lacked interest in students, that there was no cooperation between the administration and the student body, and that the new regulations were "literally crammed down our throats without [our] being consulted. Traditionally the student body has been heard in such things." After listening to the students, the board members expressed their confidence in Gilchrist, and for about a month after that, the students remained fairly quiet.

The next eruption occurred on March 19, when students demanded that two cadet officers resign. The officers turned in their resignations, but college officials rejected them and told the students they did not have the right to make such a demand. Up to this point, veterans on campus had remained silent. But on Wednesday, March 26, W. S. Andrews, president of the Veterans Student Association of Texas A&M College, called for a mass meeting of students on Thursday "to bring the truth of our college administration to the people of the state."[14]

On Thursday student veterans filled the two-thousand-seat Assembly Hall, others stood wherever they could, and hundreds massed outside. They cheered when part of a letter from the Winter Garden A&M Club, in Uvalde, was read that called for the "outright removal" of President Gilchrist. They cheered again upon hearing a letter from the Fort Worth A&M Mother's Club calling for a "strong, able leader for our sons." The students "roared approval" of a resolution calling for the removal of Gilchrist. Andrews discussed several issues the organization had with the administration, including the high profits of the college exchange store, the purchase of a Brazos River bottomland farm by the college at an inflated price, and the president's refusal to accept the free gift of Bryan Army Air Field. Andrews concluded by saying, "The administration has completely failed to measure up to its responsibilities."

Two events occurred on Friday, March 28. At an A&M board meeting, Bill McCormick, senior-class president, testified of student grievances regarding the administration. Board members peppered McCormick with questions about an open letter from the class of 1948 charging corruption in the college. Five thousand copies of the letter had been printed and paid for out of the senior-class fund. At the state capitol, Rep. Searcy Bracewell, of Houston, called on the House of Representatives to investigate the "deplorable incidents" at Texas A&M College, which "have caused great distress and consternation to the people of Texas." By a vote of 90 to 31, the House adopted a Senate resolution—Senate Concurrent Resolution 21—for the lieutenant governor to appoint five senators and the House speaker to appoint five representatives "to constitute a Joint Committee . . . to make a complete and thorough investigation of the present controversy at Texas A&M College and to inquire fully into all matters of disagreement between the student body and the administration."[15]

On Saturday the A&M board announced that students had been invited to its meetings to present "any factual information bearing upon charges . . . against the proper conduct of the office of the president. . . . We have not been able to develop one single factual charge in these hearings." The board responded in detail to the issues listed by the Veterans Student Association. All exchange-store profits went to student benefits, including a dividend to students; the Brazos River bottomland purchase was based on two separate appraisals; and the federal government had not offered the airfield to the college. The board again declared its support of President Gilchrist, and, along with the representatives of the senior class and the Veterans Student Association, welcomed the investigation by the legislature.[16]

On Good Friday, April 4, Dixon told Sen. Fred "Red" Harris, chairman of the Joint Legislative Investigating Committee, that none of the eight subpoenaed students were on campus because of Easter break but that he would return to College Station on Monday to deliver the subpoenas. On Saturday Harris told the press he was not interested in investigating A&M if the college problems were simply "schoolboys sticking their tongues out at the teacher." On Monday morning Dixon served subpoenas summoning the eight students—all members of the Veterans Student Association—to a Tuesday-night legislative-committee hearing in Austin.[17]

At the hearing, Andrews, the veterans-group president and the committee's first witness, charged that Gilchrist was "ill-equipped" to perform the duties of a college president. In his five-thousand-word prepared statement, he said the administration had failed to provide leadership and that Gilchrist was incorrect in saying that the unrest was caused by the new antihazing rules. He and his group of more than 5,500 veterans had "seen the steady deterioration of the morale and vigor of our students and faculty." At Wednesday's hearing, Sam Williams, treasurer of the association, said, "Fear exists among the students and faculty about making any comments about the administration of the college." Dixon sat in on both hearings, and he subpoenaed six members of the A&M board to appear as witnesses at Thursday evening's hearing.[18]

At no point in Dixon's career did he have the luxury of focusing on one assignment. Even though the parole-board investigation had been completed

In the lower left is a student being questioned by the joint committee investigating Texas A&M. Chairman Fred "Red" Harris is third from the right; Norman Dixon is fourth. *Author's Collection.*

and Dixon was now on the A&M assignment, Aikin continued to call on Dixon to review bills and amendments filed to fix the pardons and paroles system, and he relied on Dixon's skills for an investigation of the Texas Good Roads Association, which disagreed on the need for new rural roads, a pet project of Aikin's. By the end of the session, Aikin had obtained more funding for rural roads.[19]

That Thursday evening, after a hearing on the Texas Good Roads Association, Dixon attended Senator Harris's committee hearing on student unrest at A&M. Eight of the nine members of the A&M board testified, each stating that the student unrest was caused by the implementation of antihazing rules in January—in direct contrast to every student's statement, during the Tuesday and Wednesday hearings, that the new rules did not cause the uproar. One board member, Travis L. Smith, an A&M graduate whose three sons also had graduated from the school, said he was aware of "brutal beatings of freshmen students," including one beaten so badly he was confined to bed. George White, the board president, said that Dr. T. O. Walton, the previous college president, was not reelected because he had failed to stop hazing despite being ordered to do so by the board. The board members argued that the best way to restore peace on campus was to back up the board and the campus administration.[20]

On Saturday, April 12, Dixon served subpoenas to Dr. Walton, Gilchrist's predecessor as president, and to Frank C. Bolton, executive vice president and dean of men, to testify Monday night and Tuesday. In his testimony Dr. Walton, who was serving as postmaster at College Station, blamed the campus controversy on the "ineptness" of the board and college administrators and asserted that the hazing issue was a "smokescreen." Dean Bolton said that 509 freshmen students dropped out of school during the past year, 373 from the cadet corps. Of the freshmen who left, 75 did so as a result of hazing, 16 because of injuries incurred. He added that complaints about hazing were increasing but the college was unable to get control of it.[21]

During the next three days Dixon roamed the Aggie campus interviewing administrators, students, and faculty members, including Dr. F. C. Clark, head of the Economics Department, who in his testimony on April 21 accused the administration of intimidating students and faculty and expressed fear that the abuses might lead to a repeat of a campus controversy in 1920: "It was actually dangerous to walk down the streets. There were bullets whistling around your head. Frankly, I'm afraid the same thing will happen again." Thus far, he asserted, the stabilizing influence of the veterans on campus had prevented it. Under questioning, however, he was unable to cite a specific instance of intimidation. He also had trouble explaining what he meant when, a few weeks earlier in a speech in Dallas, he said that teaching under Gilchrist was "hell on earth." His objectivity was also brought into question by his frustration at losing his fishpond when the college had it drained as part of a mosquito-control program. In dismissing Clark, Chairman Harris said, "You know less about the things happening at the college than anyone who has appeared before this committee. You failed to give us one definite fact."

Former A&M student and Navy veteran Delbert V. Schultz testified that he was part of a group of ten students who held secret meetings in late 1945 on how to get President Gilchrist removed from office. He said that he wrote the letter, Travis Bryan, president of a Bryan bank, mimeographed it, and the senior class distributed it and that some of its criticism of Gilchrist's administration came from T. O. Walton. Shultz and other students had also planned a march on the state capitol to publicize their opposition to Gilchrist but had dropped the plan after Shultz, seeking permission for the Aggies to sleep at Camp Mabry, met with Arthur B. Knickerbocker, state adjutant general, who discouraged the idea, saying it would damage the image of A&M. Shultz explained that he had a personal grievance against Gilchrist, having been dismissed from A&M on November 16, 1946, "because of insufficient grades and Mr. Gilchrist's desire not to have me on the campus."

When President Gilchrist testified, he offered photocopies of fifty-four letters as examples of more than four hundred he had received during the past year regarding hazing. He read two letters aloud. The first said, "When my son came home for Christmas he was beat black from the belt down." The second was from a mother: "He said the seniors beat him for every letter in the words 'Merry Christmas.' Now one of his hips has no feeling whatever. I have another son who is a nervous wreck from the hazing at A&M. The seniors made him do 750 knee bends."[22]

On Friday, April 25, Dixon subpoenaed Colonel Meloy, cadet corps commandant, John Rollins, dean of men, and Col. Frank G. Anderson, track coach, to testify at Monday's hearing. At the hearing Anderson testified that the problem was "the Aggie system." He explained: "Upperclassmen at the college are interested primarily in making an Aggie out of freshmen. Other things, such as education, come second." Anderson said he had to transfer several members of the track team out of the cadet corps so they could rest and study. Dean Rollins testified that the remedy was for the committee to let the A&M board run the college and to help them do so. Colonel Meloy testified that conditions had improved somewhat.[23]

After a month of hearings, the tide of opinion seemed to tilt toward the board and college administration. However, the State Federation of Mothers Clubs of Texas A&M supported the students and called for Gilchrist's resignation, and a statewide poll in early May showed that 31 percent of those polled blamed the officials for the problems at A&M, whereas only 16 percent cast the students as the villains. A *Dallas Morning News* editorial stated, "Most of the witnesses have been anti-Gilchrist in intent, but the result thus far boils down to the astonishing fact that there simply isn't any anti-Gilchrist evidence." Weldon Hart wrote in the *Austin American* that "the two 'anti-Gilchrist' witnesses who testified Tuesday [Schultz and Clark] did Gilchrist more good than the entire array of administration and Board of Directors members." *The Battalion* published an editorial stating that the administration had satisfactorily answered most of the questions. The ex-students of Texas A&M College met on the campus, and after listening to three officers of the Veterans Student Association press their case, voted unanimously their full confidence in the A&M board.[24]

On May 13 Dixon and a highway patrolman drove two state vehicles carrying six committee members, three from each house of the legislature, to the campus for an executive session with numerous students and faculty members, many of whom had testified previously. They ate lunch at the college mess hall, which had been criticized by students for the cost and quality of its meals. As the legislators walked through the hall toward their table, a student said, "Let them sit down here and eat some of this stuff." Senator Harris, overhearing the comment, sat down by the student, saying, "Here's where I eat, boys." The hearing was held in the afternoon. In the evening the legislators attended the annual college Press Club banquet on campus, where they laughed heartily as students lampooned the committee by putting on a humorous sketch playing committee members and witnesses in a mock hearing. The student actors had attended hearings in Austin to learn the mannerisms and speaking styles of the persons they impersonated. After a full day mixed with seriousness and frivolity, Dixon and the highway patrolman drove the legislators back to Austin, arriving at 3:15 a.m.[25]

On the day after the hearing on the Texas A&M campus, Senator Harris predicted that it would take two to three weeks to complete the committee report, saying, "We have at least 2,000 pages of testimony and I personally want to go over every page of it again before I start working on the report." Dixon, the committee investigator, also had something personal he wanted to do along with finishing his work for the committee. By late May he knew his days in Company B were over. He had been on loan to the Texas Senate for almost four months, living in Austin while Leona stayed in McKinney with the boys, who were attending elementary school. He would return to the DPS payroll, retaining his commission as a Texas Ranger but, effective June 7, 1947, reporting directly to Colonel Garrison, DPS director, as a special investigator. He needed to bring his family to a new home.[26]

On June 6, Dixon's last day on the senate payroll, the Joint Legislative Investigating Committee issued its report. Seven of the ten members backed the A&M board and President Gilchrist, placing some blame on outsiders such as former president T. O. Walton and former student Delbert Schultz for contributing to student unrest and discontent. The report described "hazing" as "extremely cruel and inhuman . . . of comparative recent origin" and "never a part of the finer and more cherished traditions of the institution." The other three board members, all former A&M students, agreed that few charges were verified but faulted the board members for not "thoroughly acquainting themselves with current student problems and life on the campus of the college" and the president and his administration for failing "to command the full respect to which they should be entitled."

On June 10 Dixon submitted his report to Colonel Garrison in a two-page letter with the majority and minority committee reports attached. In his letter he wrote that the charges and allegations "were in effect that the President, Gib Gilchrist, was 'inept,' which in itself failed to be upheld by any facts presented." He wrote of the considerable time he spent at the college with students, faculty, and staff, and he concluded that there were several causes for the unrest, including the great influx of war veterans and crowded living conditions.

"The basic cause," he wrote, "no doubt being the administration's concerted attempt to stamp out the hazing practices, which had so developed as to be considered by the older students and some ex-students as 'tradition,' but which in fact had grown to an unprecedented proportion involving actual brutality." The veterans group on campus, he believed, took control of the "uprising" and "pressed the agitation" although they "had no facts." He cited Travis Bryan, the Bryan banker, T. O. Walton, the previous president, and F. C. Clark, head of the Economics Department, for "aiding and abetting the agitation." Clark seemed to Dixon "to be a mental case, appearing paranoiac to the writer."[27]

The Veterans Student Association of Texas A&M did not take the committee's report lying down. The new officers of the association, who had taken office during the summer session, issued a statement that the findings were politically motivated and that they recognized Gilchrist's qualifications as "an engineer and politician" but did "not accept his ability as an educator or leader." They charged that the "unhealthy conditions which caused this legislative investigation are still in existence on this campus today." But Gilchrist had the last laugh. In May 1948 the A&M board adopted one of the committee recommendations by establishing the Texas A&M College System with a chancellor over four colleges—Texas A&M College, at College Station; North Texas Agricultural College, at Arlington; Tarleton Agricultural College, at Stephenville; and Prairie View A&M, at Prairie View—and several other public services. The new chancellor: Gibb Gilchrist.[28]

After eating supper on July 8, Dixon returned to Camp Mabry, intending to continue working on an assignment from Colonel Garrison. Instead, at 7:30 p.m. he joined Investigator Frank Probst and Major Harper at Lake Travis, thirty miles east of Austin. They dragged the lake until 1:00 a.m. in search of the body of Cecil Prewitt, an army veteran and prominent citizen of Taylor. Prewitt was boating with his wife and a friend, and when his dog leaped into the lake, Prewitt dived in after it and drowned. The three men returned to the lake at 6:00 a.m., continuing the search for the body until 9:00 p.m. Dixon and Probst searched the lake by boat on July 15 and by plane on July 19, 21, 23, and 26. The body finally surfaced on July 27, nineteen days after he drowned and one day after a Navy diving crew from New Orleans had begun searching about 150 yards away. Major Harper was one of the searchers who found the body.

More than a decade earlier Dixon had developed a love of flying during his service in the U.S. Army Air Corps. His love of flying resurfaced during the four flights over Lake Travis, and on August 5 he and Probst visited the Austin airport to look into the possibility of purchasing a Cessna for DPS.[29]

On Saturday, July 26, after returning from that day's flight, Dixon received another assignment from Colonel Garrison: protect Governor Jester and his staff "against radical action" by Dr. William Roland Newton Jr., who on Friday, after a week of hearings, was denied a full pardon by the Board of Pardons and Paroles. Dixon was well aware of the bizarre set of events that had been swirling around Newton for the past five years, beginning late on the night of May 20, 1942, when another physician, Dr. Roy Hunt, received a series of telephone calls at his Littlefield home, north of Lubbock, where he was playing bridge with his wife and friends. According to Hunt's later testimony, a woman whose voice was familiar asked him to drive to a spot on a country road two miles from Littlefield. When he arrived there around midnight, he saw Dr. Newton's wife, Ruth, sitting in a car. As he started talking to her, Dr. Newton came running up, shooting at him and yelling, "Don't you know she's a married woman?" Wounded, Hunt fled into a field and hid in a furrow as Newton continued firing at him. As Hunt hid, Newton tried to find him by aiming his automobile headlights at the field. After the Newtons finally drove away, Hunt drove to his Littlefield clinic, where he underwent surgery performed by his brother, a doctor who drove in from Lubbock.

Dr. Newton, who lived in Cameron, Milam County, between Temple and College Station, was indicted in Lamb County on a charge of assault with intent to murder Dr. Hunt. The two doctors had been friends in college, and Hunt had served his internship at a hospital in which Ruth Newton, then unmarried, was a nurse. But at the trial Hunt testified that he had not seen Newton in ten years or Mrs. Newton in eight years and that he had no idea why they tried to kill him. Newton's claim that he was in Cameron, four hundred miles away, on the day of the shooting was backed up by prominent Cameron residents who swore under oath he was there late that afternoon, a few hours prior to the midnight assault. But at the end of the three-day trial, Newton was convicted and sentenced to seven years in prison.[30]

On October 26, 1943, seventeen months after the midnight assault, Dr. Hunt and his wife were found dead in their bedroom by their five-year-old daughter. Shot through the upper bridge of his nose, Hunt had died instantly. Mrs. Hunt had died as the result of a heavy blow, with an instrument such as the butt of a pistol, over her right eye. Rope, twine, a lamp cord, neckties, a leather belt, and a metal clothes hanger were used to tie the victims together so tightly that their wrists, throats, and ankles were cut. Blood was everywhere. Later that day a Lubbock newspaper reporter interviewed Dr. Newton, who was in Cameron, free from prison while his conviction was on appeal to the Court of Criminal Appeals in Austin. "I am terribly shocked," he told the reporter. "I've been working here day and night. First I knew of this thing was about an hour ago." Speaking of Dr. Hunt, Newton said, "I have never had any ill-feeling toward the man."

Two days later Jim Thomas, a forty-nine-year-old ex-convict, was arrested in Galveston as a parole violator. Thomas had left the state penitentiary on a sixty-day parole to have an operation on his leg that had been wounded in a gun battle near Lubbock in 1942. After interrogating Thomas about the Hunt murders, Ranger Captain Manny Gault called Captain Gonzaullas to ask that he help in the investigation by gathering some information in Mansfield, south of Fort Worth. Dixon took the assignment, and after spending most of the day in Mansfield checking records and interviewing individuals, he called Gault long distance with a verbal report on what he had learned. Six months later Dixon devoted two more days to gathering information for Gault on the Hunt case.[31]

Evidence soon surfaced that shortly after the Hunts' bodies had been found, Thomas made a long-distance call from the Panhandle to a woman friend in Galveston trying to set up an alibi that he was on the coast the day before and the day after the slayings. But eyewitnesses placed Thomas near the crime scene during that period. For example, a café operator in Littlefield said that Thomas ate at his restaurant on the two nights prior to the assault, and another person said Thomas borrowed his car during the time the attack occurred. Tests showed a match between the tire treads on the borrowed car and tracks at the crime scene. Thomas was indicted, tried, and sentenced to die in the electric chair. After that sentence was overturned on appeal, he was retried, reconvicted, and again given the death sentence. And again the appeals court overturned the conviction. Thomas was tried a third time, convicted, and this time sentenced to life imprisonment. But once more the appeals court overturned the conviction, on the basis that the evidence was insufficient to convict Thomas. Throughout his three trials Thomas remained in prison because of his earlier conviction of assault on a Lubbock policeman.[32]

At the same time the appeals court overturned Dr. Newton's seven-year sentence for assault with intent to murder Dr. Hunt. A second trial was held northeast of Littlefield in Plainview, Hale County, on a change of venue, but Dr. Hunt, the prosecution's star witness, was dead, and other witnesses were serving in the war or unavailable. For the defense, eighty witnesses supported Dr. Newton's alibi that he was in Cameron most of the day on which the assault occurred and that he drove to Houston that evening. Some witnesses placed him in Cameron late that afternoon or even early in the evening; others testified that they saw him in Houston around 11:00 p.m. Cameron was 450 miles from the crime scene; Houston was 581 miles away. After deliberating for three days, the jury declared it was hopelessly deadlocked with an eleven-to-one vote. Four months later a third trial was held in Tulia, Swisher County, north of Plainview. Again, about eighty witnesses supported Newton's alibi. This time the jury found him guilty after deliberating less than four hours and assessed a two-year prison sentence.[33]

On July 13, 1947, after the Court of Criminal Appeals upheld Newton's conviction, he received a thirty-day reprieve from Governor Jester to care for his ill mother-in-law and complete surgical treatment of some of his patients. He then turned to the Board of Pardons and Paroles and filed for additional clemency. The board began a week-long hearing on whether to approve a sixty-day extension added to the governor's thirty-day reprieve, a full pardon, or neither. All hell broke out. The board received one thousand letters, telegrams, and petitions with twenty thousand signatures in support of clemency. Supporters from Cameron argued that Dr. Newton was indispensable as a physician. Newton's wife, Ruth, appeared before the board with two of their three young children, and his mother tearfully insisted that they had left Cameron on the day of the midnight assault, driven to Caldwell, where they visited friends until dark, and then driven to Houston. He did not, she declared, shoot Dr. Hunt. Opponents from the Panhandle said that thirty-five of thirty-six jurors found Dr. Newton guilty and that they could collect one hundred thousand signatures against clemency. On Friday, July 25, Board Chairman Abner Lewis voted for a full pardon, but the other two members voted it down. On Monday Lewis voted for a two-month reprieve, which the other two rejected. Newton was going to prison.[34]

The emotions involved in the case, Newton's very vocal insistence that he was innocent, and his persistent efforts to avoid prison led Colonel Garrison to assign Dixon to guard the governor and his staff from Saturday, July 26, to Wednesday evening, July 30, when Newton was to report to the state penitentiary. For most of those days Dixon stuck close to the governor's office. On Saturday he contacted officials in Fort Worth to ensure adequate protection for the governor when he spoke at the American Legion convention on Monday. With the governor out of town on Monday, Dixon kept an eye on Newton, who was in Austin. On Tuesday he guarded the governor's office and kept in contact with parole-board members and informers regarding Newton. On Wednesday, Newton released a letter he had sent to Governor Jester. "The penitentiary holds no horrors for me," he wrote. "I'm reporting to the prison to pay a debt I do not owe." At 6:00 p.m. Dixon escorted Governor Jester to the governor's mansion, and then he returned to Camp Mabry, where he was joined by Smoot Schmidt, a member of the Board of Pardons and Paroles and previously sheriff of Dallas County. The two knew each other well and had worked together on a number of occasions. At 9:00 p.m. they received a telegram from the Texas Prison System that Newton had surrendered at the prison. Dixon called the governor's office and Colonel Garrison. His assignment was finished.[35]

But Dixon was not finished with the Hunt case. A few weeks before Newton entered prison, Jim Thomas—his five-year term for assault completed—became a free man. Three months later, in October 1947 the parole board recommended that the governor grant Newton a thirty-day parole to perform an operation, and in December the board recommended that the governor commute sixty days of Newton's sentence because he had given two blood transfusions. Convicts usually received a thirty-day sentence reduction for each blood transfusion. Thomas, the suspected murderer of the Hunts, had gone free, and Newton, convicted of assaulting Dr. Hunt with the intent to murder, was shortening his already fairly short sentence. For reasons not clarified in his diary, Dixon was asked to investigate the Hunt case anew. On October 20, sitting at his desk, he studied case files from early morning until 8:30 p.m. During the following twelve days, his investigation took him to Houston, Huntsville, Lubbock, Plainview, and Dallas. On his Houston visit, he drove to Central Farm No. 1, near Sugar Land, where Newton was serving his time as a trustee. On November 13 he contacted sources by telephone to gather information on airplanes Newton had owned in 1942 and 1943.

A few days later Dixon contacted a post-office inspector and a federal narcotics agent in San Antonio regarding the Hunt case. On November 25 he took his investigation to Cameron and Caldwell, the town where Ruth Newton said she and her husband had visited friends on their way to Houston late on the day of the midnight assault. Three days later he conferred with Governor Jester at the governor's request. On December 2 he examined records at the state board of nurse examiners—Ruth Newton had been a nurse—and on the next day he traveled to Llano, in West Texas, where he interviewed a nurse, described in his diary as an informant.

Ruth Newton was never tried for her alleged role in the midnight assault on Dr. Hunt. Jim Thomas did not undergo a fourth trial. Governor Jester turned down Newton's request for a thirty-day pardon to perform an operation, but approved the sixty-day sentence reduction for the two blood transfusions. When a prison-board member discovered Newton sitting in his wife's station wagon in a field on the prison farm eating a picnic lunch with her, his concern that Newton was being given privileged treatment led to the doctor's transfer to the more austere penitentiary in Huntsville, where he served out his term—reduced to less than a year because of good behavior and additional blood transfusions—as a bookkeeper trustee. He was released from prison on July 12, 1948, and on July 30, Governor Jester restored his citizenship rights.[36]

GAYS AND REDS ON CAMPUS

FROM FEBRUARY INTO JUNE 1947 NORMAN DIXON WAS ON SPECIAL assignment as an investigator for legislative committees, looking into alleged scandals involving the state parole board, the Texas Good Roads Association, and Texas A&M College. During those months when Norman was on a leave of absence from his Texas Ranger position overseeing several North Texas counties, Leona and their sons, Kemp and Kenneth, remained in McKinney. It was a long separation, with Norman able to return home only on occasional weekends. Long-distance phone calls were expensive, but postcards and letters were not. In one undated note during this period, Leona wrote, "Dear Norman, received, read, enjoyed your note. Have been having lots of fun and hope you have been getting lots of rest. Everything fine here. Am now on my way to town and haven't much time, but you can't say I didn't write. Will be surprised by my surprise when you get home. Love, Leona." This note, written during Norman's long absence, is considerably more cheerful than entries she wrote in her diary during his lengthy absences in previous years. Apparently she had adjusted to the life of a Ranger's wife.[1]

Dixon fully expected to return to his family at the end of the legislative session in June, but Colonel Garrison put him on the DPS payroll as a special investigator but with his payroll title "Ranger" at a private's salary, $253 a month. On such a salary the Dixons, a family of four, could not afford to purchase and maintain an automobile or buy a home. From the beginning of their marriage, Norman and Leona rented apartments, duplexes, and houses. They had lived in cities (Cleveland and Austin) and small towns (Tyler, Goldthwaite, and McKinney). Small towns were less expensive and, the Dixons thought, offered healthier and safer environments for children.

Elgin, with about two thousand residents, seemed ideal, but there were two problems. First, Norman's headquarters at Camp Mabry were about thirty miles away, and Rangers, no matter what day of the week or time of the day, were on call. Second, Norman would have to drive a state vehicle the sixty-mile round trip each day. But Colonel Garrison gave his approval, and the Dixons moved from McKinney to Elgin in early September 1947.

The family thrived in Elgin even though, during their four years there, they lived in four rental houses. On December 8, 1949, the Bastrop County Scouters met with the district committee at Elgin High School to reorganize Elgin's Troop 182, with "Ranger Norman Dixon" as the new scoutmaster. At the end of September 1950, a photographer for the Texas Department of Public Safety accompanied Scoutmaster Dixon and eight of his twenty-five Scouts on an overnight camping trip. The resulting photographs were published in a seven-page spread in the *DPS Chaparral,* a bimonthly publication for department employees. The *Austin American* published four eight-by-ten photographs of the camping trip, showing Dixon observing raccoon tracks with the boys, overseeing two scouts as they built a food-pantry rack, inspecting the completed rack suspended from a tree, and telling "true stories of the Texas Rangers" to the boys, who were circled around a campfire at night. Dixon greatly enjoyed working with the youths and spending time outdoors.[2]

In February 1951 the local American Legion post named "Texas Ranger Norman K. Dixon and the late Dr. Joe V. Fleming, Jr.," the town's "outstanding citizens of 1950." Fleming, who passed away during the year, had been Elgin's leading physician since 1933 and had established himself "in the hearts of everyone in the community." The Legion post cited Dixon as "one of our most prominent and worthy citizens," whose "efforts and energies were directed toward the youth of Elgin," and credited him as "a leader and teacher in the Methodist Church." According to the post, many civic organizations "enjoyed and profited from his talks" and the city council and law-enforcement officers "have on numerous occasions called for and received his sound advice and ready assistance in matters of law enforcement."

Six months later came word that Elgin's top citizen was leaving. In an editorial, the *Elgin Courier* stated that the departure of Norman Dixon "is going to leave a yawning cavity in the local Boy Scout organization." Filling his shoes would be difficult because "the nucleus of the organization was built around Mr. Dixon, and the excellent showing of Elgin Scouts in recent years is a direct tribute to his labors." But the troop did continue without Dixon, and he was asked back on special occasions to present awards and to serve as guest speaker.[3]

In August 1947, as Dixon was preparing for the move to Elgin, he was called upon once again to protect the governor. The first sign of a threat to Governor Jester was a phone call to the *Austin American,* which reported that the caller "in a feminine-sounding, singsong voice claimed to be Madame Peiough, an Oriental spiritualist." The governor's life, the caller said, was in "grave danger." The next call was to the governor's mansion. Again claiming to be a woman, the caller warned that the governor and his family were in danger, that there might be a shooting on Congress Avenue, Austin's main downtown street, leading from the river to the capitol.

Col. Homer Garrison, director of the Texas Department of Public Safety. *Courtesy Texas Department of Public Safety.*

In a second call to the governor's mansion, the caller, speaking in a male voice, said he understood that the governor had been threatened and that as a representative of the "Siren Detective Agency" he had been assigned to investigate the case. After the *Austin American* published an account of the first phone call, the newspaper received postcards warning it to stop publishing Madame Peiough's forecasts, and the governor's mansion received postcards saying, "Don't tell the bulls anything you know or you are liable to be gored." Each threat was followed by a phone call from "a detective" asking if any new notes had been received and saying he wanted to see them.

On Saturday, August 16, Dixon began his investigation by collecting information from Marion McLinn of the *Austin American* and Geary Wilke, the governor's secretary at the mansion, and arranging for future phone calls to be traced. On Monday he consulted with handwriting experts and psychiatrists, and they developed a plan. On Tuesday when the "detective" again called the governor's mansion, Secretary Wilke was ready. Following the agreed-upon plan, Wilke told the caller he could send a messenger to pick up the threatening postcard. With state police stationed at the governor's mansion in case a messenger showed up, Dixon rushed to the telephone company, where he learned that the phone call had been traced to a multiparty line with three residences in the same neighborhood.

With another officer, Dixon drove to the neighborhood and soon found the culprit: a fifteen-year-old boy who, as described in Dixon's diary, exhibited symptoms of nervousness, frustration, and paranoia. After the boy confessed, the Ranger put him on the phone to apologize to Secretary Wilke. Dixon convinced the boy's mother that her son needed psychiatric help, and he discussed the matter with the boy's father. The *Austin American*'s account was more sanguine, describing the boy as simply "playing detective" and having read too many detective stories. But he apparently had planned to keep playing the "detective" game. In his possession was a postcard he had written to an Austin businessman telling him to sell his interests "or else."[4]

On September 27 Dixon, Ranger Capt. Alfred Y. Allee, and San Patricio County Sheriff Alonzo Tumlinson raided Pirates Cove, near Ingleside, across the bay from Corpus Christi, seizing two slot machines and arresting E. E. Mansell, who was charged with operating a gambling establishment. The three officers attended the examining trial in Sinton, the county seat, three days later. In cross-examining Captain Allee, Mansell's attorney, Truett Barber, alluded to Allee's "innuendoes" about the defendant. That angered Allee, who yanked the revolver from his holster and lunged at Barber. Sitting at the back of the small courtroom, Barber's wife, seeing the Ranger rushing with a gun toward her husband, rose from her chair and ran screaming toward them. Sheriff Tumlinson quickly interceded, grabbing Allee's gun and separating the two men. Justice of the Peace N. F. Phillips, a retired Baptist preacher, politely asked Allee and Barber, and everyone else, to reseat themselves so that the hearing could resume. Allee and Barber apologized to the court and, later, to each other.

Two days after the incident, Joe Fletcher, DPS assistant director, came to Corpus Christi to conduct an investigation, meeting separately with Barber, Allee, and Dixon. Allee's handshake had not appeased Barber. He filed an assault-with-intent-to-murder complaint against Allee, which Justice Phillips and the county attorney rejected. Several months later the Rangers and the sheriff were back in the Sinton court for a three-day trial, facing off against Mansell, his attorneys, including Barber, and several defense witnesses. At the end of the trial, Mansell received a two-year suspended sentence. Allee, the crusty, controversial Ranger captain, survived Fletcher's investigation, continuing his service in the Ranger force until his retirement in 1970 at age sixty-five—the last Ranger to retire who had begun his service prior to the creation of the Texas Department of Public Safety in 1935.[5]

In 1948 Dixon conducted a range of investigations. Sometimes he was called on to tackle a dangerous situation, such as on March 25, when at about midnight he was called to handle an airman who had gone berserk with a butcher knife. Dixon apprehended him and turned him over to the military police at Bergstrom Air Base, near Austin. On September 1, at the request of Elgin Chief of Police George Loftus, Dixon arrested Lehman Northcutt, alias Shug Moon, taking away the knife with which he had cut his neighbor's throat, placing him in the Bastrop County Jail, and charging him with assault with intent to murder. But clearly Dixon's job was changing, and by the time of his surgery in preparation for dentures that fall, the forty-year-old Ranger was involved less and less in typical law enforcement and more and more in confronting a new perceived threat: Communism.[6]

When Dixon was told his teeth needed to be removed (he had bad teeth or gums, or both), he rejected the idea of pulling them a few at a time. Leona and the boys were shopping in downtown Elgin when Norman parked his car and walked up to them. His family was stunned: both his cheeks were hugely swollen. He explained with a manful smile that he did not want to stretch out the process. Unfortunately no dentures ever fit him comfortably.

By 1949 Dixon was serving as internal security officer for the state of Texas, although he continued to conduct occasional investigations unrelated to radical or subversive activities. For example, on July 8 he joined with A. C. Cason III of the attorney general's office on an investigation regarding charges that the Western Union Telegraph Company was furnishing horse-race information to Texas bookies. Also on the case was A. W. "Bill" Jordin, an investigator who had been put on the payroll of the DPS director's office on April 1. For the first time in his twelve-year Ranger career, Dixon had a subordinate working with him. During the next ten days Dixon, Cason, and Jordin investigated the link between Western Union and race-horse bookies in ten Texas cities. The investigation showed that *Texas Daily Sports News* had an exclusive agreement with Western Union to transmit racing information gathered from race tracks around the nation to ten racing-news ticker machines operating across Texas. The information from the ticker machines was forwarded to bookmakers and gambling houses via telephone and loudspeaker systems. Attorney General Price Daniel won a temporary restraining order enjoining Western Union and *Texas Daily Sports News* from furnishing horse-race information to Texas bookies, and on February 5, 1951, a permanent injunction was issued.[7]

Although by 1950 the drumbeat against Communism was growing louder, Dixon was called upon to investigate charges regarding the Texas Prison System. Back on March 14, 1949, Assistant Night Warden Robert L. Rucker had written to O. B. Ellis, head of the prison system, complaining that he had not been promoted as promised and stating that if he did not receive his promotion he would have to resign. In a twelve-page resignation letter to Ellis on April 9, Rucker charged the prison system with irregularities, violations, and incompetency. On May 21 he was rehired as a picket guard, and on November 22 he applied for a promotion to night warden. Instead of receiving a promotion he was fired, leading him to write a twenty-five-page letter dated February 22, 1950, to Gov. Allan Shivers, the lieutenant governor who had replaced Beauford Jester upon Jester's death in office on July 11, 1949.

Five days later Ellis asked Colonel Garrison to look into Rucker's charges that certain employees and officials of the prison system were guilty of irregularities and policy violations in performing their jobs. On Saturday, March 4, 1950, Dixon, who had become very familiar with the prison system during his investigation of the parole board three years earlier, drove with Fritz Christian, DPS personnel director, to Huntsville where they contacted Ellis, and then to Conroe, where they interviewed Mary Lou Gebhard, whom Rucker had paid to type his twelve and twenty-five page letters. She was sure no one had helped him compose the letters. The investigators agreed, finding the letters full of "unconventional punctuation; misspelling; faulty grammar, rhetoric and composition; the rambling style and broken continuity."

On Sunday the investigators interviewed Rucker, whose criticisms against "employees and officials" were primarily directed at Andrew C. Turner, the warden who had "promised" him a promotion. According to Rucker, a guard saw Turner deliver whiskey to a convict; convicts had seen whiskey go into Turner's office through the window; convicts claimed they could buy clemency through Turner; Ellis and members of the parole board did what Turner told them to do; Turner ran everything except the Eastham Farm; and Turner built a house on Highway 75 using prison material and convict labor.

Rucker gave the investigators the names of individuals who knew Ellis had been told that red clay was found in the 11th Street sewer, indicating convicts were digging their way out. But during interviews on Monday, the individuals disputed Rucker's story, saying they thought the clay came from nearby construction, never said a word to Ellis, and did not give it another thought until an escape did occur several weeks later on December 26, 1949, when seven convicts crawled through a tunnel under the prison wall and through a hole about a foot in diameter in the outside wall.

As Dixon knew quite well, escapes from Texas prisons occurred frequently. Two months after the Huntsville tunnel escape, Ellis spoke to a gathering of 250 citizens in Fort Bend County concerned about convicts escaping from prison farms, including an escape of ten prisoners five days earlier. Ellis did not give the crowd much comfort, telling them that prison-farm buildings were "poorly planned," fences were too low, and lighting of prison yards was too weak. It simply was not hard, he said, for a determined prisoner to escape.

On Tuesday through Friday Dixon and Christian interviewed all the convicts, prison guards, and officials named by Rucker as involved in or knowing of improper activities. One interviewee was Andrew Turner. Regarding Rucker's charge that convicts helped build his house, Turner explained that the house was built ten years before he moved to it from government housing in May 1948. While living there, his son painted part of the porch, but no convicts were involved. A year later he moved back to a state house. As to Rucker's charge that he was promised a promotion, Turner said the promise was conditioned on Rucker's proving he was capable while working for the system for a few months. After a couple of months, Turner said, prison officials knew Rucker did not have what it took.

In their report to Colonel Garrison, dated March 14, Dixon and Christian stated that at the request of Ellis, they "strolled around the lower yard and chatted with a few of the convicts, and observed the general demeanor and labors of others. Investigator N. K. Dixon spent about two weeks in the Walls [the main prison in Huntsville] about 3 years ago, and . . . judging by . . . the outward and expressed attitude of the convicts, their apparent spirits, conviviality, cheerfulness etcetera, there is no doubt whatever that there is currently a marked change over the general moral [*sic*] of 3 years ago." Morale had improved. Rucker's accusation that Ellis knew a tunnel was being dug "collapsed on checking." Turner's delivery of whiskey "did not stand up" and Turner's building a house on convict labor "failed to hold." The investigators did find that some of the older guards thought convicts were being "coddled," and they favored returning to "sterner and harsher methods." The investigators recommended that officials make the older guards feel they are a part of the new methods and help them understand the aims. All in all, they wrote, the prison officials are "sincerely endeavoring to do a real job, under considerable difficulties."[8]

A few days later after reading the report, Ellis spoke to the press about the investigation. He clarified the statement in the report that "a number of employees have been relieved of duty in the past two years" by explaining that more than fifty prison employees had been fired during the past eighteen months because they helped smuggle dope and whiskey to inmates and had been careless in searching and guarding prisoners. Ellis had every reason to be pleased by the report, and when Dixon wrote to him on June 15, 1951, asking if he could bring some Boy Scouts to see the penitentiary, Ellis responded that the prison had a blanket rule against letting groups go through but wrote, "Bring your boys down anytime that you want to. I want to ask you to ask the boys not to advertise the fact that they have been down."[9]

Norman Dixon's ties to Scouting began during his childhood in New Jersey, where the Dixon family had settled in 1917, when Norman was nine years old and his father was beginning his service in World War I. In the same year the Bolsheviks set up a Marxist republic in Russia, leading to a Communist movement in the United States. According to Harvey Klehr and John Earl

Haynes, authors of several books on American Communism, those attracted to the movement viewed capitalism as "an outmoded, irrational, and exploitative system that benefited a small minority of wealthy people at the expense of the vast majority of Americans." Disagreements among American Communists and difficulty keeping up both with Soviet policy shifts and with changes in Russian leadership kept the number of members low. According to Klehr, American Communists were "fighting [more] among themselves than . . . against capitalism."

During the Great Depression of the 1930s, the Communist Party USA (CPUSA) was frustrated by its inability to take advantage of the worst economic crisis in American history. It tried fighting to reform capitalism as a tactic to win over workers, but by 1933, after four years of the Great Depression, the party membership stood at about eighteen thousand, only three thousand more than ten years earlier. Most who joined the CPUSA left after a brief period. They came looking for answers to the Depression but found none, and they were bored by the bureaucratic nature of party meetings and their assignments, mostly standing on street corners selling party newspapers and passing out leaflets. New members were also turned off by party veterans who distrusted them, suspecting they might be informants. To gain more influence, the CPUSA turned to "mass organizations"—known as "fronts" in the United States—which appeared independent and were composed mostly of non-Communists but in fact were party controlled, by a Communist leader or by a Communist faction that manipulated its activity.

In 1935 half the party members were jobless, one-third belonged to a union, and one-third lived in New York City. The typical member was white, foreign born, unemployed, and between thirty and forty years of age. Few lived in Texas. Nevertheless, in the fall of 1935 the Texas Communist Party was organized and its Houston headquarters staffed with a chairman, a secretary, and a handful of field workers. It operated openly in Texas through the 1940s, its statewide membership never exceeding a thousand, always small and ineffective. But the Communist logo and literature could be found up and down the Texas coastline, especially during strikes. The Texas party never had more than a small number of dues-paying professionals. Most of its members were laborers in CIO (Congress of Industrial Organizations) unions along the coast. There was a scattering of lawyers, teachers, and University of Texas (UT) students in the party, along with some residents from black neighborhoods in Houston and Mexican-American barrios in San Antonio.[10]

Most Texans—and many other Americans—were hostile toward Communism. A January 1940 Gallup Poll reported that 70 percent of Americans believed it was more important to investigate Communism than Nazism—even though a world war against fascism was under way. One reason was Martin Dies, a racist, isolationist, and anticonservationist congressman from rural East Texas. Dies and his rural East Texas constituency, 90 percent of Anglo-Saxon descent, did not trust foreigners, and anyone trying to upend segregation was their enemy. As chairman of a U.S. House committee created in 1938 to investigate un-American activities, Dies showed little interest in Nazis, focusing instead on the "Trojan Horse," the enemy within. The Soviet Union, he would say repeatedly, has a well-organized spy network in the United States with secret agents seeking military and industrial secrets. He charged that "fifth columnists," supporters of Soviet Communism, were infiltrating key positions in Pres. Franklin Roosevelt's New Deal administration.[11]

During the summer of 1940, Dies held closed hearings in the South. In most of the hearings he was the only committee member present. On Friday, August 2, Dies sent Robert Stripling, committee secretary, and Jim Steadman, committee investigator, to Austin to look into alleged Communist activities at UT. The *Austin Tribune* noted that radical groups had been on the campus for years, giving as an example a group that proposed a few years earlier to "invite negroes, of both sexes, to a dance and party they were planning." Wick Fowler, a liaison between Colonel Garrison and the Dies committee, and Dixon, in the Bureau of Intelligence at the time, worked with the committee representatives during their two-day unannounced visit on the UT campus. Dixon subpoenaed several students and an economics instructor for questioning by Stripling and Steadman, and he obtained handwriting samples from some students and another economics instructor to determine the authorship of a letter written to a Communist official.

When Stripling and Steadman had finished their two-day investigation on campus, Dixon drove three UT students to Beaumont for a Dies committee hearing. The *Dallas Morning News* characterized the three as the "alleged ringleaders in Communist activities" at the university. The students said that they had seen no "isms" on campus but that students generally opposed going to war and were against the draft. Homer Brooks, head of the Texas Communist Party, was scheduled to testify but was excused after he said he feared for his life and asked for protection from a U.S. marshal, which Dies refused to provide, saying, "You couldn't come to a safer place than Beaumont." After the hearing Dixon returned the three students to Austin, ending his first involvement with alleged Communists. Two days later Dies interrupted his hearings in Beaumont to send Stripling and Steadman to the West Coast to investigate charges of sabotage.[12]

UT President Homer Rainey had challenged Dies to prove his assertions that there were revolutionary groups on campus. The investigators did find that one professor held regular meetings with several students to discuss Karl Marx, but Dies announced that the situation had been taken care of, that no subversive activities existed at the university. For the next four years, until his retirement in 1944, Dies continued to investigate people and groups, especially those allied with the New Deal coalition that he suspected of un-American activities. His committee, which came to be known as HUAC (House Un-American Activities Committee), existed until 1975.[13]

Not satisfied that the campus was free of Communists after the Dies committee conducted its investigation, in 1941 the Texas Senate set up a "Little Dies Committee." Although the new committee found no Communists at UT, it sponsored a bill to fire any professor or teacher in the state whose teachings were "inimical" to the Constitution. But the primary suspects among the teaching profession remained the same through the years: professors and instructors in the UT Economics Department.[14]

The Economics Department acquired its radical reputation mostly because it supported New Deal legislation. Members of the UT Board of Regents tried repeatedly to have one or more economics professors fired, but President Rainey protected them. In the spring of 1942 three young UT economics instructors attended a mass meeting in Dallas held to attack the New Deal law requiring the forty-hour workweek. The organizers had been spreading false information about the law, and at the meeting the instructors asked for two minutes to explain it. They were not allowed to speak, although it had been labeled as an open meeting, and after the meeting they made a public statement about not being allowed to speak. The board fired them.[15]

In 1941 Governor O'Daniel appointed railroad and banking businessman Orville Bullington to the board. The state senate confirmed his appointment only after determining that he was against Communism and willing to fire professors. For the next three years, Bullington was on the attack against UT. He railed against the inclusion of the third volume of John Dos Passos's *U.S.A.* trilogy in English classes because it employed sexual language and supported labor unions. He demanded the firing of an economics instructor who was a conscientious objector. And he attacked President Rainey for tolerating a homosexual ring on campus.

At a faculty meeting on October 12, 1944, Rainey issued a list of sixteen grievances against the board, including efforts to fire economics professors and instructors, removal of the Dos Passos book, and refusal to allow a school of social work on the basis that it would nurture socialism. The board responded by firing Rainey. At that, several thousand students boycotted classes for a week and marched from the campus to the capitol and the governor's mansion with the Longhorn band playing Chopin's "Funeral March." The sensational events led a state senate investigating committee to inquire into the situation. At a hearing in November Bullington testified that one reason for firing Rainey was that he was not diligent in ridding the university of "a nest of homosexuals in the faculty." He said Rainey had discovered the "nest of homosexuals" as early as September 1943 but had neglected to mention it to the board until eight months later. He credited Rainey with asking the DPS to investigate but faulted him for allowing homosexuals to be hired in the first place.[16]

At the time Dixon was headquartered in McKinney, serving in Company B under Captain Gonzaullas. On May 1, 1944, Dixon drove from McKinney to Dallas, where he conferred with Gonzaullas, then to Austin per orders of Colonel Garrison. On May 2 he wrote in his diary that he was "detached and on special confidential investigation pertaining to the internal security of the U.S." He added in parentheses that he was conducting a morals investigation of a homosexual club at UT. His investigation would further acquaint him with growing fears of Communism. Gays *and* Reds on campus!

Dixon stayed on the assignment until July 15, when he submitted his report to Colonel Garrison. He conducted many interviews and interrogations, listing the names in his diary. During the majority of the interviews, he was accompanied by A. J. Norstrom, an FBI agent. Some individuals were interviewed or interrogated more than once, and on several occasions he wrote in his diary that he interviewed "and broke" the individual, or "took statement."

He was able to get away from Austin for a couple of weekends, joining Leona and the boys in Smiley at the family farm. As always throughout his Ranger career, his special assignments were punctuated by emergencies. On May 24–25 he chased after and helped apprehend escaped German soldiers Hans Jung and Heinz Daberko. On June 12 he investigated the accidental shooting of Bill Jackson, a DPS employee, by Cleo Nipper, another DPS employee, in the office of the secretaries to Colonel Garrison and the assistant director. On June 21 he joined a manhunt for prisoners who had escaped a prison farm by killing a guard. Two days later he and two highway patrolmen escorted Jesse James, the state treasurer, to the Federal Reserve Bank in San Antonio where he deposited ten million dollars. On June 24–27 he played host to a group of law-enforcement officers from Chile, showing them the sights, taking them to a rodeo, escorting them to restaurants, and helping Captain Gonzaullas show them the Lone Wolf's extensive collection of firearms taken from criminals. On June 30 Dixon and Col. Royal Phillips were the Chileans' guests of honor at a dinner in San Antonio.[17]

The existence of the "nest of homosexuals" that Dixon investigated was not the only reason the board gave for having fired Rainey. Board members also charged that he wanted to let blacks into UT and that Communism was being taught in the Economics Department. One board member had told a UT official that there were a thousand Communists on campus, but Rainey countered by testifying to the senate investigating committee that there were no Communists at UT, that the board's real concern was liberalism, not Communism. He also stated that he had cooperated fully with the board and DPS on the homosexual issue.

Colonel Garrison testified that he and Rainey had agreed the homosexual investigation needed to be conducted "with the greatest of secrecy. . . . In any investigation, many persons are accused, and once the cloak of suspicion falls on a person, it is hard to remove. Many persons are accused and only a few found guilty. . . . This type of investigation is most difficult. . . . Many of these people are psychopathic liars and their statements must be corroborated and substantiated." Garrison told the committee that the investigation had begun in October 1943, when Rainey requested it, and that it was still in progress at the time of his testimony, in November 1944. He said, "I assigned one man full time to work on it." But Dixon did not work on it before May 1, 1944, nor after July 15, 1944. Obviously Garrison had assigned more than one person to the investigation, though apparently at different times.

In 1945 the membership of the UT Board of Regents changed, and the four economics instructors who had been fired were offered their jobs back. Two accepted. Nevertheless the Southern Association of Colleges and Secondary Schools put the university on probation, and in 1946 the American Association of University Professors blacklisted UT. In 1947 Texas Ranger Norman Dixon became a special investigator for Colonel Garrison, and by 1948 his position began to evolve. State politicians and the public were becoming increasingly concerned about radical movements that seemed to threaten their way of life. It was becoming Norman Dixon's job to protect the citizens of Texas from those forces.[18]

A LONE RANGER

In his 1947 diary Norman Dixon lists two items connected to radical activity. He spent the bulk of one Friday reading old and current issues of *Daily Worker,* the CPUSA newspaper, and he covered a speech given by Henry Wallace at Gregory Gym on the UT campus. Dixon also covered a Wallace for President Club meeting in April 1948. Wallace, who previously had served as a cabinet member and vice president under Pres. Franklin D. Roosevelt, was running for president on the Progressive Party ticket. A supporter of civil rights and friendly relations with the Soviet Union, Wallace was not a Communist or a Socialist. He was an idealist and eccentric. He insisted, for example, that his audiences be integrated at his campaign stops in the South, which led to his being harassed by hecklers at many Southern appearances.[1]

Dixon was keeping an eye on Wallace's campaign because the Texas Communist Party supported him and because some of Wallace's closest advisors had ties to the CPUSA. At a campaign event during a two-day visit to Houston in September, Wallace attracted a crowd of four thousand—although some pelted him with tomatoes and eggs. Two months later, in the election in Texas, Wallace received only 3,764 votes for president. Beauford Jester, a Democrat, won the gubernatorial election with better than a million votes.[2]

In 1948 Dixon began writing "propaganda" items for DPS. By "propaganda," a word he routinely used in his diaries, he meant press releases, internal memoranda, and reports issued by Colonel Garrison on subversive or Communist activities. For example, in June Garrison wrote a report on the National Maritime Union local in Galveston, which the national union leaders were trying to purge of Communist influence. Galveston seamen, armed with brass knuckles, clubs, and guns, fought back in meeting halls and on the docks, but CPUSA members were purged from the union, though only after plenty of back-and-forth gunfire between national and local union members.[3]

On January 4, 1949, Dixon noted in his diary, "Completed report of Party-Line propaganda for Director." On the following day Colonel Garrison distributed the report to DPS division chiefs, Ranger captains, and highway-patrol captains. In his cover memorandum he explained that the attached commentary "has been prepared for your benefit, to help you keep currently posted on the Communist Party Line as it shifts and changes, and enable you to more quickly recognize the Red Fronts, Fellow Travelers, Party Workers, and Communist Sympathizers, whose actions and words must adhere to the Party-Line." The intent, Garrison stated, was to provide such commentaries "approximately twice a month" and to add "information including lists of subversive organizations and suspect persons, with particular reference to those thought to be located or operating in your respective areas, or districts." In his report Dixon described the current party line as focusing on "the growing mass unemployment and the coming depression." The report provided brief summaries of propaganda in *Daily Worker* articles and a list of *Daily Worker* headlines, such as "Mexicans in Colorado Live in Box Cars," reflecting the party's "anti-American attitude."[4]

Dixon's second "subversive intelligence" report, issued by Colonel Garrison on January 20, listed additional examples of party propaganda in *Daily Worker* articles and headlines (e.g., "Los Angeles Newsboys Fight Police State Bill"). The report also estimated the strength of the CPUSA to be thirty-three districts with 75,000 members and "around 40,000 non-registered Communists under strict Party discipline." District 23, representing the State of Texas, with headquarters in Houston, had a total membership "at about 800, with at least forty per cent Negroes." Among the officers listed was "Wendell Addington, Youth Director and acting South Texas Regional Director."[5]

Wendell Addington first came to the attention of the public when, as a University of Texas student, he actively supported Heman Sweatt's effort to enroll in the university law school after being rejected because he was black. In December 1946 Addington joined the famous writer and UT professor J. Frank Dobie and an overflowing mixed crowd of blacks and whites at a campus rally to raise funds to help finance Sweatt's ultimately successful lawsuit against the school. Addington was a World War II veteran, as were 63 percent of the seventeen thousand students attending UT in 1946.[6]

The cover of the February 1948 issue of the *Ranger*, a UT student publication, featured a profile of Wendell Addington with an enlarged reproduction of his 1948 CPUSA membership card. Inside the magazine was an article he wrote, titled, "Why I Am a Communist." Addington grew up in Lubbock during the Great Depression and began to find out, he wrote, "that alongside the old and dying capitalist world, there was being born a new world, the world of socialism. . . . I became proud of the job the workers and farmers of Russia were doing in constructing the first socialist state known to man." While going to Texas Tech he had a part-time job at a theater that was part of a chain, and there he saw the projector operators, who were earning about thirty-five cents an hour, fired when they organized into a union. He met his first Communists among the soldiers he served with in World War II, and back in Texas after the war he read Communist publications, attended Communist lectures, and joined the party.[7]

In writing about the *Ranger* article, the *Dallas Morning News* reported that Addington, then a junior economics major, identified himself as secretary of the Communist Party of Austin and said there were around five hundred party members in Texas of whom about forty were in Austin and half of those at UT. Two months later Addington appeared before seventy-five delegates from twenty-six Texas colleges who had gathered in the chambers of the Texas House of Representatives to campaign for a state bonus for veterans. The delegates listened quietly as Addington, described by the *Dallas Morning News* as "a tall, neatly-dressed youth with pinkish red hair" representing the youth committee of the Communist Party, called for a state bonus of $500 to $750, to be paid for by taxing natural-resource consumption or corporate income, which, he said, would help prevent a possible depression. After Addington had finished speaking, a Texas A&M student moved that the delegates reject any association of the bonus movement with the Communist Party. When the motion carried "amid loud applause," Addington picked up "his bulging, shiny leather briefcase" and left.[8]

A month later Addington appeared before the Austin City Council requesting permission for the Communist Party to use the city library auditorium for a meeting. The council denied the request unanimously, going on record as opposing use by the Communist Party of any tax-supported city facility. Two months later, in July 1948, Addington participated in a debate at Southern Methodist University (SMU), in Dallas, on whether the Communist Party should be outlawed. The *Dallas Morning News* reported that "Addington, a slim, soft-spoken fellow who often could hardly be heard, took the brunt of his audience's attack," which included "hoots and catcalls . . . hoots of disbelief . . . laughter and roars of protest . . . [and] more yelling." The last words the newspaper reporter heard were from an old man to a neighbor: "Can you understand what that fellow's getting at?" Then the meeting broke up.[9]

At a February 15, 1949, meeting of the House Criminal Jurisprudence Committee, W. A. Kirk, a black professor of government at Tillotson College, a school for blacks in Austin, spoke in support of Rep. S. J. Isaacs's anti-lynching bill. One by one, committee members voiced approval of Kirk's testimony, but when Wendell Addington spoke in favor of the bill, Rep. Eugene Williams walked out of the hearing, saying, "I don't think we ought to listen to him," and Representative Isaacs asked that his bill be sent back to a subcommittee for further consideration and study. A week later Dixon accompanied Colonel Garrison to the Senate chamber for a hearing on a bill sponsored by Sen. John Bell that would prohibit members of the CPUSA from voting. After Garrison's testimony they watched intently as Addington spoke against the bill. The bill passed the Texas legislature and became law without any other opposition.[10]

On March 3 Dixon again watched Addington speak, this time on the UT campus at a meeting of the Young Progressives of America, the youth organization of the Progressive Party. The next day Dixon prepared his biweekly "subversive intelligence" report with Addington on his mind. "One of our greatest concerns with COMMUNIST PARTY activities," he wrote, "is their attack upon our youth. . . . They will *infiltrate* any existing youth organization or movement that they can." He warned of the threat of Communist teachers, and of Communist students who will "infiltrate student organizations, and inaugurate new movements."

On March 14 Addington *and* Dixon testified before the House State Affairs Committee on Rep. Marshall Bell's bill to forbid the state from employing any member of a "subversive organization" and to authorize the state to compile a list of forbidden organizations. Addington, who made frequent appearances before legislative committees, was not allowed to finish his testimony. Although Representative Bell's loyalty bill would die in the Senate, Dixon prepared for its possible passage by collecting lists of subversive groups from the House Un-American Activities Committee (566 "Communist or Communist Front" organizations) and from the U.S. Attorney General (82 "Communist" organizations). On March 23 he wrote a subversive intelligence report and attached the combined list of subversive organizations (ten single-spaced legal-size pages). "The legislatures of many states," Dixon wrote in the report, "including Texas, have anti-Communist bills before them. . . . It will fall upon us, not the Federal agencies, to enforce these acts, and to provide the state-wide intelligence that will be required." He cautioned DPS division heads and captains to avoid putting "the wrong label on the wrong package."[11]

On March 23, as Dixon was preparing his list of subversive organizations and his biweekly subversive intelligence report, the Senate adopted a resolution, passed unanimously by the lower body, authorizing presidents of all state-supported colleges to investigate and expel any student or teacher "found to be disloyal to this nation." Wendell Addington went on the attack, calling it a "vicious witch-hunting proposal" and a "sweeping destruction of basic civil liberties." A week later he commented on a bill requiring college students and faculty to sign a loyalty oath that they did not belong to or work for any subversive organization. "It is a matter of common knowledge and judicial record," he said, "that the Communist party has never advocated the overthrow of the government by force and violence."

Dixon attended most hearings on the various bills on subversive matters. He did so not just to track the status of proposed legislation but also to observe those in attendance. At an April 7 House committee hearing on Senator Bell's bill to prohibit Communists from voting, he noticed several "Commies from Houston" and tailed them around town after they left the hearing. At a follow-up hearing on the bill five days later, he noted in his diary, "No CPs showed." As Dixon scanned the hearing room looking for subversives, Colonel Garrison testified that in 1948 he had set up a special division to investigate Communist infiltration in Texas. (Until five days before Garrison's testimony, the division consisted solely of Dixon and his secretary, Doris Smith. On April 5, 1949, A. W. "Bill" Jordin had been assigned to work with Dixon.)[12]

In late April Dixon was at the capitol covering the activities of a group of blacks pressuring UT and the legislature regarding the right of blacks to attend medical school. He identified Communists in the crowd, and over the next two days he investigated a "Negro petition" given to the governor, in the process acquiring a photograph taken by an Amarillo newspaper photographer of three Communists associated with the Negro efforts. He also interviewed a history professor at Tillotson College after Wendell Addington spoke to her class. The efforts by Addington and other members of the CPUSA to reach out to blacks were very much on Dixon's mind.[13]

In 1949 Addington was twenty-four years old, a college senior, and married. He was featured in a *Time* magazine article that, in referring to his frequent appearances before legislative committees, said, "His favorite tactic seemed to be tactlessness. . . . The angrier the legislators got, the more Addington seemed to like it." The legislative resolution instructing college presidents to expel those "found to be disloyal to this nation" was aimed at Addington as much as anyone. *Time* quoted one sponsor of the resolution, Ralph "Peppy" Blunt, as having said, "Academic freedom, huh? The only isms we want in Texas are Texasism and Americanism."[14]

At a legislative hearing on the bill to require every teacher and student to sign a loyalty statement, Dixon watched as Addington, representing the state Communist Party, said in his soft voice: "Political parties cannot have their principles tested anywhere but the polls. The issue is whether the Legislature has the right to determine political thoughts of students." That angered Rep. Sam Hanna, who, said the *Dallas Morning News,* "was all for locking the Communists up in asylums. He said they were screwballs." The bill passed and became law, and in August, UT officials mailed loyalty-oath forms to all preregistered students, including Wendell Addington, identified by the *Dallas Morning News* as the only "avowed Communist" on the UT campus. The pledge stated that the signer would support the United States in war and is not a member of any group advocating overthrow of the government. Addington said he would sign it.[15]

After the close of the 1949 spring semester at UT and the adjournment of the legislature, Dixon would briefly mention Wendell Addington in two of his subversive intelligence reports. In the May 31 report, Dixon attached a list of ninety-two names "of those considered the most active members of the Communist Party in Texas today." The word "CONFIDENTIAL" was stamped in large red print on each page. First on the alphabetical list was "Addington,

Wendell G." In his July 8 report Dixon wrote that Addington had been placed on a national organizing committee to form a new Communist youth organization, temporarily called a "YOUTH LABOR LEAGUE." Dixon's last mention of his nemesis in his diaries was on June 23, 1949, when a state senator complained that two men and a woman were distributing leaflets in the Lake Austin UT student-housing unit. Dixon ran a check on their car's license-plate number. The car was registered to Wendell Addington. Although Dixon does not mention him again, Addington graduated from UT the following academic year and moved to New Orleans, where he served as the southwest director of the CPUSA's youth commission.[16]

A controversial movie came to Austin's Paramount Theater in August 1949. *Home of the Brave* is a film about a paralyzed black veteran who learns to walk again only when he learns not to kowtow to bigotry. In the controversial climactic scene, when the doctor yells a racist slur at him, the black veteran rises in anger and as he moves toward the doctor, he realizes he is walking. The Young Progressives of America picketed the theater, demonstrating for a showing of the movie in front of an integrated audience. Nearby, Dixon observed their actions and a DPS photographer took their pictures. In his September 26 subversive intelligence report, Dixon quoted part of an article about the incident that appeared August 3 in the *Daily Worker*: "A gang of hate-inflamed high school students from well-to-do areas assaulted the pickets, attempting to destroy the leaflets, shouting the vilest obscenities, and knocking down a passing soldier who came to the support of the Young Progressives." Dixon's response was that the attackers were "mostly town loafers and store employees. There was practically no shouting and no obscenities, unless the term 'Nigir [*sic*] lover' is an obscenity. There was a minor affray, and an alleged soldier was knocked down after definitely asking for it (and he lied about his identity—no doubt a comrade). We were there."

Dixon lived by a highly ethical and moral code, but he also lived by the Jim Crow code that most white Texans accepted and seldom questioned. He saw no contradiction. He believed in treating blacks fairly—as long as they did not "agitate" against white supremacy. He also believed, as did most white Texans, that blacks were satisfied with their status. Thus any blacks "agitating" for change or to end Jim Crow were under Communist influence. They were "dupes" (a term he used often in his subversive intelligence reports) of Communism.[17]

But agitation also came from another direction. Republicans, frustrated by Franklin D. Roosevelt's four terms as president and Truman's unexpected win in 1948, badly needed an issue. The Cold War became that issue, and no one took greater advantage of it than Joseph McCarthy, senator from Wisconsin. According to Klehr and Haynes, McCarthy was "partisan and irresponsible," and he was guilty of "unsubstantiated testimony, anonymous informants, outright lies, and abusive assaults on witnesses." McCarthy biographer Thomas C. Reeves writes that experienced anti-Communist activists "were astonished or sometimes amused to learn of McCarthy's ignorance of Communism." Though he appeared to know nothing of Communist history, theory, or strategy, his admirers felt that "McCarthy could do no wrong . . . fighting to keep America free from the enemy within." In 1950 he received up to twenty-five thousand letters a day, many with tips about perceived Communist activity.[18]

At the same time that McCarthy was launching his crusade against Communism, Ida Darden (who years earlier had battled against woman suffrage as a socialist plot to weaken white supremacy) began publishing the *Southern Conservative,* an eight-page anti-Communist newspaper in Fort Worth. She believed that all branches of the federal government were saturated with Communist thinking, that Protestant churches were turning atheistic by accepting the social gospel, that Edna Ferber's novel *Giant* was Communist propaganda, and that all taxes should be abolished. One of her daughters, Helen Darden Thomas, was an organizer of the Houston chapter of Minute Women of the U.S.A. The Minute Women, with Texas chapters in Dallas, San Antonio, and Wichita Falls as well as Houston, were mostly upper-middle-class and upper-class white women who opposed Communism and labor unions and supported segregation, the oil industry, and patriotism. The Houston chapter was the most active in Texas, growing to five hundred members by 1952. The members undertook letter-writing campaigns, heckled speakers, and promoted anti-Communist, anti-New Deal, and anti-Semitic literature. They put their supporters on the Houston school board and caused a number of teachers and school officials to be fired or to resign. Thomas devoted much of her time to building a list of individuals she believed were Communists or leaned toward Communism.[19]

With the atmosphere against Communism heating up in Texas, Dixon's job was to keep the giant state and its millions of citizens safe. He retained his Ranger commission, and he was indeed a "lone Ranger." He even had a faithful companion, A. W. "Bill" Jordin, assigned to work with him. During 1950 Dixon drove to U.S. Air Force bases across the state to meet Office of Special Investigations (OSI) officers and to share information on subversive issues with them. He looked into charges of subversive activity at SMU. In Fort Worth he checked "for threatened Communist activities during the Labor Day celebration at the Will Rogers memorial." He investigated the burning of a field at Bergstrom Air Force Base, in Austin. He looked into charges of homosexual activity among students of colleges in Houston. At the high schools in Dallas he investigated charges that a youth organization, "Young Life," was subversive.[20]

The United States Immigration Service was conducting deportation proceedings against aliens in Texas for alleged membership in the CPUSA. During the proceedings, subpoenas were issued to U.S. citizens associated with the defendants to force them to testify about their political beliefs. This served two purposes: the deportation of Communist aliens and the exposure of their radical associates. Deportation proceedings against aliens led to subpoenas and contempt trials of such nonaliens as James Green, head of the Texas Communist Party. Green was convicted and sentenced to jail, but appeals courts overturned the conviction in the summer of 1950. Green, his Houston house stoned and his life threatened, moved his family to Brooklyn, but Sheriff C. V. "Buster" Kern seized his Communist Party records—including financial statements, names and addresses of subscribers to the *Daily Worker,* and notes on dues and memberships—before they could be shipped out of state. The records revealed that, in December 1949, 210 dues-paying CPUSA members were in Texas, 73 of them in Houston. But the records did not show the members' names, which was very disappointing for Dixon who spent three days in Houston immediately upon learning of the seizure of the records.[21]

After a New York trial of eleven top Communists revealed that the FBI had informants in Communist cells across the country, the Texas cells broke into small units and many members went underground. When Fred Estes, leader of the forty-member Dallas chapter, replaced James Green as head of the Texas Communist Party, Gov. Allen Shivers told the *Dallas Morning News,* "Texas is one of the biggest places in the world, but there isn't room here for a single Communist." DPS, he said, had a division keeping close watch on Reds in Texas, and he expected that the next legislature would pass legislation to deal with people like Estes and Addington.[22]

In complete agreement with the governor were Texas' wealthy oil barons Clint Murchison, Hugh Roy Cullen, and H. L. Hunt. All three were fervent anti-Communists fully supportive of any legislation that would attack the enemy within. Murchison opposed Communism along with "egg heads" and "long hairs." In a June 1950 speech to the graduating class of Baylor University Medical Center in Houston, Cullen said, "Both socialism and communism are gaining on us. . . . Joe Stalin has a great fifth column in this country, which is being trained in the underground for future use." He called Joseph McCarthy "the greatest man in America." Hunt founded Fact Forum, which produced a radio broadcast that eventually was on 222 stations, a magazine with a circulation of sixty thousand, and a newspaper column in 1,800 newspapers. All three used millions of their dollars to fight Communism, integration, and "creeping socialism."[23]

On January 29, 1951, Rep. Marshall Bell of San Antonio presented a Communist-control bill to the House State Affairs Committee. The one concern of committee members was whether the bill was constitutional. Colonel Garrison, with Dixon in attendance scanning the audience, told the committee members that he felt it could be enforced, and that it would help

DPS guard against threats of sabotage. The members listened attentively, but what caused them to pass the bill out of committee were two hostile witnesses. First to speak against the bill was Todd Lowry, whom Dixon had identified as a Communist in his May 31, 1949, subversive-intelligence report and as one of the Young Progressives who picketed the movie *Home of the Brave* in his September 1949 report. Second was Fred Estes. Lowry told the committee that he represented the Progressive Party in Texas. Estes said he represented only himself. When Estes finished his prepared statement, the committee members tore into him, and then quickly and unanimously voted to send the bill to the floor of the house for passage.

Representative Bell's bill passed the House 127–7 with opponents labeling it a "storm-trooper, goose-stepping gesture." On February 13, after a five-minute hearing (during which Colonel Garrison called it a necessary aid to enforcement of the Federal Communist Control Act), the bill passed unanimously out of the Senate Committee on Privileges and Elections. On February 27, after the bill passed the full senate unanimously, Governor Shivers signed it into law—effective immediately. A few days later Colonel Garrison distributed Dixon's subversive-intelligence report, attaching the bill and exhorting DPS division heads and captains to "instruct each person under your command that any information received suspected of involving subversive activity be immediately submitted to the office of the director. Too many times this office has learned of information that came into the hands of personnel of this department, which was either ignored or passed on to a federal agency without forwarding to this office."[24]

The Texas Communist Control Act required that any Communist or person who was knowingly a member of a Communist Front organization and was in the state for five consecutive days must register with the DPS by the fifth day. The penalty for not registering was a fine of one to ten thousand dollars or two to ten years in prison. Anyone committing sabotage against national-defense facilities was subject to penalties up to and including the death penalty, and the names of Communists or nominees of the CPUSA were prohibited from being printed on primary- or general-election ballots.[25]

In May a United Press reporter interviewed "N. K. Dixon, a former Ranger who has specialized since 1947 in subversive-control work" and was head of the DPS "Internal Security division, a tight-knit, close-mouthed intelligence unit." He quoted Dixon as saying, "The Communist conspiracy isn't confined to a state or a nation. It is worldwide. There is no reason to believe Texas would be overlooked." According to the release, Governor Shivers hailed the law "as a sharp blow at Red activities in Texas." Originally he endorsed the death penalty for convicted Communists, but he did not seek to put it in the legislation. By October, eight months after the law became effective, no

Communists had registered. An Associated Press article asked: "Seen a Communist lately? The state police haven't. If there were any Communists lurking in the Lone Star State, they hit for cover faster than a gun-shy hound in the middle of a Fourth of July fireworks barrage." Colonel Garrison responded, "We're making constant investigation, but as far as we know, there's certainly no real organized Communist activity in Texas now." A lone Ranger and his faithful companion were determined to keep it that way.[26]

THE CHIEF

For several years after passage of the Texas Communist Control Act in 1951, Norman Dixon served as chief of the Internal Security Section of the Texas Department of Public Safety. When he walked the hallways of the headquarters building, he was greeted as "Chief," as in "Good morning, Chief," or "How are you today, Chief?" There were few actual Communists in Texas, but the government was as vigilant and concerned about the threat of subversive activities as were states with greater numbers of suspected CPUSA members and fellow travelers. As the years advanced, more investigators were added to the Internal Security Section and stationed around the state, though Chief Dixon knew that stationing a few men in different parts of Texas was insufficient. As Colonel Garrison would say, "Policing is based on information, and, without adequate information, law enforcement breaks down." In a talk delivered to a men's supper club at a Presbyterian church on November 20, 1951, Dixon said: "We have subversives strongly aided by all who do not take interest, much less action. . . . Communist activities *are* confined. But this cannot hold without a fuller cooperation of the general public. What can you do?" he asked. "It is you we need to back us up, to aid us and to contribute your information." His last words to the supper-club members were, "Why not you?"[1]

On the very next day, Dixon received a phone call from a young man wanting to meet with him. That afternoon in the chief's office, the visitor explained that he had entered the University of Texas in 1946 and was working on his doctorate. He was almost twenty-nine years old and married but with no children. In the spring of 1948, he said, he went with another student to a beer joint on Speedway near 22nd Street, where they met Wendell Addington. He did not know it at the time, but he now thought the meeting with Addington had been prearranged. The three men ate a meal and drank four or five beers, and by the end of the evening, all three had signed applications for membership in the Communist Party. Addington, of course, was a well-known Communist, and the other student, the visitor said, might also have been a member. In a statement two days later, the young man told Dixon,

Internal Security agents Jim Boutwell, Horace Douglas, and John Kelley with Chief Norman Dixon, second from right. *Author's Collection.*

"Now knowing how they plot and work to win a recruit I suspect that this was primarily staged to bring me into the Party."

In that first meeting he told Dixon that he soon received a membership card (which he later would burn), paid thirty-five cents in dues for his first month, and attended two party meetings, one in an apartment and the other in a city park. He received two assignments: to sell the *Daily Worker* in the black section of town and to seek signatures for a petition at campus church organizations. He never carried out the second assignment, did not attend any more meetings, and paid no more dues. As far as he was concerned, he was no longer a member of the Communist Party. His wife, he explained, had no sympathy for his involvement in the party and now, in 1951, was employed by the State of Texas. His concern that his past membership could embarrass or hurt her had led him to contact Dixon. He felt guilty, he told the chief, and he felt an obligation to the State of Texas and his country.

Chief Dixon had an answer, and the visitor quickly accepted, volunteering to try rejoining the party "for the purpose of aiding the Texas Department of Public Safety in its investigation of subversive activities." He would be an informant "without consideration of any compensation of any kind other than my own satisfaction of doing something towards righting a wrong I felt I had done." The chief did say that whenever possible he would be compensated for expenses he incurred "helping the Department of Public Safety in their official duties." Dixon suggested he try renewing his "former acquaintanceship with people suspected of being engaged in Communist Party activities, and becoming versed in the Party's interests and goals, and reporting any programs to Mr. Dixon." For the next four years and four months, the young man would be an informant for Dixon. Talking periodically into a wire recorder, he would give detailed information about every relevant meeting, encounter, and activity. Transcribed onto paper, his recordings total one hundred five pages.[2]

For several months in 1952 Dixon was confined to his home with tuberculosis. On January 31 Fred McIntire, the FBI agent in charge of the San Antonio office, wrote a sympathy letter, stating, "I am sorry to learn of your illness, and I am hoping for your speedy recovery." On April 8 Lt. Col. James Hay of the Fourth Army headquarters at Fort Sam Houston in San Antonio, wrote, "I was terribly shocked to hear of your illness. All of your friends in the office are . . . hoping for an early and complete recovery." On June 3 a naval intelligence officer named Phil, referring to Dixon as "old buddy," "chum," and "old boy," wrote, "I hope by now you are well on the road to recovery." A friend loaned the sick chief a newfangled television set, and because Austin did not yet have a television station, he installed an antenna on the roof so that Dixon could watch programs transmitted from a San Antonio station eighty miles distant. The screen was small and the picture quality poor, but the Dixon family were transfixed by this new form of entertainment. They would gather in chairs in the parents' bedroom, where Norman lay on the bed, and watch variety and comedy shows and the national nominating conventions of the Republican and Democratic parties. Dixon was not pleased that Adlai Stevenson was the Democratic Party candidate, preferring Senator Richard Russell of Georgia, a conservative segregationist.[3]

As the state official responsible for keeping Texas safe from sabotage, espionage, Communism, and subversive activities in general, Chief Dixon would devote increasing amounts of his time to lecturing and speaking throughout the state to church groups, club meetings, law-enforcement conferences, and any other gathering willing to put him on their agenda. As was true of anything he undertook, he was meticulous in learning the rules of "Speech Making," the title of a short, handwritten set of notes in his personal files, which included, "160 words per minute as speaking speed for professional delivery . . . 150 words average ruled tablet longhand (1 minute per page) . . . 340 words typed, double spaced 1" margins on sides & bottom, 2" at top (2 min per page) . . . deduct for adlibbing, demonstrations, reading quotes, etc.—write balance for 160 wpm speed."[4]

In September, having recovered from his illness, Dixon was in San Antonio with E. J. Jacobson, executive assistant attorney general, to head off a "fishing expedition" for Communists by a Bexar County grand jury. For a month jurors, or a juror, had been leaking information about the grand jury going after Communists. After Jacobson and Dixon appeared before the jurors, Jon Ford, a reporter for the *San Antonio Express,* revealed that "reports from behind the locked doors indicated a majority was unimpressed with alleged efforts of Executive Asst. Attorney General E. J. Jacobson and Public Safety Dept. Internal Security Chief N. K. Dixon to stall a probe of local Communists. Harsh words were reserved for Jacobson and Dixon's efforts on the state level for the last 18 months." In other words, after a year and a half, Jacobson and Dixon still had not convicted any Reds under the Communist Control Act. The grand jury, according to Ford, just might "hand down into court a case or two under the red control bill, let the judges, not the investigators, decide whether it is constitutional or not."

But a few days later, after a leak that the jurors were preparing an anti-Communist report, Judge W. W. McCrory of the criminal district court read the jurors the riot act for investigating matters outside their purview, warning them that anyone responsible for a leak was subject to being fined or jailed. "If you indict a man," he told them, "you've got to prove not only that he is a Communist but that he is controlled by the Soviet Republics. I don't see how anyone on earth could prove that." The judge told them that any indictment "would just be a burden on the district attorney's office and the district attorney would have a hard time trying to make a case. It's not against the law to be a Communist." After the judge's rebuke, the jury did not release any anti-Communist report or indict anyone for violating the Communist Control Act.[5]

On the UT campus Dixon's youthful informant slowly worked his way into a Communist Party group, which, like the other groups on campus, was limited to three members for security reasons. The informant's group leader said he would pay monthly dues of one dollar and would have to pledge some additional amount to the state party plus pay a fifty-cent initiation fee. At the first group meeting, in March 1953, the leader explained that the Communist Party was not developed in Texas, though Texas did have a full-time Communist official, paid from the pledges. The group would meet every two weeks. At an April meeting, the informant fulfilled an assignment by giving a prepared talk on "Party Vigilance," which "led to a lively discussion of how to detect 'stoolies.'" The fact that the speaker himself was a "stoolie" must have seemed ironic to him, but he told Dixon, "I believe that their reaction indicated that there was no suspicion of me, or if there was it has been erased." The informant left a May meeting with a carbon copy of two chapters of a novel the group leader was writing; he gave them to Dixon as "a sample" of the leader's typewriting. As the young man well knew, Alger Hiss, accused of

Norman Dixon giving a lecture on subversive activities at the training school for military-intelligence agents in Fort Sam Houston. *Author's Collection.*

being a Soviet agent, was found guilty of perjury three years earlier partly on the basis of documents proven to have been typed on his typewriter.

In the evening of June 1, 1953, the informant climbed into the backseat of the Austin group leader's car at 11th and Congress. In the front seat was a passenger introduced as "Mike Adams," the sole full-time paid member of the CPUSA in Texas. Adams—short, chubby, and soft-spoken and looking like a regular businessman—had come to Austin from Dallas to collect dues and pass out propaganda literature to the Austin Communist groups. Adams told the informant he wanted to meet him and see what he looked like in case he or his wife ever needed to contact him. His wife, he said, would introduce herself as "Eve." Adams explained it was "rather corny but it was easy to remember—Adam and Eve." His wife was "an excellent worker for the Party," and if he was not available, she would make his contacts for him.

On the following day, the informant met with the chief, who, after hearing of the encounter with Adams, showed him a photograph. It was "Mike Adams." Dixon did not explain who he really was, but when Sam Hall died in a hospital in New York the following January, the informant realized he was "Mike Adams," which was confirmed by his group leader. A native of Alabama and an idealistic intellectual who opposed segregation and was disillusioned by the Great Depression, Hall had joined the CPUSA in the late 1930s and fought in World War II, and by 1950 he had built a reputation in Birmingham as "the City's Top Commie." Hall, who looked more like a Rotary Club member than a hard-core Communist, received the tough assignment of rebuilding the Texas Communist Party. With his wife Sylvia (not "Eve"), Hall was trying to do just that—under the watchful eye of Chief N. K. Dixon and his Internal Security investigators.[6]

After an early July meeting, the informant passed on to Dixon the new monthly dues structure: $0.15 for youth and the unemployed, $0.50 for housewives and those making under $40.00 a week, $1.25 for those earning $40.00 to $60.00 weekly, $2.50 for those earning $60.00 to $80.00 weekly, $3.25 for those earning $80.00 to $100.00, and $10.00 for income above $100.00. Dixon also learned of a report from "Mike Adams" on the progress of the CPUSA in Texas, which revealed that the total dues collected from members in May was $38.61, of which $6.50 came from Austin. The informant's group of three had contributed $2.50, meaning that the other Communist groups in Austin paid a total of $4.00 in dues. And in the same month $215.60 was paid statewide in pledges. State expenditures for the month included $244.21 for transportation, $81.00 for car maintenance, and $24.00 for stationery, office supplies, and the like. Apparently the Texas party had a surplus going into May, because at the end of the month it still had a balance of $10.00.

On December 10, 1953, the informant and the group leader met for coffee at the Chuck Wagon on the UT campus. As they sipped their coffee, the informant suggested someone in the group should write an article for the *Daily Worker* on the Industrial Commission hearings regarding the Distributive Processing and Office Workers Union (DPOWU), the International Union of Mine, Mill and Smelter Workers, and the International Fur and Leather Workers. The informant was told to draft the article, and in it to discuss both the commission's intent to break the unions and the governor's adoption of McCarthyism to perpetuate his power.[7]

The "union-busting" campaign had begun in Houston on November 24, when the state attorney general, John Ben Shepperd, told reporters, "Texas is now faced with an invasion of shrewd, scheming envoys from New York who are backed by a $1 million slush fund and unlimited support from Moscow" and whose aim was to secure a stranglehold on ports and mineral and petroleum operations in Texas and thereby enable the Soviet Union to paralyze the area on a moment's notice. "This was," he charged, "one of the most diabolical plots I have ever seen." The next day in a major speech to the Galveston County Rotary Clubs, Shepperd charged that a Communist plot was under way to take over the oil industry and the main Gulf Coast ports. It began, he said, twelve days earlier, when the DPOWU called a strike during an organizing drive in Port Arthur and picketed twenty-two Port Arthur department stores, hotels, and eating places. He asserted that several DPOWU officers had "a long record of pro-Communist activities, friendships and sympathies." When they continued refusing to "affirm or deny" that they were, or had been, Communists, Shepperd said, he sent them 402 questions, which they also did not answer.[8]

Two days after Shepperd's speech in Galveston, Governor Shivers, whose hometown was Port Arthur, appointed a five-man Industrial Commission to hold hearings on "alleged Communist domination of certain labor organizations in Texas." In his press release announcing the appointments, he said, "There can be no place in Texas organized labor for Communists. There is no place in Texas for Communists, period." The targets of the commission were the three unions lambasted by the attorney general.[9]

The anti-Communism movement was riding high across the nation. The House Un-American Activities Committee gained considerable attention looking for Communist infiltration in New York City schools, the motion-picture industry, and the clergy. As chairman of a subcommittee on State Department spending, a committee on government operations, and a subcommittee on investigations, Joseph McCarthy was receiving tips and leaks regularly and had several probes going on simultaneously. In February 1954 more than a thousand Texans attended a one-hundred-dollar-a-plate dinner for McCarthy in Dallas. The Minute Women were at the height of their influence in Texas. About five hundred of their members in Houston and more than four hundred in San Antonio rallied against the United Nations, "subversive" literature in school libraries, and federal aid to education.[10]

On November 30, in a highly anti-Communist atmosphere, the Industrial Commission held its first meeting in Governor Shivers's office. Assisting the commission were the attorney general and his staff and Dixon and his Internal Security investigators. The 450 members of the Port Arthur DPOWU local chapter reacted quickly, voting to withdraw from the union and reorganize as the Sabine Industrial Union Local 1814. The leaders of the First Methodist Church and of St. James Catholic Church in Port Arthur were asked to head a watchdog committee of local citizens to ensure that the new CIO local was not tainted by Communism.

Shepperd and two assistant attorneys general took two hours to introduce to the commission thirty-one exhibits in support of the charge that the three unions were Communist dominated. Included were clippings from the *Daily Worker*, most likely provided by Chief Dixon and his staff, and a congressional subcommittee report that reached the same conclusion. Maurice Malkin, who had joined the CPUSA in 1919 and was expelled in 1937, testified that he helped organize and lead all three unions. But when asked if he had specific knowledge of Communist activity in Texas, he said he did not. In his testimony Malkin added the cattle industry as an area of interest for the Party, stating, "In time of war they could poison the cattle, cut off the meat supplies in the armed forces."[11]

Dixon probably snickered at the idea of Communist cowboys, but he understood clearly that the main focus of CPUSA interest in Texas was the Gulf Coast industrial areas, as he told a *Daily Texan* newspaper reporter in April 1951. Of the ninety-eight known Texas Communists Dixon listed in his subversive-intelligence report in May 1949, 56 percent lived on the Gulf Coast, mostly in Houston, Galveston, and Port Arthur. In February 1954, a few weeks after the death of Sam Hall, the only full-time paid party member in Texas, Dixon's informant asked his group leader if he was being considered for the job. No one from Austin would be picked, the leader answered. It was the Gulf Coast and oil-field workers who were important.[12]

In its preliminary report, dated December 7, the Industrial Commission stated: "The overwhelming preponderance of evidence presented conclusively shows that these three isolated labor unions . . . are either Communist controlled, dominated, or influenced; that through the Communist Party and/or front organizations these unions are linked together; that these unions either are now operating in or attempting to enter Texas; that there is a clear and present danger." The commission found no evidence of Communists in any other labor union in the state. It commended the efforts of the attorney general and his assistants, and stated that the Internal Security Section of DPS "was most helpful." The report concluded that "the present laws of Texas are inadequate to deal with this menace" and that in its final report to the governor and legislature the commission would recommend "adequate legislation" that will "have teeth and will forever prevent the recurrence of this threat."[13]

At a state youth and government program, the attorney general told 440 teenagers he was proposing to outlaw the Communist Party, to prohibit unions from affiliating with organizations that advocate overthrowing the government, to require that unions sign nonsubversive affidavits, and to ban subversives from serving as union officers or organizers. On January 13, 1954, Governor Shivers wrote identical letters to M. B. Morgan, Bureau of Labor Statistics; Maj. Gen. K. L. Berry, Adjutant General's Department; and Howard Carney, Secretary of State: "I hereby request that your department render whatever possible assistance to the Internal Security section of the Texas Department of Public Safety in its efforts in investigating, screening, and ferreting out all subversive elements that would seek to overthrow the government of this State and Nation by force or violence. . . . We have no choice in the fulfillment of our public trust but to do everything we can to rid Texas of Communists."[14]

On January 21 Governor Shivers declared: "I am presently trying to chase three Communist-dominated unions out of Texas. . . . There is no room for them here. Period." In March Shivers called the legislature into special session to pass the anti-Communist legislation that he, Attorney General Shepperd, and the Industrial Commission had proposed. According to Governor Shivers, 75 percent of those who wrote to him approved his call for the death penalty for convicted Reds. A Baptist pastor supported it, writing, "I'm highly in favor of seeing them under ground, far under, all the way to Hell where they belong."[15]

The Baptist preacher did not get his wish. The bill sailed through the legislature without a death penalty, the final version passing the Senate 29–0 and the House 127–7. The Communist Suppression Act, signed by the governor on April 15, declared: "An international Communist conspiracy . . . committed to the overthrow of the government of the United States and of the several States, including that of the State of Texas, by force or violence . . . constitutes a clear and present danger to the government of the United States and of this state." The act outlawed all subversive organizations and subversive activities. Communists and fellow travelers convicted of violating the law were subject to up to twenty thousand dollars in fines and twenty years in jail. Opponents in Texas argued that the provision permitting searches and seizures was in violation of state and federal constitutions, and as the law was being passed, U.S. Attorney General Herbert Brownell warned the U.S. Congress not to pass a similar law because of constitutional questions. A few months later, ignoring Brownell's counsel, Congress passed a similar law.

To aid in the enforcement of the Communist Suppression Act, Section 9a appropriated seventy-five thousand dollars to hire several more Internal

Security investigators and station them around the state, to add clerical staff in the section headquarters office, and to pay for section travel and operating expenses. In a February interview prior to the special session, Chief Dixon spoke with a reporter for the *Daily Texan,* the UT student newspaper: "As for the various Texas laws aimed at Communists, the party, and its front organizations, there is much more to enforcement than simply going out and arresting someone." His investigators, he said, were stationed all over the state, and they worked with various branches of the federal government and with other states. "Just to satisfy one person by going out and arresting one suspected of suspicious activities can do more harm than good." He explained: "If we go out and pick up someone on a subversive charge, then the subversive organization's work will stop. Suspects we have had our finger on for many years will be rushed out of the state by the hierarchy. Then we have to start all over again." In an ordinary criminal case, he said, the guilty party is arrested as soon as possible. Not so with Dixon and his staff. "This work has to be pursued quietly for we can't afford to tip off the enemy as to our action. Also, we believe it is our responsibility to protect the individual's right by not accusing a person of wrongdoing before thorough investigation.[16]

As Colonel Garrison said in his testimony to the Industrial Commission, Texas had a law on its books requiring Communists in Texas to register by their fifth day in the state, but no one had registered. Dixon, who worked directly for Garrison as chief of the Internal Security Section, knew the names and addresses of members of the Communist Party who lived in Austin, Dallas, Galveston, Houston, Port Arthur, San Antonio, and other locations in Texas and not just for five days but for months and years. Garrison knew that Dixon had arrested none of them, and he understood. An arrest might not lead to a conviction. A conviction might not withstand court appeals questioning the constitutionality of the Communist Suppression Act. Even if an arrest led to a conviction and was upheld by higher courts, the state would pay a high price: the cover would be blown; subversives not arrested would go underground; informants would be discovered and expelled; and the gathering of intelligence would become extremely difficult.

On April 15, 1954, the Communist Suppression Act, supported by the vast majority of legislators, went into effect. The two politicians leading the effort were the attorney general, who aspired to become governor, and the present governor, who had his eye on an unprecedented third term. Chief Dixon was not a politician. He was at the pinnacle of his career, but the seeds of his fall had been planted.

THE FALL

According to Chief Dixon's informant, in a January 1954 meeting, the leader of his Communist group joked about a *Daily Worker* article stating that "they" had microphones that could receive voices clearly through a brick wall. But he was bothered by DPS head Colonel Garrison's recent statement that Communists in Texas were under observation. (In fact the head of the Industrial Commission made the statement.) The group, he said, had been too lax. They should not mention "names, dates, places or meetings" in phone calls. He asked if everyone had a habit of "looking to see if we were being followed when coming to the meetings." And the group was careless about "mentioning names" in meetings. Of course people at the leader's residence were under observation, and the informant, as usual, gave the chief a detailed record of the meeting.

Later in the month the group leader, worried about anti-Communist legislation, told the informant he had been reading *Worker* articles about committee hearings in Philadelphia in which many teachers had broken from the party because they had to sign loyalty oaths and wanted to protect themselves from perjury. There might be an advantage, he said, to severing all "official connections" to the party. He could truthfully say, "I am not a member of the Communist Party." He then discussed the "stoolie menace," saying it was an important matter, but not as serious in Texas with its small groups as it was in places such as Philadelphia and New York, where groups had hundreds of members. He was sure, he told Dixon's informant, that there were no stoolies in "our" little group. In April, after the Communist Suppression Act sought by Governor Shivers, Atty. Gen. Ben Shepperd, and the Industrial Commission had been enacted, the informant's group went inactive.[1]

On April 21, 1954, one week after Governor Shivers had signed Texas' legislation essentially outlawing the CPUSA, Joseph McCarthy came to Houston as the guest of oil millionaire and friend Hugh Roy Cullen and gave a speech to five thousand Texans as the principal speaker at the San Jacinto Monument during ceremonies put on by the Sons of the Republic of Texas. Only three hundred had attended the previous year's event. Calling McCarthy "a great patriotic American," Cullen said, "It is fitting he should speak on the battleground where Texas won its independence. . . . He is doing more than any other man to fight the Communist conspiracy in this country."

On the day after McCarthy's San Jacinto speech, the McCarthy-Army hearings began in the U.S. Senate. The senator had charged the army with harboring Communists, but it was McCarthy who found himself on trial. By the time the hearings ended on June 17, the transcript contained more than two million words and 187 hours had been aired on television across the nation. As a consequence, McCarthy's support among the American people plummeted. Two weeks later Dixon was in Houston speaking at the annual Texas Police Association Conference, and McCarthy must have been on his mind. "I deplore exploitation of the Communist problem as a bandwagon to success," he said. "The headline hunter is no help. Swatting everything that looked like a mosquito never whipped malaria."[2]

At the same conference, Dixon announced that in July the DPS Internal Security Section, using funds provided by the recent legislation outlawing the Communist Party, was sponsoring an anti-Communist school for officers from police and sheriff departments across the state, with federal and state experts teaching "subversive ideologies, economics, propaganda, espionage, security investigation, counter-intelligence and sabotage." He described it as "the first school of its type in the country, as far as we know." According to the *New York Times,* it was a school to teach city and state police that "all red rashes are not measles." The school ran from July 6 through July 23, during which more than thirty instructors provided a total of 120 hours of classroom instruction, discussion, and demonstration.[3]

In October Dixon told one hundred peace officers at a regional meeting of the Texas Police Association in Odessa that local officers must work together with Dixon and his Internal Security officers, and that "we, in turn, must work with the FBI." He issued a warning, one he had given before: random arrests of a few Communists "will hurt more than it will help." He explained that premature arrests of suspected Communists "will expose our hand and that would be disastrous." In McAllen, sponsored by the local American Legion post, Chief Dixon spoke to a Veterans Day audience of seventy-five people, telling them that the CPUSA had been exploiting numerous issues, including anti-McCarthyism. He warned that Americans were more divided than at any time since 1864. But, he said, "We can win it peacefully. . . . We do not need to employ demagoguery to fight demagoguery."[4]

In December Dixon told a reporter for the *Texas Observer,* a liberal publication, that his investigators have to be "particularly sensitive to the presumed allegation or the false allegation." He said: "We have to be aware in this division that there are a lot of groups who exploit an issue for their own benefit and are prone to put the emphasis where it doesn't belong. Our investigators have got to recognize the motive behind the allegation." Asked if his division had found any disloyal people in state government, Dixon said, "We have no knowledge of anybody in State Government whose allegiance is not to the State of Texas and the United States." Acknowledging that no Communists had registered with the State, Dixon explained that they had not been expected to register because they had been instructed by the Party not to comply. "We are not pointing the accusing finger at anyone," he said, "but are establishing facts."[5]

Senator Joseph McCarthy did point his accusing finger at others. He did so many times, including at those who dared question his methods or charges. Unwisely for him, the targets of his finger-pointing were at times other U.S. senators. A movement among senators to censure McCarthy picked up steam after the McCarthy-Army hearings, severely damaging his reputation and image. Six senators, three Democrats and three Republicans, all Southerners and Westerners, were appointed to a special committee to consider forty-six allegations against him. Hearings began August 31 and ended September 13. Two weeks later the committee issued a sixty-eight-page report recommending that McCarthy be censured. The senator showed no remorse, calling the committee a "lynch bee." On December 2, 1954, the Senate voted 67–22 to condemn Joseph McCarthy for contempt and abuse. His colleagues had turned on him, and a month later Dixon took one more slap at him, telling 200 police officers at a South Texas conference, "We can't say the Communists are wrong and then adopt their tactics." The public lost interest in McCarthy, the press ignored him, and in 1956 when he sent letters to every Republican candidate in his home state of Wisconsin offering to help in their campaigns, only one accepted. A year later he died a broken man.[6]

Dixon viewed the demagoguery of McCarthy as irresponsible and harmful to national and state efforts to keep the American people safe from subversive threats. In the chief's mind, Communists were taking full advantage of McCarthy's tactics, which turned the American people against each other rather than uniting them against a radical enemy. Of course many politicians used the fear of Communism for their own political advantage, especially when campaigning for office. In 1954 Shivers was running for an unprecedented third term, and his push to outlaw the Communist Party and strap Reds to the electric chair garnered him much favorable attention among voters. His opponent in the primary was Ralph Yarborough, a liberal Democrat and a serious threat to Shivers's reelection. But during the campaign, the U.S. Supreme Court issued *Brown v. Board of Education of Topeka*, which ruled that segregated schools were unconstitutional, giving the governor two hot issues: race and Communism.

"If we bow down to the Supreme Court decree, if we artificially and arbitrarily enforce the mixing of white and colored children in the classroom," Shivers warned, "we are going to blight the education of whole generations of children from both races. While I'm governor, this is not going to happen."

Gov. Allan Shivers. *Author's Collection.*

Shivers supporters sent a well-dressed black man through East Texas in a new Cadillac with Yarborough bumper stickers. Stopping at gas stations and acting obnoxious, he said he was in a hurry to get back to work for Yarborough. They also doctored a photograph of Yarborough to make him look like a Negro and sent it to newspapers across the state.

Shivers tied Yarborough to Communism, saying he didn't have to look under the bed for Communists: they were in bed with him. On one occasion the Shivers campaign sent a crew to Port Arthur at 5:00 a.m. to film the city empty of shoppers and activity, falsely depicting it as a ghost town that had been destroyed by a Communist-led strike and warning that the viewer's town would be next if Shivers were not reelected. Television documentaries and pamphlets showed falsified pictures of white women and black men walking picket lines together. Shivers defeated Yarborough, but the vote was close even though ninety-five of one hundred daily Texas newspapers endorsed Shivers, and even though he had considerably more campaign funds than Yarborough. After the election an aide said, "Allan really doesn't like to demagogue, but he was about to lose the race. He had to have a white charger to ride in order to win."[7]

Chief Dixon probably was uncomfortable with Shivers's anti-Communist demagoguery during the 1954 campaign, but that did not affect his close working relationship with the governor and his staff. As previously noted, the chief sent the governor issues of the *Daily Worker* containing articles about Texas. He forwarded other information that he believed would interest the governor, and the governor's office routinely sent him correspondence and other materials that the Internal Security Section should review or investigate. Keeping close tabs on the activities of Communists and their sympathizers in Texas was a major function of Dixon's section, but he and his staff also conducted special investigations for Colonel Garrison, Dixon's immediate superior.

In 1952 James F. Boutwell, an Internal Security investigator (and later sheriff of Williamson County), found that John F. Leahy, head of the Cotton Research Committee of Texas (created by the Texas Legislature to find new uses for cotton fiber and to improve the quality of cotton), had committed forgery against the state. Leahy confessed to altering travel vouchers, filing mileage expenses for trips he never took, and putting his girfriend on the payroll in a job that did not exist so she could have money to buy furniture and household goods.

In 1953 Chief Dixon and two of his staff—Special Investigator A. C. Cason III and Administrative Assistant Bill Kavanaugh—appeared in a front-page story and photograph in the *Austin Statesman* after a six-month investigation into "a widespread East Texas traffic in fake college credits and degrees, in which names of seven Negro colleges were fraudulently used." None of the colleges were implicated, and all cooperated in the investigation, but some of their teachers and former employees were charged with misdemeanors and felonies for having worked with outsiders using stolen and counterfeit forms to sell fraudulent college credits and degrees.[8]

Besides chasing radicals and lawbreakers, Chief Dixon served occasionally as host to visitors from law-enforcement programs around the world. In September 1953 Col. Thomas Eric St. Johnston, a former Scotland Yard officer and England's equivalent to Colonel Garrison, arrived in Texas to finish a three-month tour of American police agencies. He was pleased to learn that his host, N. K. Dixon, was a former Ranger (his last commission as a Ranger had expired earlier that year), telling the press, "I was delighted the Rangers still exist."[9]

In October the chief played host to three visiting high-level police officials from Germany. Dixon entertained them with tours of Marshall Ford Dam, a ranch near Llano, a rodeo, and a football game, where their eyes stayed focused on the cheerleaders and the band. The host and the Germans bonded, and they kept in touch for several years. Four years after the visit,

Col. Oberst Werner Haag (who at the time of his visit was head of the federal police school in which officers and cadets were trained as border guards) wrote to Dixon, updating him on his and the other officers' lives. In his closing paragraph, he said, "I always like to remember those days in Austin, during which you cared so much about us and where we have seen so much of your beautiful country."[10]

By the time of Colonel Haag's letter, Dixon was no longer chief of the Internal Security Section, and Allan Shivers was no longer governor. A major scandal had taken place, leading to a Pulitzer Prize for a reporter for the *Cuero Record,* a small-town newspaper in South Texas with a circulation of 3,800. The scandal, investigated by Chief Dixon and his team of state agents, tainted Shivers as governor, hurting his prospects for yet another term. The investigation began following the elections in 1954 when reporter Roland Kenneth Towery saw two white businessmen socializing with black veterans at the country club in Cuero. It made no sense. Looking into it, Towery learned that the white men were paying the country club's black caretaker ten dollars for every veteran he could recruit into their land scheme. The white men then paid each veteran about one hundred dollars (one got a set of new tires instead) to sign an application. Most were illiterate and did not understand that by signing the form they were buying land. Those who did understand had no clue where the land was located. Towery's first article appeared in the *Cuero Record* on November 14, 1954, nine days after Shivers had won his unprecedented third term. Before long, three district attorneys, the state attorney general, the state auditor, special House and Senate Investigating Committees, and Chief Dixon's Internal Security Section were finding widespread abuse.

The state land program for veterans began in 1836, the year Texas won its independence from Mexico and the General Land Office was established. The Republic of Texas, and later the State of Texas, never had much cash, but each was rich in land. Bascom Giles, who earned his wealth building eight hundred homes in Austin and selling acreage that became part of the Austin airport, was elected land commissioner in 1938, defeating the incumbent William McDonald, whose reputation had been weakened by allegations of a scandal involving the leasing of oil lands. Dixon and his partner Bob Crowder had investigated the charges against McDonald for the state in 1938. Now, in 1954, Dixon was investigating charges against Giles, who was serving his eighth two-year term.

The Veterans' Land Act, proposed by Giles in 1945 and enacted in 1946, used proceeds from bonds to buy land and resell it to veterans at 3 percent interest on forty-year loans. The Veterans' Land Board, made up of the governor, the attorney general, and the land commissioner, administered the program. On December 27, 1954, in a special Senate Investigating Committee hearing on the allegations, Dixon read into the record affidavits from numerous veterans who said they were paid to sign up for the program. Few knew they were purchasing land. On the following day the Veterans' Land Board rejected a block application for forty veterans to buy land. Thirty-seven of the forty gave statements they had not applied to buy land; the other three could not be located.[11]

Giles, who had won a ninth term in office as land commissioner in November 1954, submitted a letter of resignation to Governor Shivers on January 1, 1955. It would not be a good year for him, the governor, or the attorney general. Shivers and Atty. Gen. John Ben Shepperd seldom attended meetings of the Veterans' Land Board, routinely sending substitutes in their place. Nor did they read meeting minutes. They were not implicated, but the scandal took place under their noses, and the Senate Investigating Committee rebuked both for their negligence. In March 1955 grand juries in Travis and Bexar Counties indicted Giles, and in June he was indicted in Zavala County. Dixon was testifying to grand juries on the land scandal as late as March 16, 1956, when a picture of him waiting to testify was on the front page of the *Corpus Christi Caller*. In all, Giles faced fifteen felony indictments. Investigators discovered that some of his bribe money had been hidden as payments to a ten-thousand-acre ranch in Minnesota, and other payments had gone directly from land promoters to people to whom Giles owed money.[12]

In his trials Giles received thirteen sentences totaling seventy-five years, to be served concurrently. His final sentence was six years in the state penitentiary. He served one and one-half years of the sentence and paid eighty thousand dollars in civil-suit judgments. All together, 318 criminal indictments were brought against eighteen individuals in nine counties, one of whom was John Bell, a U.S. congressman who had sponsored the Veterans' Land Act as a state representative. Only two of those indicted served prison sentences, but the land promoters involved in the scandal were forced by civil suits to buy back the land at the artificially inflated prices, allowing the state to recover most of its money.

On May 8, 1955, a letter from Dixon to Towery was published in the *Cuero Record:* "The entire Internal Security Section of this Department wishes to extend to you its heartiest congratulations for the receiving of the well-earned Pulitzer Prize. The personnel of this section are probably more aware than most people of the sacrifices you made for the sole purpose of cooperating unselfishly with those of us who were striving to conduct a criminal investigation." Many years later, in 2005, the *Dallas Morning News* reported, "Last year the honored journalist officially donated his papers to the General Land Office Archives, the same state agency whose crooked commissioner's career he had destroyed."[13]

Dixon's UT campus informant had little to report in 1955. The Communist group was moribund. The informant did, however, see his former group leader once in June and again in July, at which time the leader gave him fifty-plus Communist Party books, reports, pamphlets, and periodicals. When the two met again for a couple of hours in January 1956, the informant was preparing to move to Chicago. The leader warned him that Communists would make up only 50 percent of those attending meetings. The rest would be FBI agents. According to author Walter Goodman, the "FBI agents" were actually nominal or disillusioned members of the Party.

In June 1955, when Dixon told his informant that the Internal Security Section was planning to prosecute the other group members, the informant said he would testify. Dixon contacted him again on February 20, 1956, outlining the plan to prepare prosecution cases, file charges, and inform a grand jury how the other group members had violated state law. The informant again told Dixon he would testify. On March 9 as the informant was preparing to leave Texas, Dixon contacted him again. Once more he assured the chief he would testify, and at that time he turned over to the chief a pillowcase filled with the books, pamphlets, reports, and periodicals his former group leader had given him the previous July. In turn, Dixon reimbursed him $143.90 for expenses from October 29, 1952, through April 23, 1954, including expenditures for dues, pledges, gas, a subscription to the *Daily Worker*, and fifty cents for beer.[14]

On April 18, 1956, a few weeks after Dixon's last meeting with his informant, the *Austin American*, the morning newspaper, stated: "Another investigation of statewide import may be under way by the grand jury. The jury held an extraordinarily long session Monday with two high ranking police officials." That was a reference to DPS Director Homer Garrison and Internal Security Chief N. K. Dixon. Dist. Atty. Les Procter told the reporter that the session "may or may not" prove important. The *Austin Statesman*, the afternoon paper, followed up by stating, "The air of mystery in which the Travis County grand jury is working thickened Wednesday." That morning, two groups of witnesses were kept apart so neither would see the other. One group waited in a jury dormitory adjoining the grand jury room and would leave by a route that would keep them from passing the other group outside the jury room. Speculation in court circles ran rampant. It seemed clear, one source told the reporter, that the inquiry had nothing to do with the veterans' land scandal, nor did it have anything to do with the insurance scandal. "Just what it is, however, is the year's best kept secret."[15]

And it remained the year's best-kept secret. Nothing came of it. The informant's two comrades were not indicted. And there was yet another secret: Dixon, referred to as "Chief" in both articles, was no longer chief. On February 9 all internal security agents had been called to Austin for individual meetings with Garrison. Dixon, at College Station giving a talk on defense-plant protection, returned to Austin midafternoon, as the interviews were under way. On February 28 he was called into the director's office and asked to discuss why there had been no arrests under the state's anti-Communist legislation. The chief gave the director the same explanation he had given in speech after speech, and which in fact was the same explanation the director himself had given publicly: putting the spotlight on individual Communists drives the rest underground; their activity becomes hidden; agents lose their informants, who are sought out and expelled; and all intelligence is lost. And given the questionable constitutionality of some provisions, arrests might not lead to convictions, or convictions might be overturned. Dixon might have reminded the colonel both that the Pennsylvania Supreme Court had struck down a Pennsylvania act outlawing the Communist Party on the basis that federal law superseded it and that the U.S. Supreme Court had heard arguments on the case (*Pennsylvania v. Nelson*) and was expected to render a decision soon. Arresting Communists before the court ruled would be risky. Texas Communists, he felt, were contained and under control, which Garrison had also told the public.

In a personal note, Dixon wrote, "Placed on shelf and Kavanaugh called in & told to take over—affair appeared cut and dried." As Bill Kavanaugh, the section administrative assistant, returned to the office to call the agents around the state, telling them he was taking over, Dixon drove home, stunned. He had not seen it coming. He had always thought he and Garrison were on the same page. He said nothing to Leona that night, but she knew something was dreadfully wrong. In bed next to him, she watched as he tossed and turned, and she listened as he let out deep-throated sighs. Neither slept. In the middle of the night he left the bed. He wrote her a note: "It is after 3:00 a.m. & I haven't slept yet—I took pill & hot cocoa—If you don't want to wait, feel free to go on, or you can wake me. I'll go along with whatever you want to do—beg you to forgive me, and not condemn me. I am what I have left, and can't stand going by other people's rules. I love you better than it looks like, and my hate is for myself, in fact."

Calling the agents into Austin on February 9 and meeting with each one of them individually was a very unusual step. Something had precipitated Garrison's action, and Dixon concluded that the colonel was under heavy political pressure to make headlines. Both Governor Shivers and Attorney General Shepperd had their political futures thrown into disarray by the veterans' land scandal—which Dixon and his staff had investigated. Coming on the heels of that scandal was another, this one involving the state insurance agency. Shivers's approval ratings had plummeted. Throwing a few Reds in jail would make big headlines and might resurrect his career. But the colonel, a proud and principled man, could not tell Dixon, his longtime top investigator, to arrest some Reds so Shivers can be reelected. Dixon's "hate for himself" was due to his failure to understand what was at stake. He told Leona that all he needed to do was tell Garrison, "If you think it best to arrest some Communists, we will do that." There were, he could have said, a couple of prospects a few miles down Guadalupe Street on the UT campus. Two months later, those two "prospects" were indeed targeted, though not indicted.[16]

Allan Shivers apparently did want a fourth term despite his drop in popularity. On February 21, one week before Dixon lost his job, Shivers announced that he was "seriously considering" running for a fourth term. He said that friends across the state were urging him to run and that he would make a decision within two weeks. On March 2, a few days after Dixon's demotion, Shivers spoke to voters on statewide radio, defending himself from the veterans' land board and insurance scandals but announcing he would not run again.[17]

Shivers may or may not have been breathing down Garrison's neck. There is another possible explanation. Some of Dixon's own agents, frustrated that no action had been taken against Communists, might have rebelled. In June 1955 Dixon had told his informant that his section was preparing a case against the other group members, but eight months passed with no action, even though recorded statements by Dixon's informant laid out in great detail the actions and statements of the Communists in his group. Most likely Dixon's hesitation to seek grand-jury indictments was based on the following considerations: First, the group members had dropped their party membership two years earlier, when the group disbanded. Second, nowhere does the informant's 105-page transcript indicate that any group member had taken an action or made a statement supporting the violent overthrow of the federal or state government. (The members' main concerns seemed to be protecting the rights of workers and blacks.) And third, the Pennsylvania Supreme Court ruling that that state's anti-Communist law was unenforceable had been taken to the Supreme Court, whose decision—which could affect Texas anti-Communist statutes—was expected at any time.

After his demotion to research assistant (at no loss in pay through September), Dixon's personal notes indicate a strained and awkward atmosphere in the internal security headquarters: "Girls instructed to stop being so friendly etc., then complaint made about everyone being so cold." He wrote of the "girls'" frustration that agents Newt Humphries and A. C. Cason III were unable to "explain contradictory decisions." He received a note from the clerical staff: "Here is the invite to come into our room / No matter what obstacle may loom / Because to us you're a friend / And to us make no amends / Tho we'll take our orders from an Ol' Hoss / To us you're still our only boss!" It was signed by Peggy, Butch, Mary, and Jenny.

On April 2 the U.S. Supreme Court issued its ruling on *Pennsylvania v. Nelson,* banning state prosecutions for sedition against the United States. Steve Nelson, openly Communist, had been sentenced to twenty years in jail and fined heavily for violating the Pennsylvania Sedition Act. But, as the Pennsylvania Supreme Court had ruled and the U.S. Supreme Court affirmed, Nelson had committed no act of sedition against the State of Pennsylvania, and the state had no jurisdiction regarding sedition against the United States. In his notes Dixon wrote, "This ruling I wanted before acting—eliminated hearing cost to find out something we found out free." In other words, Dixon saw no sense in spending time, effort, and money trying to indict and convict Communists in Texas when a court decision that was imminent could render all the expenditures wasted. Even so, later that month Garrison and Dixon, ever the good soldier, attempted to indict the Communist Party group members. It was a wasted effort.

Another effort to indict Communists was being made in Harris County. In a note Dixon mentioned Kavanaugh's concession that the county district attorney shared Dixon's concern about proving that the Communist Party violated Texas law regarding intent to overthrow the government. That concession, along with the *Nelson* case, led Dixon to reflect further on Governor Shivers's role in his demotion. Dixon had worked closely for years with Shivers and his staff. He knew the governor had indulged in some anti-Communist demagoguery in the 1954 election campaign, but his working relationship with the governor and his aides had always been good. In his notes, he wrote: "Gov. never (to my knowledge) asked for any conference on the detriments, risks, disadvantages etc. in prosecution action. Appears strictly forging ahead for political (only) reasons."[18]

On October 1 Dixon's pay was reduced from the $425 he had received monthly as section chief to $375 as a research analyst. He enjoyed researching and writing reports, partly because research satisfied his intellectual curiosity and because producing well-organized reports was intellectually challenging. Research also allowed him to work mostly in isolation in the section he had created and headed for several years, where relationships now proved awkward. Fritz Christian, former head of the DPS Personnel Department, who years earlier had worked with Dixon on the investigation of the prison system and who since had moved to Washington, D.C., encouraged his friend to take a job in the nation's capital, where he could fully utilize his skills and expertise. But Norman and Leona had built their dream house in Austin in 1956 and did not want to move. Besides, Harry Ransom, his close friend at the University of Texas, was optimistic that UT might create a security-officer position that would be tailor-made for him. But it never materialized.[19]

On July 30, 1958, Dixon transferred from Internal Security to the Statistics Division in DPS with his pay restored to $425 a month. He was fifty years old, and his law-enforcement career was over.

AN OLD RANGER LETS GO

NORMAN DIXON BEGAN WRITING PLAYS, FICTION, AND POETRY LONG before he became a Texas Ranger. After his law-enforcement career ended, he began writing again. Tucked away in his files are many short stories, some poetry, a few nonfiction pieces, and a novel, "Sagacity of a Savage," based on historical events in Texas in the 1830s. The old Ranger may have been raised in the Northeast, but he had long ago become a Texan. He tried many times, but none of his works was ever published. In 1961, however, in the 27th Annual Writer's Digest Short Story Contest, he placed 193rd out of 4,750 participants, winning a bookrack. In an article in the September 1964 issue of *Texas Public Employee*, Dixon explained his interest in writing as "a part of me before I stopped growing." He wrote short stories "to learn word economy" and poetry or verse "to learn or accomplish a rhythmic flow." The time devoted to his writing, he said, was sporadic. His rewards were "awareness of progressive learning, accomplishment in creating, relaxation, enthusiasm, escape and hope of a new future in his later years."

On February 29, 1972, Dixon retired from the Texas Department of Public Safety. For the next twenty years, in Austin's mild climate he spent as much time as possible outdoors, where he developed a perpetual tan working on his yard, gardening, woodworking, and pursuing other projects. In one corner of the backyard he built a large greenhouse; in the opposite corner he placed a storage shed so large that it became known as "the barn" and filled it with tools and equipment. Whenever he felt like it, he relaxed on a bench under a shade tree or at the patio table, reading magazines, books, and newspapers. One magazine that he kept in his files but was unable to read was the July 1952 issue of *Die Neue Polizei*, a German publication with an article on Texas Rangers and a photograph of Ranger N. K. Dixon standing at the top of Mt. Bonnell, west of Austin, overlooking the Lake Austin portion of the Colorado River. His rifle is in his right hand; in his left are the reins of his horse, which is standing behind him. It is the most reproduced photograph of the Ranger, appearing in books, DPS brochures, pamphlets, and the like.[1]

Norman and Leona drove up to Waco each year for the retired Texas Rangers reunion at the Texas Ranger Hall of Fame and Museum at Fort

Taken in 1951 at Mount Bonnell, overlooking Lake Austin, this is the most reproduced photograph of Texas Ranger Norman Dixon. It appeared on the back cover of a book on Texas Rangers, in a German magazine, and in a widely distributed pamphlet on Texas Rangers. *Courtesy Texas Department of Public Safety.*

Fisher Park, where he greatly enjoyed visiting with his fellow retirees. In 1973, the Texas Ranger Sesquicentennial, the Ranger Hall of Fame opened with a big celebration at Fort Fisher. Among the sixty-eight signatures Dixon collected on the inside covers of his sesquicentennial celebration book—most from current, retired, and special Rangers—were those of movie and television star Clint Walker, Lt. Gov. Ben Barnes, DPS Director Pat Speir, and a great-great-nephew of Big Foot Wallace, a Texas Ranger from the previous century.[2]

During the 1980s Dixon's hearing deteriorated badly. Hearing aids were little help, especially during family gatherings, when conversation came from different directions, sometimes all at once. By the late 1980s his health had worsened. Even though he gave up cigarettes in midlife and his pipe after only a few years, the decades of chain smoking had taken their toll. Emphysema began robbing him of his vitality. He thoroughly enjoyed every visit with his five grandchildren, his sons, and their wives, but this once-proud athlete had to watch as Leona mowed the lawn and maintained the yard. Occasional injections of steroids boosted his energy, allowing him to go shopping in a mall or eat out at a restaurant, but by 1991 his lungs were giving out on him.

He began thinking of his student years at the University of Florida sixty years earlier, in the midst of the Great Depression, when he was able to attend college only because of a student-athlete scholarship. Without any solicitation he sent $300 to the University of Florida Foundation, assuming, he wrote, "that you do have a source funded by contributions through which you can advance loans to students in need of financial aid." Dan Ott, director of Planned Giving, sent Norman a handwritten response: "Thank you for your generous gift. . . . I'm sure just as you have vivid memories of the hard times of the 1920s and 1930s and what a saving miracle it was for some students to be able to get a loan then—I'm equally sure some student(s) today will feel the same way when they benefit from the gift you have made." That act of generosity seemed to bring his life full cycle.[3]

In 1992 he used a portable oxygen tank to get around until he became bedridden—and miserable. With no sense of day or night, he placed unending demands on Leona. By late summer he was bellowing, "I want to go! I want to go!" But his heart was too strong. Finally, Leona could no longer handle him, and on September 1 the old Ranger was taken by ambulance to a nursing home, where, lying in a bed, he grumbled in a weak voice to his older son, "Why wasn't I taken on a tour of this place before being moved here?" Those were among his last words. Before dawn the next morning, Leona received a call to hurry to the nursing home, where her two sons joined her. As they stood by his bedside, Norman Kemp Dixon, aged eighty-four, knowing it was time to let go, took his last breath.[4]

NOTES

Chapter 1

1. Interviews with Tommie Spellman Bullock, February 22, 2010, and Leona Spellman Dixon, February 23, 2010.

2. Norman Dixon, "Chronology: The Life of Norman Kemp Dixon," Norman Dixon Personal Papers (hereafter "DPP"). Written during Dixon's retirement years, the Chronology contains a paragraph or so on each year of his life from 1908 to 1956. Frederick W. Dixon, "Synopsis of Report on Athletic Department, YMCA, United Kingdom," January 1, 1919, DPP; Ronald Dixon (Norman's brother) wrote a short essay titled "Boyhood Memories: The Flood," June 1993 (DPP); *Newark Advocate,* March 28, 1913.

3. Dixon, "Chronology."

4. *Florida Alligator,* undated, DPP; *Mobile Register,* March 27, 1928, DPP; *Florida Alligator,* May 4, 1929.

5. Shirley Reiff Howarth, *C. Paul Jennewein: Sculptor* (Tampa: The Tampa Museum, 1980), 5, 97; Norman Dixon wrote a short essay titled "Carl Jennewein–Sculptor," DPP; autographed photograph of Indian and Eagle sculpture, DPP.

6. Dixon, "Chronology"; Air Corps Transcript of Flying Records of Norman K. Dixon, DPP; Honorable Discharge papers of Norman K. Dixon, DPP.

7. Dixon, "Chronology."

8. Leona Dixon, Diary, January 1932; interview with Leona Dixon.

9. Interview with Tommie Spellman Bullock; Louis Spellman to author, June 5, 2010.

10. Louis Spellman to author, June 5, 2010; Norman Dixon to author, date unknown.

11. Interviews with Bullock and Leona Dixon.

12. Gene Ellen Dixon and Norman K. Dixon divorce papers, DPP; Norman K. Dixon and Leona V. Spellman marriage license, DPP.

13. Interviews with Bullock and Leona Dixon.

14. Dixon, "Chronology"; interview with Bullock.

15. Dixon, "Chronology"; interview with Leona Dixon.

16. Kenneth B. Ragsdale, *The Year America Discovered Texas: Centennial '36* (College Station: Texas A&M University Press, 1987), 48–60, 127–28, 224–25.

17. Norman and Leona Dixon's 1936 Days of Real Sports concessionaire identification passes, DPP.

18. Norman Dixon to Ronald Dixon, December 4, 1936, DPP.

19. Mike Cox, *Time of the Rangers: From 1900 to the Present* (New York: Tom Doherty Associates, 2009), 155–56; Ragsdale, *The Year America Discovered Texas,* 145–53.

20. Norman Dixon to Homer Garrison, January 16, 1937, DPP; Cox, *Time of the Rangers,* 178.

21. *Houston Chronicle,* August 16, 1936; *Dallas Morning News,* August 24, 1936.

22. Cox, *Time of the Rangers,* 179–80; *Dallas Journal,* August 20, 1936.

23. Dixon to Garrison, January 16, 1937, DPP; H. H. Carmichael to Norman K. Dixon, January 18, 1937, DPP; Carmichael to Dixon, April 29, 1937, DPP.

24. Norman K. Dixon to C. G. McGraw, April 30, 1937, DPP; McGraw to Dixon, May 4, 1937, DDP; Norman K. Dixon to L. G. Phares, May 13, 1937, DDP; J. A. Jones, Secretary, Dallas Claim Men's Association to All Members, May 12, 1937, DPP.

25. Norman K. Dixon to Col. H. H. Carmichael, May 31, 1937, DPP.

26. L. G. Phares to Norman K. Dixon, June 18, 1937, DPP; Phares to Dixon, July 26, 1937, DPP.

27. *Houston Chronicle,* August 8, 1937, DPP; S. E. Spinks, *Law on the Last Frontier: Texas Ranger Arthur Hill* (Lubbock: Texas Tech University Press, 2007), 25.

28. *The Houston Chronicle,* August 22, 1937; *Dallas Morning News,* October 31, 1937; *Philadelphia Inquirer,* June 26, 1938, DPP.

29. Questionnaire completed by Dixon for the Retired Texas Ranger Reunion of 1986, DPP. A newsletter for the training class of 1937 lists Norman Dixon as a "special student," separate from the '37 class roster because he had accepted a position with the Bureau of Intelligence prior to the highway patrol training, DPP; Texas Peace Officers Training School certificate, DPP; Oath of Service, dated August 2, 1937, notarized by Clarence K. Krueger, DPP; DPS appointment of Norman K. Dixon as a Junior Criminal Investigator, September 1, 1937, DPP; DPS appointment of Norman K. Dixon as a Private in the Texas Ranger Force, September 2, 1937, DPP.

Chapter 2

1. Cox, *Time of the Rangers,* 24, 164–69; Ben Proctor, *Just One Riot: Episodes of Texas Rangers in the 20th Century* (Austin: Eakin Press, 1991), 11–12.

2. Norman Dixon Ranger Diary (hereafter "NKD Diary"), January 1, 1938.

3. Leona Dixon Diary (hereafter "LSD Diary"), January 1–May 31, 1938.

4. Lewis C. Rigler and Judyth Wagner Rigler, *In the Line of Duty: Reflections of a Texas Ranger Private* (Houston: Larksdale, 1984), 163–65; Robert Nieman, "Twentieth-Century Shining Star: Capt. Bob Crowder," *Texas Ranger Dispatch* 14 (Summer 2004). See http://www.texasranger.org/dispatch/Backissues/Dispatch_Issue_14.pdf

5. NKD Diary, January 3–4, 1938; *Longview Daily News,* January 9, 1938.

6. Robert M. Utley, *Lone Star Lawmen: The Second Century of the Texas Rangers* (New York: Oxford University Press), 368.

7. NKD Diary, January 8, 1938.

8. Most details regarding the Sojourner case come from an essay, "Justices," that Dixon drafted about his experiences with justices of the peace, DPP; *Dallas Journal,* November 6, 1937; *Dallas Morning News,* January 14, 1938.

9. NKD Diary, January 13–15, 1938; *Dallas Morning News,* January 16, 1938.

10. LSD Diary, January 13–19, February 14, 1938.

11. LSD Diary, March 13, 1938; NKD Diary, March 13, 1938; *Tyler Courier-Times,* March 14, 1938, NKD Collection.

12. Cox, *Time of the Rangers,* 135–37.

13. *Tyler Courier-times,* March 15, 1938; *San Antonio Express,* April 10, 1938; NKD Diary, March 14–15, 1938.

14. Cox, *Time of the Rangers,* 145–46; Brownson Malsch, *Captain M. T. Gonzaullas, Lone Wolf: The Only Texas Ranger Captain of Spanish Descent* (Austin: Shoal Creek Publishers, 1980), 103; *Dallas Morning News,* May 17, 1938.

15. George Norris Green, *The Establishment in Texas Politics: The Primitive Years, 1938–1957* (Westport, Connecticut: Greenwood Press, 1979), 14; *Austin Statesman,* January 4, 5, 1938.

16. *Dallas Morning News,* January 10, 1938; NKD Diary, January 12, 1938; Land Office Irregularities, Department of Public Safety Records, Texas State Archives (hereafter "TSA").

17. Land Office Irregularities, TSA; NKD Diary, January 20–23, 1938.

18. NKD Diary, January 24–26, 1938; Land Office Irregularities, TSA; N. K. Dixon to H. W. Fowler, January 28, 1938.

19. NKD Diary, January 26–February 6, 1938.

20. LSD Diary, January 24, 26, 29, February 2–6, 1938.

21. NKD Diary, February 16–18, May 18, 1938; Land Office Irregularities, TSA.

22. NKD Diary, February 19–22, 1938.

23. Land Office Irregularities, TSA.

24. *Dallas Morning News,* January 22, 26, February 9, March 3, 1938; *Austin Statesman,* January 26, March 4, 1938.

Chapter 3

1. Roger M. Olien and Diana Davids Olien, *Life in the Oil Fields* (Austin: Texas Monthly Press, 1986), 1–2, 6, 13, 35.

2. A fence buys and sells stolen goods. *Theft Prevention Handbook for the Texas Oil Industry* (Dallas: The Texas Mid-Continent Oil & Gas Association, 1944), 9–10. The handbook was prepared by Norman Dixon and three oil-industry investigators and representatives.

3. NKD Diary, January 3–5, 1938; *Theft Prevention Handbook,* 11.

4. Dixon, "The Tong Thief," DPP. Much of this article is unpublished, although portions of it appear in the *Theft Prevention Handbook.*

5. *Theft Prevention Handbook,* 12.

6. NKD Diary, February 7–8, 17, 1938; *State of Texas v. Walter Ratliff,* District Court Records, Hopkins County, Texas; *State of Texas v. Lester Orr,* District Court Records, Hopkins County, Texas.

7. A roller bit is a drilling bit with hardened rotating rollers. NKD Diary, March 10, 17–18, 29, 1938.

8. LSD Diary, March 31 and April 3, 7, 9–10, 1938.

9. NKD Diary, April 1–14, 27–28, 1938; *Longview Daily News,* April 28, 1938; similar articles appeared on April 28 in the *Corpus Christi Times* and the *San Antonio Light* and on April 29 in the *Dallas Morning News,* the *Dallas Times-Herald,* and other newspapers.

10. A rock bit is similar to a roller bit. NKD Diary, April 30, May 1, 3, 1938; LSD Diary, April 30, 1938; *Denton Record-Chronicle,* August 29, 1938; *San Antonio Express,* September 2, 1938.

11. NKD Diary, May 9, 1938; N. K. Dixon to M. T. Gonzaullas, May 11, 1938, DPP.

12. NKD Diary, May 10–11, 1938.

13. NKD Diary, May 15, 1938.

14. NKD Diary, May 16, 1938.

15. NKD Diary, May 19–28, 1938; LSD Diary, May 28, 1938.

16. NKD Diary, May 29, 1938. In a parenthetical note dated October 14, 1938, Dixon

entered the information about the grand-jury no bill and about Crowder's later encounter with Stewart.

17. NKD Diary, May 30–31, June 1, 1938; LSD Diary, May 31, June 1–2, 1938.

18. Dixon to McGraw, April 30, 1937, DPP; NKD Diary, June 1–4, 1938.

19. Malsch, *Captain M. T. Gonzaullas,* 122–25; M. T. Gonzaullas to Col. H. H. Carmichael, Director, Department of Public Safety, *Annual Report,* September 1, 1936, DPP.

20. NKD Diary, June 6–12, 14–18, 1938.

21. M. T. Gonzaullas address to the Joint Annual Convention of the Texas Division of the International Association for Identification and the City Marshals and Chiefs of Police Association of Texas, El Paso, June 20–22, 1938, DPP.

22. LSD Diary, June 22, 25, 1938; NKD Diary, July 1, 1938.

23. LSD Diary, July 15–16, 23, 1938; NKD Diary, July 15, August 1–5, 1938.

24. *Austin Statesman,* August 15, 1938; NKD Diary, August 15–19, 24, 1938; *Austin American,* August 16, 1938; LSD Diary, August 17, 19, 1938; *Galveston Daily News,* August 17, 1938; *Paris News,* September 11, 1938.

25. NKD Diary, September 2, 5, 7, 11, 1938.

26. LSD Diary, August 27, 31, September 1, 3, 5–6, 10, 13, 1938; Western Union telegram from Norman Dixon to R. F. Dixon, September 14, 1938, DPP; Norman Dixon to Ronald and Isabel Dixon, September 18, 1938, DPP.

27. LSD Diary, September 15, 17, 21, 23, 24, 26–30, October 2, 1939; NKD Diary, September 24, 1938; *Austin American-Statesman,* September 25, 1938; Utley, *Lone Star Lawmen,* 190–91.

28. Utley, *Lone Star Lawmen,* 193–94, 331.

29. According to his diary, Dixon spent parts of thirty-one days between September 15 and November 7, 1938, working on Oscar.

30. *Dallas Morning News,* August 12, 1984, DPP; Michael Charney to Norman K. Dixon, September 14, 1984, DPP.

31. LSD Diary, October 30, November 3, 1938; NKD Diary, November 20, 1938.

32. *Austin Statesman,* November 2, 1938.

33. *San Antonio Light,* November 3, 1938; *Austin Statesman,* November 3, 4, 1938; NKD Diary, November 3, 1938; *Dallas Morning News,* November 4, 1938.

34. LSD Diary, December 9, 11, 19, 25–27, 1938; NKD Diary, December 25, 1938; *Syracuse Post-Standard,* August 14, 1938.

Chapter 4

1. LSD Diary, December 28, 1938, January 1, 4, 6, 13, 17, 1939.

2. LSD Diary, May 13, 19–20, 1939.

3. *Corsicana Daily Sun,* April 18, 1939; NKD Diary, April 18, 1939; *Galveston Daily News,* April 19, 1939.

4. NKD Diary, April 18, 21–25, May 24–25, 1939.

5. NKD Diary, June 6–14, 1939; Wick Fowler, "Hunch Leads to Quick Arrest," *Sheriff's Association of Texas Magazine* 8, no. 4 (June 1939): 13; *Corsicana Daily Sun,* June 15, 1939.

6. NKD Diary, June 15, September 4, 1939; *The Austin Statesman,* June 16, 1939; *San Antonio Light,* June 16, 1939.

7. NKD Diary, June 19, 1939; *Dallas News,* January 7, March 8, 1939.

8. LSD Diary, June 19–20, 1939; NKD Diary, June 20–21, 1939; *San Antonio Light,* July 16, 1939; *San Antonio Express,* December 5, 1939; *Lubbock Morning Avalanche,* December 8, 1939.

9. LSD Diary, June 21–22, 1939; NKD Diary, June 27–July 12, 1939.

10. *Laredo Times,* July 24, 26, 1939; NKD Diary, July 23, 1939.

11. NKD Diary, July 24–28, 1939; LSD Diary, July 24, 1939; *Laredo Times,* July 28, 1939.

12. NKD Diary, July 29–August 1, 1939; LSD Diary, July 29, August 1, 1939.

13. *Laredo Times,* February 18, 1940; NKD Diary, February 11–17, 1940.

14. NKD Diary, August 23, September 25–29, 1939; *Denison Herald,* September 29, 1939.

15. A marble table is a pinball machine of chance. A punch board generally is a square of wood or cardboard with hundreds of sealed holes each filled with a slip of paper containing a number or a symbol. The player punches through the seal and extracts the paper to see if he has won a prize. NKD Diary, October 2–5, November 10–17, 1939; *Austin Statesman,* December 4, 1939.

16. NKD Diary, October 7, December 10–12, 1939.

17. NKD Diary, December 23, 1939, February 6, 8, March 2, 4, 7, 1940; Rigler and Rigler, *In the Line of Duty,* 120–21.

18. NKD Diary, December 4–8, 1939, January 1, February 19, 22–24, 28, 1940.

19. *Kerrville Mountain Sun,* December 14, 1940; NKD Diary, March 18–April 17, 1940; Alfred Petsch to Colonel Homer Garrison Jr., April 17, 1940.

20. NKD Diary, May 22–24, June 21, 1940; *San Antonio Light,* June 10, 1940.

21. NKD Diary, June 28–29, August 27, 28, 31, 1940; *San Antonio Light,* August 28, September 3, 1940.

22. Laurance Spellman to author, May 14, 2009.

23. LSD Diary, October 15–17, 1939.

Chapter 5

1. NKD Diary, September 2, 27–28, 1940; *San Antonio Evening News,* September 3, 1940; *San Antonio Express,* September 4, 5, 1940.

2. *Corpus Christi Caller-Times,* September 29, 1940; *Corpus Christi Times,* December 16, 1940; *Houston Chronicle,* December 16, 1940; Mike Cox, *Texas Ranger Tales: Stories That Need Telling* (Plano: Republic of Texas Press, 1997), 242–45.

3. Panguinge, generally called "pan," is a gambling form of the game Rummy. NKD Diary, September 29–30, October 3–7, 1940; *Corpus Christi Times,* September 30, October 1, 7, 9, 1940.

4. Chuck-a-lucks is a game played with three dice. NKD Diary, October 8, 11–12, 20–21, 1940; *Corpus Christi Caller,* October 23, 25, 1940.

5. NKD Diary, November 1–30, December 1–11, 15–17, 1940; *Corpus Christi Times,* December 17, 1940.

6. NKD Diary, November 28, 1940–January 21, 1941; *San Antonio Light,* September 15, 1940; *Valley Star-Monitor-Herald,* September 15, 1940; *Big Spring Daily Herald,* February 2, 1941; *Corsicana Daily Sun,* February 15, 1941.

7. NKD Diary, December 21, 1940; Russell Morton Brown to J. Edgar Hoover, December 10, 1940.

8. NKD Diary, January 22, 1941; Homer Garrison Jr., to N. K. Dixon, January 24, 1941; Norman Dixon to Ronald Dixon, September 3, 1941.

9. NKD Diary, January 23–24, February 25, 27, 1941; "Liquor Control in Texas Outlined in Talk by Joe Sharp of the Liquor Control Board," *Sheriff's Association of Texas Magazine* 8, no. 5 (July 1939): 13, 22; Joe Sharp, "Liquor Control in Texas" *Sheriff's Association of Texas Magazine* 8, no. 7 (September 1939): 17–18; Thad Sitton, *The Texas Sheriff: Lord of the County Line* (Norman: University of Oklahoma Press, 2000), 147.

10. NKD Diary, February 2, 1941; Utley, *Lone Star Justice,* 413; Spinks, *Law on the Last Frontier,* 14; McWilliams's draft is dated January 30, 1941; Dixon's edited version is dated February 2, 1941, DPP.

11. NKD Diary, February 3, 8, 18–21, 25–28, 1941.

12. NKD Diary, February 3, 11, 15–17, May 15, 1941; *Lubbock Morning Avalanche*, December 16, 1939, April 15, 1941; *Big Spring Daily Herald*, October 9, 1940.

13. NKD Diary, March 10, 19, 26, April 2, 10–11, 1941; Homer Garrison Jr. to T. E. Middlebrooks, April 30, 1941, DPP.

14. Sitton, *The Texas Sheriff*, 97–98.

15. NKD Diary, March 24–25, 1940; Rigler and Rigler, *In the Line of Duty*, 79; Sitton, *The Texas Sheriff*, 143.

16. NKD Diary, April 4–7, 1941; H. Joaquin Jackson with James L. Haley, *One Ranger Returns* (Austin: University of Texas Press, 2008), 30.

17. NKD Diary, May 9–14, 17, 25–30, June 5, 1941; *Brownwood Bulletin*, May 28, 1941; *Ft. Worth Star-Telegram*, May 29, 1941.

18. NKD Diary, June 24–25, 1941; *Big Spring Daily Herald*, June 25, 1941.

19. NKD Diary, July 3–4, 12, 15–17, 1941; *Temple Daily Telegram*, July 17, 1941.

20. NKD Diary, July 19–20, 1941; Norman Dixon to Ronald Dixon, September 3, 1941; Cox, *Time of the Rangers*, 190–91; *Brownwood Bulletin*, August 11, 1941.

21. NKD Diary, July 25–August 12, 1941; Norman Dixon to Ronald Dixon, September 3, 1941.

22. *Brownwood Bulletin*, August 11, 1941; Cox, *Time of the Rangers*, 191.

23. Dixon, "The Law, the Cop and You," undated, DPP.

24. Norman Dixon to Ronald Dixon, September 3, 1941; NKD Diary, August 26–28, 1941.

25. NKD Diary, September 10–12, 19, 27–October 20, 1941.

Chapter 6

1. W. E. Neely, "No More Human Man than Sheriff Harney," *Sheriff's Association of Texas Magazine* 8, no. 5 (July 1939): 9–10; Rev. Bill Crook, "Preacher Sees Harney's Good-Bad Traits," *Sheriff's Association of Texas Magazine* 8, no. 5 (July 1939): 23.

2. "Sheriff Harney Is Exonerated," *Sheriff's Association of Texas Magazine* 9, no. 4 (June 1940): 4; "Harney Alert for Political Curve Tossing," *Sheriff's Association of Texas Magazine* 9, no. 4 (June 1940): 11; *San Antonio Light*, April 4, 1941; *San Antonio Express*, April 10, 1941.

3. *Corpus Christi Caller*, March 22, 1942.

4. NKD Diary, October 26–29, 1941.

5. Sitton, *The Texas Sheriff*, xii, 97, 105–108.

6. A boatswain's mate supervises personnel in ship-maintenance duties. NKD Diary, October 30–November 5, 1941.

7. *Austin Statesman*, February 11, 1942.

8. A "relator" provides information relevant to an attorney general's petition. NKD Diary, February 15–19, 1942; *Corpus Christi Times*, February 19, 1942.

9. The Mann Act is a federal statute making it a crime to transport a woman across state lines for "immoral" purposes. *Corpus Christi Caller*, March 22–29, April 8, 1942; NKD Diary, March 23–28, April 4–5, 1938.

10. Gerald C. Mann to Homer Garrison, June 10, 1942, DPP.

11. NKD Diary, December 30, 1941; *San Antonio Express*, April 4, 1938, *New York Times*, April 3, 1938; *Los Angeles Times*, April 4, 1938.

12. *Berkeley Daily Gazette*, April 2, 4, 1938; *New York Times*, April 4, 1938, April 5, 1942; "Famous Frome Murder Case Unsolved after Year," *Sheriff's Association of Texas Magazine* 8, no. 3 (May 1939): 37; Jackson, *One Ranger Returns*, 47–5; Clint Richmond, *Fetch the Devil:*

The Sierra Diablo Murders and Nazi Espionage in America (Lebanon, NH: University Press of New England, 2014), 36, 50, 56–57, 101.

13. *Berkeley Daily Gazette,* April 4, 6, 1942; *Prescott Evening Courier,* April 6, 1938; *San Antonio Express,* April 7, 1938; *New York Times,* April 6, 1938; Jackson, *One Ranger Returns,* 53–54.

14. *San Antonio Express,* April 11, 16, 1938; *New York Times,* April 10, 12, 1938.

15. *San Antonio Light,* April 11, 1938; *El Paso Herald-Post,* April 12, 15, 1938; NKD Diary, August 12, 1938.

16. *Big Spring Daily Herald,* April 14, 1938.

17. *Prescott Evening Courier,* April 27, 1938; NKD Diary, April 26, 1938.

18. *Big Spring Daily Herald,* May 1, 1938; *Abilene Reporter-News,* May 2, 1938; *San Antonio Express,* May 7, 1938; *Spokane Daily Chronicle,* May 9, 1938. During a long criminal career, Trotsky was deported at least nine times, used thirty-five aliases, and had ties to a Nazi spy ring that might have been involved in the Frome murders. Richmond, *Fetch the Devil,* 313.

19. *El Paso Herald-Post,* May 16, 1938.

20. *St. Petersburg* (FL) *Evening Independent* August 2, 1938; *Berkeley Daily Gazette,* August 2, 1938; *Ellensburg* (WA) *Daily Record* August 3, 1938; Jackson, *One Ranger Returns,* 54–55; *Lubbock Avalanche Journal,* May 14, July 30, 1939.

21. *Austin American-Statesman,* September 13, 1938; "Frome Murder Case to Be Solved," *Sheriff's Association of Texas Magazine* 8, no. 7 (September 1939): 38; "Frome Murder Case Will Be Cleared Up," *Sheriff's Association of Texas Magazine* 9, no. 5 (July 1940): 6; "Safety Department Persists in Search for Slayer of Mrs. Frome and Daughter," *Sheriff's Association of Texas Magazine* 14, no. 5 (August 1945): 23.

22. NKD Diary, December 30–31, January 1–10, 1942; *Bakersfield Californian,* January 14, 1942.

23. *Berkeley Daily Gazette,* January 13, 1942; *Dallas Morning News,* January 13, 1942.

24. NKD Diary, January 12–17, 1942.

25. *Dallas Morning News,* January 13, 1942; *Berkeley Daily Gazette,* January 13, 1942; *Bakersfield Californian,* January 14, 1942; *El Paso Herald-Post,* January 14, 19, 1942.

26. NKD Diary, January 23–25, 1942; *El Paso Herald-Post,* January 14, 26, 1942; *Berkeley Daily Gazette,* January 13, 1942; *Oakland Tribune,* January 14, 1942; *Sheriff's Magazine of Texas* 14, no. 5 (August 1945): 23.

27. NKD Diary, September 14–19, 1950; Jackson, *One Ranger Returns,* 58–62.

Chapter 7

1. *San Antonio Express,* May 21, 1940; *Corsicana Daily Sun,* May 21, 1940.

2. A fifth columnist is a subversive who supports the enemy. Anti-American Activities, Gov. W. Lee O'Daniel Papers, TSA.

3. The Texas Colorado River is not the river that courses through the Grand Canyon. NKD Diary, May 31, June 13–July 5, 8–9, 1940.

4. Jennifer Toth McIntyre, "Allegiance and Heritage: The German-Americans of Fredericksburg, Texas, in the Nazi Era, 1933–1945" (master's thesis, Texas Tech University, 2004), 3, 9, 16–18, 21; Green, *The Establishment in Texas Politics,* 72.

5. McIntyre, "Allegiance and Heritage," 46–48, 60, 80.

6. NKD Diary, February 6–8, 10–11, 13–14, April 9, August 17–21, September 13–17, 21–25, October 3, 6, 16, 25, 1941; January 29, February 3, April 21–24, May 6, 12, 15, 18–23, 27–28, June 3–28, July 15–30, 1942.

7. M. W. Acers to Colonel Homer Garrison Jr., June 15, 1942, DPP.

8. NKD Diary, July 27–August 5, 1942; Dwight Whitwell to M. T. Gonzaullas, August 20, 1942, DPP; *McKinney Daily Courier Gazette*, October 6, 1942.

9. M.T. Gonzaullas to Col. Homer Garrison Jr., September 26, 1942; Homer Garrison Jr. to N. K. Dixon, September 29, 1942, DPP.

10. *San Antonio Express*, May 21, 1940.

11. Anti-American Activities, TSA.

12. NKD Diary, November 19, 1942.

13. Utley, *Lone Star Lawmen*, 203; McIntyre, "Allegiance and Heritage," 85–87; "World War II Internment Camps," *Handbook of Texas Online*, Texas State Historical Association (hereafter TSHA).

14. Utley, *Lone Star Lawmen*, 203; Cox, *Time of Rangers*, 197; N. K. Dixon to Maj. George D. Thomas, June 8, 1942; George D. Thomas to Captain Taft, June 9, 1942, DPP.

15. Kennedy, *Freedom from Fear*, 633–37; John W. Storey and Mary L. Kelley, eds., *Twentieth-Century Texas: A Social and Cultural History* (Denton: University of North Texas Press, 2008), 175; Frederica Burt Wyatt and Hooper Skelton, *Coke R. Stevenson: A Texas Legend* (Junction: Skelton Press, 1976), 65.

16. NKD Diary, March 29, June 28, 1943.

17. Cox, *Time of the Rangers*, 202; NKD Diary, September 17–18, 1941; *Eastland County Weekly Record*, September 19, 1941; *Cross Plains Review*, September 26, 1941; *Fort Worth-Star Telegram*, October 7, 1941.

18. NKD Diary, July 30, August 26–27, September 11, October 3–9, 1943.

19. Proctor, *Just One Riot*, 14.

20. Cox, *Time of the Rangers*, 194–95; NKD Diary, February 4–12, 1942.

21. *Dallas Morning News*, February 4, May 11, June 29, 1942, February 1, 1943; "Federal Bureau of Investigation: Sabotage," *Sheriff's Association of Texas Magazine* 14, no. 4 (July 1945): 39.

22. NKD Diary, July 2–3, 10, 1941, September 30, 1942, November 16, 1943, April 28, 1944.

23. Cox, *Time of the Rangers*, 202; Richard P. Walker, *The Lone Star and the Swastika* (Austin: Eakin Press, 2001), xi, 1–2, 112–13; Mark Choate, *Nazis in the Pineywoods* (Lufkin: Best of East Texas Publishers, 1989), 43, 47, 74; Arnold P. Krammer, "When the Afrika Korps Came to Texas," *Southwestern Historical Quarterly* 80, no. 3 (January 1977): 255–56, 272.

24. With up to ninety thousand soldiers and ten thousand German POWs, Camp Swift was one of the largest training camps in Texas. NKD Diary, February 5, 19, April 24, May 24–25, 1944, February 5, 1945; *San Antonio Light*, May 23, 1944; *Harlingen Valley Morning Star*, May 26, 1944.

25. www.perrinairforcebase.net/history.htm; "Camp Howze," *Handbook of Texas Online*, TSHA.

26. "Majors Field," *Handbook of Texas Online*, TSHA; *Corsicana Daily Sun*, March 5, 1943; "Oral History, N. K. Dixon," Texas Ranger Research Center Archives, Texas Ranger Hall of Fame and Museum, Waco; NKD Diary, March 4, 1943.

27. *San Antonio Express*, May 19, 1943; "McKinney, Collin County, Texas," *Sheriff's Association of Texas Magazine* 12, no. 10 (January 1944): 7; "McKinney, Texas," "Veterans Administration Hospital, McKinney," *Handbook of Texas Online*, TSHA.

28. Storey and Kelley, *Twentieth-Century Texas*, 176; Kennedy, *Freedom from Fear*, 645. The US Office of Price Administration issued Norman and Leona Dixon *War Ration Book Four* numbers 298747 and 298748, respectively, DPP; N. K. Dixon to Nocona Boot Co., November 1, 1944, DPP; N. K. Dixon to Ab Riggs, 1944, DPP; B. W. Shudde to N. K. Dixon,

February 12, 1944, DPP; "Bravery! How about the Battle of Nylons," *Sheriff's Association of Texas Magazine* 14, no. 7 (October 1945): 89.

29. *Dallas Morning News,* September 12, 1942; Address of Gov. Coke Stevenson, January 9, 1943, *Coke Stevenson Papers (Address & Pamphlets),* Center for American History, University of Texas at Austin; *New York Times,* November 26, 1942.

30. Lewis W. Bailey, "Peace Officers' Duties in Furtherance of the Tire Conservation Program," *Sheriff's Association Magazine of Texas* 11, no. 8 (November 1942): 29; NKD Diary, November 30, 1942.

31. NKD Diary, March 20, 1943–November 29, 1946.

32. NKD Diary, August 25–27, 1942; *Sherman Daily Democrat,* August 26, 1942.

33. NKD Diary, April 10, 19, 23–27, 1945.

34. *Dallas Morning News,* February 2, March 7, April 20, 1945; NKD Diary, March 26, April 30, May 25, 1945; *Mexia Weekly Herald,* March 23, 1945; *Paris News,* May 16, 1945.

35. NKD Diary, August 14–15, 1945; *New York Times,* August 15, 1945; "First Time in History Denton's Office Closed," *Sheriff's Association of Texas Magazine* 14, no. 5 (August 1945): 15; *Dallas Morning News,* August 15, 1945.

Chapter 8

1. NKD Diary, November 29, 1943.

2. Storey and Kelley, *Twentieth-Century Texas,* 76, 79–81, 84; Utley, *Lone Star Lawmen,* 100–101; Kennedy, *Freedom from Fear,* 765.

3. Malsch, *Captain M. T. Gonzaullas,* 93–102; Utley, *Lone Star Lawmen,* 134–40.

4. "Anti-Lynch Law," *Sheriff's Association of Texas Magazine* 8, no. 11 (January 1940): 20; "Senator Tom Connally Opposed Bill Inspired by Eastern Politicians," *Sheriff's Association of Texas Magazine* 9, no. 2 (April 1940): 15; Green, *The Establishment in Texas Politics,* 79; *St. Petersburg* (FL) *Evening Independent,* July 13, 1942.

5. James A. Burran, "Violence in an 'Arsenal of Democracy': The Beaumont Riot, 1943," *East Texas Historical Journal* 14 (Spring 1976): 39–44; "Beaumont Riot of 1943," *Handbook of Texas Online,* TSHA; Malsch, *Captain M. T. Gonzaullas,* 151–52.

6. Malsch, *Captain M. T. Gonzaullas,* 152–54; *Dallas Morning News,* June 17, 1943; *Dallas Morning News,* undated.

7. Malsch, *Captain M. T. Gonzaullas,* 154–56; NKD Diary, June 16, 1943.

8. *Beaumont Enterprise,* June 17, 1943; *Beaumont Journal,* June 17, 1943; *Dallas Morning News,* June 17, 18, 1943; Burran, "Violence in an 'Arsenal of Democracy,'" 45.

9. NKD Diary, June 18–22, 1943; *Dallas Morning News,* June 21, 1943; Burran, "Violence in an 'Arsenal of Democracy,'" 46–47.

10. *Paris News,* December 17, 1943.

11. NKD Diary, November 29, December 1–3, 1943; *Denton Record-Chronicle,* November 30, 1943; *Paris News,* December 17, 1943.

12. NKD Diary, December 13, 1943; *State of Texas v. Allen Murray,* District Court Records, Denton County.

13. *State of Texas v. Allen Murray,* District Court Records, Denton County; *Paris News,* December 17, 1943; NKD Diary, December 16, 1943.

14. *State of Texas v. Allen Murray,* District Court Records, Denton County; *Dallas Morning News,* December 18, 1943; NKD Diary, December 17, 1943.

15. *State of Texas v. Allen Murray,* District Court Records, Denton County; *Lubbock Morning Avalanche,* December 25, 1943; *Pampa News,* May 10, 1944; *Denton Record-Chronicle,* December 21, 1944, January 1, 1945.

16. James W. Marquart, Sheldon Ekland Olson, and Jonathan R. Sorenson, *The Rope, the Chair, and the Needle: Capital Punishment in Texas, 1923–1990*, (Austin: University of Texas, 1994), 29, 32; *State of Texas v. Allen Murray*, District Court Records, Denton County.

17. NKD Diary, February 7, 1946; *State of Texas v. Clyde Moore*, District Court Records, Henderson County; *Big Spring Daily Herald*, February 8, 1946; *Dallas Morning News*, February 27, 1946; *Lubbock Morning Avalanche*, April 4, 1946; *San Antonio Express*, May 7, 1946; *Paris News*, May 8, 1946.

18. *Dallas Morning News*, April 17, May 4, June 20, 1947.

19. Marquart, Olson, and Sorenson, *The Rope, the Chair, and the Needle*, 130.

Chapter 9

1. Malsch, *Captain M. T. Gonzaullas*, 1, 5–7, 13, 20, 26, 42–43, 57–58, 62, 65, 119, 122, 138–40, 189; Bob Stephens, "Manuel Trazazas 'Lone Wolf' Gonzaullas," *Texas Ranger Dispatch* 7 (Summer 2002). See http://www.texasranger.org/dispatch/Backissues/Dispatch_Issue_07.pdf; *Dallas Morning News*, May 25, 1963; *Houston Chronicle*, July 10, 1951.

2. Rigler and Rigler, *In the Line of Duty*, 178–79.

3. J. Lee Stambaugh and Lillian J. Stambaugh, *A History of Collin County, Texas* (Austin: Texas State Historical Association, 1958), 3, 46–51, 56; https://texasalmanac.com/population.

4. https://texasalmanac.com/population.

5. *Texarkana Gazette*, September 7, 1942.

6. Homer Garrison Jr., to N. K. Dixon, June 30, 1943, DPP.

7. Cox, *Time of the Rangers*, 139; "Dallas Police Get Two-Way Radio," *Sheriff's Association of Texas Magazine* 9, no. 4 (June 1940): 13; "Denison Police Get Two-Way Radio," *Sheriff's Association of Texas Magazine* 9, no. 5 (July 1940): 27.

8. Department of Public Safety Biennial Report for the Fiscal Years 1938–39 and 1939–40, pp. 40–43; Cox, *Time of the Rangers*, 187, 428.

9. Rigler and Rigler, *In the Line of Duty*, 27.

10. A Photostat was an early type of photocopy. NKD Diary, April 6–9, 1945; June 19–20, July 6, 1946; Federal Communications Commission Restricted Radio Telephone Operator Permit, Issued to Norman Kemp Dixon on May 7, 1945, DPP.

11. "10-Signals Used by Texas Department of Public Safety," 4" × 5" DPS card, DPP; Homer Garrison Jr., "Review of the Personnel Strength of the Texas Department of Public Safety, September 1, 1949," DPP.

12. NKD Diary, November 27, December 4, 10, 1942; Joaquin Jackson, *One Ranger: A Memoir* (Austin: University of Texas Press, 2005), xiii; Cox, *Time of the Rangers*, 245.

13. NKD Diary, January 9–12, 1943.

14. More populous counties, such as Dallas County, had multiple district courts. Sitton, *The Texas Sheriff*, 5, 23, 43, 48–49, 56, 66.

15. "The Denison Police Department," *Sheriff's Association of Texas Magazine* 9, no. 6 (August 1940): 37.

16. Allen G. Hatley, *Texas Constables: A Frontier Heritage* (Lubbock: Texas Tech University Press, 1999), xi, xii, 54.

17. "Robnett, Frisco Special Agent at Sherman, Has Solved Notable Cases," *Sheriff's Association of Texas Magazine* 14, no. 9 (December 1945): 27–28; J. M. Rooney, "The Rail Police," *Sheriff's Association of Texas Magazine* 8, no. 3 (May 1939): 13–16; "Frisco System," *Handbook of Texas Online*, TSHA; Cox, *Time of the Rangers*, 113.

18. A honky-tonk is a bar that caters to lower-class men. NKD Diary, November 25, 30, December 2, 4, 1942; *Denton Record-Chronicle*, December 5, 1942.

19. NKD Diary, December 5–14, 1942.

20. NKD Diary, December 17–26, 1942, February 1, March 1, 29, April 12, September 30, 1943, December 15, 1944–January 2, 1945; *Denton Record-Chronicle,* December 22, 1942, March 29, April 14, 1943; *Abilene Reporter News,* September 30, 1943.

21. NKD Diary, September 14–October 10, 19, 24, 30-November 3, 1942; May 24, October 11, 1943.

22. NKD Diary, March 17–18, 1943.

23. NKD Diary, July 31–September 30, 1943.

24. *Abilene Reporter-News,* January 31, 1945; NKD Diary, April 25–28, 1945; *Dallas Morning News,* April 28, 1945.

25. "Two Swindlers Sought after Jail Escape," *Sheriff's Association of Texas Magazine* 14, no. 8 (November 1945): 95; *Dallas Morning News,* July 21, 1946; *Ada* (OK) *Evening News,* July 31, 1946; NKD Diary, February 24, 1946; "Robnett, Frisco Special Agent at Sherman, Has Solved Notable Cases," *Sheriff's Association of Texas Magazine* 14, no. 9 (December 1945): 28.

Chapter 10

1. NKD Diary, August 17–20, 24–25, 28, October 3–4, 1942; *Denison Herald,* August 25, October 7, 1942; *Denison Press,* August 25, 1942; *Sherman Daily Democrat,* August 26, 1942.

2. NKD Diary, October 18–21, 1944; *San Antonio Express,* October 22, 1944; *San Antonio Light,* February 9, 10, 11, 1945.

3. NKD Diary, February 5–12, 1945; *San Antonio Light,* February 11, 12, 13, 1945; NKD Diary, February 12, 1945; www.lrl.state.tx.us.

4. "Retrieve Plantation," *Handbook of Texas Online,* TSHA; *Freeport Facts,* April 22, 1943; *Dallas Morning News,* June 6, 1943; Malsch, *Captain M. T. Gonzaullas,* 148–50; NKD Diary, June 3–5, 1943.

5. NKD Diary, June 5–7, 1943; *Dallas Morning News,* June 7, 11, 17, July 19, 23, 1943.

6. *Sherman Daily Democrat,* June 13, 1943; *Dallas Morning News,* June 13, 17, July 8, 1943.

7. *Dallas Morning News,* November 2, 1943; NKD Diary, November 1, 1943.

8. NKD Diary, November 20–23, 1945; *Gainesville Daily Register,* November 21, 24, 1945; "Dead Gainesville Sheriff Victim of Long Hours," *Sheriff's Association of Texas Magazine* 14, no. 8 (November 1945): 110.

9. NKD Diary, November 23–28, December 4–7, 1945, January 8, 1946; "Horn is Appointed Sheriff to Succeed Late Carl Wilson," *Sheriff's Association of Texas Magazine* 14, no. 9 (December 1945): 19; *Gainesville Daily Register,* December 7, 1945.

10. *State of Washington v. Richard Britton, Appellant,* Washington Supreme Court, March 13, 1947; *Reno* (NV) *Evening Gazette,* December 14, 1945.

11. NKD Diary, December 26–27, 1945.

12. J. D. Thomas, "Death Parks a Clue," *Timely Detective Cases* 3, no. 3 (December 1946): 75; Stanley Swanson, "Hat Fits a Killer," *Inside Detective* 25, no. 1 (January 1948): 41.

13. NKD Diary, December 27–31, 1945, January 1–3, 1946.

14. NKD Diary, June 1–9, 1946; *Seattle Post-Intelligencer,* June 7, 1946.

15. NKD Diary, January 24–25, 29, 1947; *Walla Walla* (WA) *Union-Bulletin,* January 14, 16, 17, February 17, 1948.

16. NKD Diary, February 18–April 3, 1946; M. T. Gonzaullas to Rangers R. A. Crowder, etc., March 20, 1946, DPP; M. T. Gonzaullas to All Members of Company "B" Texas Rangers, December 20, 1946.

Chapter 11

1. *Lubbock Evening Journal,* May 10, 1946; *Lubbock Morning Avalanche,* May 11, 1946; *Kansas City Star,* June 2, 1946; Malsch, *Captain M. T. Gonzaullas,* 159–63.

2. *Paris News,* March 25, April 15, 1946; *Kansas City Star,* June 2, 1946; Malsch, *Captain M. T. Gonzaullas,* 163–64.

3. NKD Diary, April 14–July 31, 1946.

4. *Kansas City Star,* June 2, 1946; Cox, *Time of the Rangers,* 205; Malsch, *Captain M. T. Gonzaullas,* 164–65.

5. NKD Diary, April 17–18, 27, May 2, 1946; *Big Spring Weekly Herald,* April 26, 1946; *Paris News,* April 28, 1946.

6. *Corsicana Daily Sun,* May 4, 1946; *Paris News,* May 8, 1946; Cox, *Texas Ranger Tales,* 253–55; Malsch, *Captain M. T. Gonzaullas,* 165–66; NKD Diary, May 3, 1946.

7. Michael Newton, *The Texarkana Moonlight Murders: The Unresolved Case of the 1946 Phantom Killer* (Jefferson, NC: McFarland, 2013), 81; *Paris News,* May 9, 12, 1946; *Dallas Morning News,* May 6, 9, 31, 1946.

8. NKD Diary, May 4, 7, June 24, 27–28, July 12, 22–25, 1946; *Texarkana Gazette,* July 23, 1946; *Texarkana Daily News,* July 27, 1946; *Port Arthur News,* May 15, 1946.

9. NKD Diary, August 4, 17, 1946. Dixon's diary shows he spent parts of forty-seven days between August 19 and December 24, 1946, on the Kreager case. *Abilene Reporter-News,* August 12, December 22, 1946, November 3, December 19, 1948; *Corsicana Daily Sun,* August 7, 8, 9, 1946; *San Antonio Light,* August 11, 1946.

10. *Dallas Morning News,* October 30, 31, 1946; *Paris News,* October 31, 1946; NKD Diary, October 31, 1946; Malsch, *Captain M. T. Gonzaullas,* 166–67.

11. NKD Diary, October 25–30, 1946; M. T. Gonzaullas to N. K. Dixon, October 28, 1946, DPP; *Big Spring Daily Herald,* November 1, December 17, 1946.

12. *McKinney Daily Courier-Gazette,* December 12, 1946; Don Graham, *No Name on the Bullet: A Biography of Audie Murphy* (New York: Viking, 1989), 101, 143–44; NKD Diary, December 11, 1946.

13. NKD Diary, June 21, July 2, 31, August 26, 1947; N. K. Dixon to Box D-10, *Sherman Daily Democrat,* December 14, 1946.

Chapter 12

1. NKD Diary, December 23, 1946; *Abilene Reporter-News,* December 23, 1946; Booth Mooney, *Mister Texas: The Story of Coke Stevenson* (Dallas: Texas Printing House, 1947), 1, 21.

2. "Board of Pardons and Paroles," *Handbook of Texas Online,* TSHA; "Question of Paroles and Pardons Still Subject of Heated Debate in Texas," *Sheriffs' Association of Texas Magazine* 14, no. 5 (August 1945): 3; "Pardon Board Official Says Members Act within Law," *Sheriffs' Association of Texas Magazine* 14, no. 7 (October 1945): 51.

3. *Abilene Reporter-News,* December 31, 1946; *Hearne Democrat,* January 3, 1947.

4. *San Antonio Light,* January 22, 29, 1947; NKD Diary, January 31, 1947; *San Antonio Express,* February 4, 1947.

5. NKD Diary, February 3–26, 1947.

6. *The Austin American,* February 27, 1947, DPP; *Houston Press,* February 27, 1947, DPP.

7. NKD Diary, February 27–April 3, 1947.

8. *Houston Press,* May 5, 1947; *Dallas Morning News,* May 6, 1947.

9. *Dallas Morning News,* June 7, 22, 1947.

10. "Texas A&M University," *Handbook of Texas Online,* TSHA.

11. Kennedy, *Freedom from Fear,* 786–87; *San Antonio Light,* March 4, 1947.

12. *San Antonio Light,* January 29, 30, 1947; *San Antonio Express,* January 31, February 2, 1947.

13. *San Antonio Express,* February 1, 1947.

14. *San Antonio Light,* February 22, 1947; *San Antonio Express,* March 26, 27, 1947.

15. *The Battalion* (Texas A&M student newspaper), March 29, 1947; *San Antonio Express,* March 28, 1947; Texas A&M Investigation, 1947, Department of Public Safety Records, TSA.

16. *Dallas Morning News,* March 30, 1947.

17. NKD Diary, April 4–7, 1947; *Austin Statesman,* April 3, 1947; *Dallas Morning News,* April 6, 1947.

18. *Port Arthur News,* April 9, 1947; *Amarillo Globe,* April 9, 1947; NKD Diary, April 8–9, 1947.

19. NKD Diary, March 31–April 1, 10, 1947 (regarding Texas Good Roads Association); NKD Diary April 7, May 12, 1947 (regarding Pardons and Paroles bills); *Abilene Reporter-News,* April 11, 28, 1947; *San Antonio Express,* June 6, 1947.

20. *Houston Chronicle,* April 11, 47.

21. NKD Diary, April 12, 1047; *San Antonio Light,* April 15, 1947; *San Antonio Express,* April 15, 1947.

22. NKD Diary, April 17–19, 1947; *San Antonio Express,* April 22, 1947; *San Antonio Light,* April 22, 23, 1947; *Austin American,* April 23, 1947.

23. NKD Diary, April 25, 28, 1947; *San Antonio Express,* April 29, 1947.

24. *Dallas Morning News,* April 24, 1947; *Austin American,* April 27, 1947; *The Battalion,* May 3, 6, 1947; *San Antonio Express,* May 3, 1947; *San Antonio Light,* May 12, 1947.

25. NKD Diary, May 13, 1947; *Dallas Morning News,* May 14, 1947. (Dixon's diary notes that the *News* reporter spent May 5–7 on the A&M campus with him.)

26. *Dallas Morning News,* May 15, 1947.

27. *Dallas Morning News,* June 7, 1947; *Austin American,* June 7, 1947; Texas A&M Investigation, 1947, TSA.

28. *Dallas Morning News,* June 30, 1947, July 11, 1948; "Gibb Gilchrist," *Handbook of Texas Online,* TSHA.

29. NKD Diary, July 8–9, 15, 19–23, 26, August 5, 1947; *Pampa Daily News,* July 9, 1947; *Amarillo News-Globe,* July 28, 1947.

30. NKD Diary, July 26, 1947; *Dallas Morning News,* July 26, 1947; *Lubbock Morning Avalanche,* October 27, 1943.

31. *Lubbock Morning Avalanche,* October 27, 29, 1943; NKD Diary, October 29, 1943, April 14–15, 1944.

32. *Port Arthur News,* November 3, 1943; *Dallas Morning News,* August 31, 1944; *Dallas Times-Herald,* September 23, 1944, January 12, 1945; *Abilene Reporter-News,* October 20, 1946; *Amarillo News-Globe,* June 29, 1947.

33. *Lubbock Morning Avalanche,* May 10, October 5, 1946; *Lubbock Avalanche-Journal,* June 2, 1946; *Lubbock Evening Journal,* June 4, 1946.

34. *Amarillo News-Globe,* June 29, 1947; *Amarillo Globe,* July 21, 1947; *Dallas Morning News,* July 22, 1947; *Lubbock Evening Journal,* July 23, 1947; *Austin American,* July 29, 1947.

35. NKD Diary, July 26–30, 1947; *Lubbock Evening Journal,* July 21, 1947.

36. NKD Diary, October 20–November 1, 13, 25, 28, December 2–5, 1947; *Lubbock Morning Avalanche,* January 16, October 30, 1947; *Lubbock Evening Journal,* December 17, 1947; *Lubbock Avalanche Journal,* August 1, 1948.

Chapter 13

1. Leona Dixon to Norman Dixon, undated note, DPP.

2. Dixon, "Chronology"; *Elgin Courier,* December 15, 1949, January 5, 1950; *DPS Chaparral* 3, no. 6 (November–December 1950): 5–11; *Austin American,* October 5, 1950.

3. *Elgin Courier,* February 15, August 2, 1951, February 26, June 18, 1953; *Austin American,* October 13, 1953.

4. Multiparty lines, usually called party lines, were less expensive than individual lines and were in widespread use during the 1940s. NKD Diary, August 16–19, 1947; *Austin American,* August 23, 1947.

5. NKD Diary, October 3, 1947, March 21–24, 1948; *Corpus Christi Caller,* October 1, 3, 1947, March 25, 1948; *Austin American* clipping, late September 1970, DPP.

6. NKD Diary, October 20–21, 1947, March 25, September 1, October 21–23, 1948.

7. NKD Diary, April 1, July 8–18, 1948; *Lubbock Evening Journal,* August 22, 1949; *El Paso Herald-Post,* September 30, 1949, February 5, 1951.

8. N. K. Dixon and Fritz Christian to Col. Homer Garrison Jr., March 14, 1950, DPS Records, Box 2008/054–19, TSA; NKD Diary, March 4–10, 1950; *Lubbock Morning Avalanche,* December 27, 1950; *Lubbock Evening Journal,* February 17, 1950.

9. *Galveston Daily News,* March 21, 1950; N. K. Dixon to O. B. Ellis, June 15, 1951; Ellis to Dixon, June 18, 1951.

10. Harvey Klehr and John Earl Haynes, *The American Communist Movement: Storming Heaven Itself* (New York: Twayne Publishers, 1992), 6–7, 49–52, 74; Harvey Klehr, *The Heyday of American Communism: The Depression Decade* (New York: Basic Books, 1984), 10, 90–92, 104–107, 165; Merline Pitre, *In Struggle against Jim Crow: Lulu B. White and the NAACP, 1900–1957* (College Station: Texas A&M University Press, 1999), 71; Don E. Carleton, *Red Scare! Right Wing Hysteria, Fifties Fanaticism, and Their Legacy in Texas* (Austin: Texas Monthly Press, 1985), 27–28.

11. August Raymond Ogden, *The Dies Committee: A Study of the Special House Committee for the Investigation of Un-American Activities, 1938–1944* (Westport, CT: Greenwood Press, 1984), 47, 179, 208; Green, *The Establishment in Texas Politics,* 69; Walter Goodman, *The Committee: The Extraordinary Career of the House Committee on Un-American Activities* (New York: Farrar, Straus & Giroux, 1968), 21.

12. Ogden, 210; NKD Diary, August 2–4, 1940; *Austin Statesman,* August 4, 6, 1940; *Austin Tribune,* August 4, 1940; *San Antonio Express,* August 6, 1940; *Port Arthur News,* August 9, 1940.

13. Green, *The Establishment in Texas Politics,* 72–73; Jeff Woods, *Black Struggle, Red Scare: Segregation and Anti-Communism in the South, 1948–1968* (Baton Rouge: Louisiana State University Press, 2004), 26.

14. Green, *The Establishment in Texas Politics,* 73; "Martin Dies," *Handbook of Texas Online,* TSHA.

15. Carleton, *Red Scare,* 22; Susan Richardson, "Reds, Race, and Research: Homer P. Rainey and the Grand Texas Tradition of Political Interference, 1939–1944," in *Perspectives on the History of Higher Education,* vol. 24, ed. Roger Geiger (New Brunswick, NJ: Transaction Publishers, 2005), 145, 148–49; Ronnie Dugger, *Our Invaded Universities: Form, Reform and New Starts* (New York: W.W. Norton, 1974), 39–43.

16. Richardson, "Reds, Race, and Research," 145, 151–53, 158; Dugger, *Our Invaded Universities,* 45–46, 49; Green, *The Establishment in Texas Politics,* 87; *San Antonio Express,* November 18, 1944; *Dallas Morning News,* November 18, 1944.

17. NKD Diary, May 1–July 15, 1944.

18. Green, *The Establishment in Texas Politics,* 86–89; Dugger, *Our Invaded Universities,* 50; *Paris News,* November 19, 1944.

Chapter 14

1. NKD Diary, May 17, September 19, 1947, April 23, 1948; *San Antonio Express,* May 18, 1947; Carleton, *Red Scare,* 44; Woods, *Black Struggle, Red Scare,* 28.

2. Carleton, *Red Scare,* 52–53; "Elections of Texas Governors, 1845–2006," *Handbook of Texas Online,* TSHA.

3. NKD Diary, June 19–24, 1948; Carleton, *Red Scare,* 49–51.

4. Homer Garrison Jr., to Division Chiefs, Ranger and Patrol Captains, January 5, 1949, "Subversive Intelligence," DPP (hereafter "Subversive Intelligence Report").

5. Subversive Intelligence Report, January 20, 1949, DPP.

6. *Dallas Morning News,* December 17, 1946; *Austin American-Statesman,* October 17, 2010; Michael L. Gillette, "Blacks Challenge the White University," *Southwestern Historical Quarterly* 86 (2): 322, 338–40.

7. Wendell Addington, *Why I am a Communist!* (New York: The Youth Commission, Council of Student Clubs, Communist Party of the United States, 1948), 1–4.

8. *Dallas Morning News,* February 15, 1948; *Paris News,* February 15, 1948; *Lubbock Avalanche Journal,* April 18, 1948.

9. Minutes of the City Council, City of Austin, Texas, May 13, 1948; *Dallas Morning News,* July 22, 1948.

10. *Lubbock Evening Journal,* February 16, 1949; NKD Diary, February 22, 1949; Carleton, *Red Scare,* 96.

11. NKD Diary, January 25, March 3–4, 14, 23–24, 1949; Subversive Intelligence Report, March 8, 30, 1949; *El Paso Herald-Post,* March 15, 1949; Carleton, *Red Scare,* 95–96.

12. *San Antonio Light,* March 23, 24, 1949; *Dallas Morning News,* March 31, April 13, 1949; NKD Diary, April 7, 12, 1949.

13. NKD Diary, April 20, 27–29, 1949; *Corsicana Daily Sun,* April 20, 1949.

14. "Education: Lone Star v. Red," *Time,* April 4, 1949. See http://content.time.com/time/magazine/article/0,9171,800010,00.html

15. NKD Diary, April 6, 1949; *Dallas Morning News,* April 7, August 26, 1949.

16. Subversive Intelligence Report, May 31, July 8, 1949; NKD Diary, June 23, 1949; *Dallas Morning News,* October 22, 1950.

17. NKD Diary, August 4–7, 1949; Subversive Intelligence Report, September 26, 1949.

18. Klehr and Haynes, *The American Communist Movement,* 132–34; Thomas C. Reeves, *The Life and Times of Joe McCarthy: A Biography* (New York: Stern and Day, 1982), 249, 315–16.

19. "Darden, Ida Mercedes Muse," "Minute Women of the USA," *Handbook of Texas Online,* TSHA; Pitre, *In Struggle against Jim Crow,* 141–42.

20. NKD Diary for 1950.

21. Carleton, *Red Scare,* 55–63; NKD Diary, July 18–20, 1950.

22. *Dallas Morning News,* October 22, 1950.

23. Carleton, *Red Scare,* 91–93; Woods, *Black Struggle, Red Scare,* 42.

24. *San Antonio Express,* January 30, February 14, 28, 1951; Subversive Intelligence Report, March 8, 1951.

25. Art. 6889–3, Texas Communist Control Law, Revised Civil Statutes of Texas.

26. Clipping of untitled United Press International release, dated May 1951, DPP; *Paris News,* October 18, 1951.

Chapter 15

1. *Dallas Morning News,* August 23, 1964; Norman Dixon, "Talk to the First Southern Presbyterian Church Men's Supper Group," November 20, 1951, DPP.

2. Statement of Confidential Informant (hereafter "Informant Statement"), November 21, 1951, DPP.

3. Fred McIntire to Mr. Norman K. Dixon, January 31, 1952, DPP; James Hay to N. K. Dixon, April 8, 1952, DPP; Phil _____ to Norm, June 3, 1952, DPP.

4. Dixon, "Speech Making," undated, DPP.

5. *San Antonio Express,* September 19, 21, 26, 1952.

6. Informant Statement, March 13–May 22, June 1–2, 1953, DPP; Gregory S. Taylor, *The History of the North Carolina Communist Party* (Columbia: The University of South Carolina Press, 2009), 147; John Egerton, *Speak Now against the Day: The Generation before the Civil Rights Movement in the South* (Chapel Hill: The University of North Carolina Press, 1995), 457–58; Sarah Hart Brown, *Standing against Dragons: Three Southern Lawyers in an Era of Fear* (Baton Rouge: Louisiana State University Press, 1998), 95–96.

7. Informant Statement, June 24–July 29, December 10, 1953, DPP.

8. *Corpus Christi Caller,* November 25, 1953; *Fort Worth Star-Telegram,* November 26, 1953.

9. Green, *The Establishment in Texas Politics,* 135; Industrial Commission Folder, Allan Shivers Papers, TSA; *Houston Post,* November 26, 1953.

10. Reeves, *The Life and Times of Joe McCarthy,* 476, 507, 534, 539; Green, *The Establishment in Texas Politics,* 127–30; "Minute Women of the USA," *Handbook of Texas Online,* TSHA.

11. *Fort Worth Star-Telegram,* November 28, December 5, 1953; *Houston Post,* November 30, 1953; *San Antonio Express,* December 3, 1953; *Austin American,* December 4, 5, 1953; *Wichita Falls Record,* December 5, 1953.

12. Carleton, *Red Scare,* 99; Subversive Intelligence Report, May 31, 1949; *Daily Worker,* January 10, 1954; Informant Statement, February 12, 1954, DPP.

13. Industrial Commission Folder, Allan Shivers Papers, TSA.

14. *Houston Post,* December 12, 1953; Executive Dept.–Communism, 1954, Allan Shivers Papers, TSA.

15. *San Antonio Express,* January 22, 1954; Executive Dept.–Communism #2, 1954, Allan Shivers Papers, TSA.

16. Communism–Correspondence, TSA; *Daily Texan,* February 26, 1954.

Chapter 16

1. Informant Statement, January 7, 10, April 23, 1954, DPP.

2. Reeves, *The Life and Times of Joe McCarthy,* 593–96, 604, 635, 639; Carleton, *Red Scare,* 267–71; *Houston Post,* June 30, 1954; N. K. Dixon, "Dixon Urges United Fight against Reds," *Texas Police Journal* 2, no. 6 (July 1954): 15–16.

3. *Houston Chronicle,* June 29, 1954; *New York Times,* July 5, 1954.

4. *Odessa American,* October 4, 1954; "Red Tactics Outlined at TPA Meeting," *Texas Police Journal* 2, no. 10 (November 1954): 7, 15; N. K. Dixon, "Combating Communist Mind-Control Plots," Veterans Day speech, November 11, 1954, DPP; *McAllen Monitor,* November 12, 1954.

5. *Texas Observer,* December 13, 1954.

6. Reeves, *The Life and Times of Joe McCarthy,* 645, 648–52, 660–62, 665–71; "Chief Dixon Speaks," *Texas Police Journal* 3, no. 1 (February 1955): 6.

7. D. B. Hardeman, "Shivers of Texas: A Tragedy in Three Acts," *Harper's Magazine,* November 1956, 49–56; Green, *The Establishment in Texas Politics,* 151, 156–62; Kinch and Long, *Allan Shivers,* 157–59.

8. Executive Dept.–Communism, 1954, TSA; *Austin American,* March 28, April 12, 1952; *Austin Statesman,* May 23, 1953; *Dallas Morning News,* May 23, 1954; DPS Press Release, May 22, 1953.

9. *Houston Chronicle,* September 20, 1953; *Houston Post,* September 20, 1953.

10. *Austin Statesman,* October 20, 1953; Oberst Werner Haag to N. K. Dixon, August 2, 1957, DPP.

11. Ross McSwain and Harold Byler, *Texas Politics and Greed: A Historical Story of the Veterans' Land Scandal in the 1950's* (Bloomington, Indiana: AuthorHouse, 2005), 1–4, 7–8, 13–15, 20–21; "Veterans' Land Board Scandal," *Handbook of Texas Online,* TSHA; *San Antonio Express,* December 28, 1954.

12. McSwain and Byler, *Texas Politics and Greed,* 21, 24–25, 29; Green, *The Establishment in Texas Politics,* 168; *Corpus Christi Caller,* March 16, 1956; "National Affairs: Bonus for the Boys," *Time,* August 8, 1955. See http://content.time.com/time/magazine/article/0,9171,807395,00.html

13. "Veterans' Land Board Scandal," *Handbook of Texas Online,* TSHA; McSwain and Byler, *Texas Politics and Greed,* 44, 112, 162; *Cuero Record,* May 8, 1955; *Dallas Morning News,* May 18, 2005.

14. Informant Statement, June 28, 1955–March 9, 1956, DPP; Goodman, *The Committee,* 436.

15. *Austin American,* April 18, 1956; *Austin Statesman,* April 18, 1956.

16. "NKD–Personal Notes," February 9, 28, 1956, DPP; Interview with Leona Spellman Dixon, February 23, 2010; *Pennsylvania v. Nelson,* 350 US 497 (1956), US Supreme Court.

17. *San Antonio Express,* February 22, 1956; *Waco News-Tribune,* March 2, 1956.

18. "NKD–Personal Notes," Undated, DPP; *Pennsylvania v. Nelson,* US Supreme Court.

19. "NKD–Personal Notes," February 20–June 2, 1958

Chapter 17

1. "Die Texas-Rangers," *Die Neue Polizei* 6, nr. 7 (Juli 1952): 110–11.

2. *Texas Rangers Sesquicentennial Anniversary 1823–1973: Pictorial Edition* (Forth Worth: Heritage Publications, 1973).

3. N. K. Dixon to University of Florida Foundation, June 7, 1991, DPP; Dan Ott, Director of Planned Giving, to Mr. Dixon, June 13, 1991, DPP.

4. "Norman Kemp Dixon," Obituary, *Austin American,* September 3, 1992.

BIBLIOGRAPHY

Addington, Wendell. "Why I am a Communist." New York: The Youth Commission, Council of Student Clubs, Communist Party of the United States, 1948.

Berry, Lewis E., ed. "Botany, Beetles, or Butterflies." *DPS Chaparral* 3, no. 6 (November-December 1950): 5–11.

Brown, Sarah Hart. *Standing against Dragons: Three Southern Lawyers in an Era of Fear.* Baton Rouge: Louisiana State University Press, 1998.

Bullock, Tommie Spellman. Interview by author, February 22, 2010.

Burran, James A. "Violence in an 'Arsenal of Democracy': The Beaumont Riot, 1943." *East Texas Historical Journal* 14 (Spring 1976): 39–44.

Carleton, Don E. *Red Scare: Right Wing Hysteria, Fifties Fanaticism and Their Legacy in Texas.* Austin: Texas Monthly Press,

Choate, Mark. *Nazis in the Pineywoods.* Lufkin: Best of East Texas Publishers, 1989.

Communism–Correspondence, Allan Shivers Papers, Texas State Archives.

Communist Informant. Transcript, 1951–1956. Dixon Personal Papers.

Cox, Mike. *Texas Ranger Tales: Stories that Need Telling.* Plano: Republic of Texas Press, 1997.

———. *Time of the Rangers: From 1900 to the Present.* New York: Tom Doherty Associates, 2009.

Dixon, Leona Spellman. Diaries, 1936 and 1938–1939.

———. Interview by author, February 23, 2010.

Dixon, N. K. "Dixon Urges United Front against Reds." *Texas Police Journal* 2, no. 6 (July 1954): 15–16.

———, and Fritz Christian. Letters to Col. Homer Garrison Jr. Department of Public Safety Records, Box 2008/054–19, Texas State Archives.

Dixon, Norman K. "Chronology: The Life of Norman Kemp Dixon."

———. "Ranger Diaries," 1938–1950.

———. "Subversive Intelligence Reports," Texas Department of Public Safety.

Dugger, Ronnie. *Our Invaded Universities: Form, Reform and New Starts.* New York: W. W. Norton, 1974.

Egerton, John. *Speak Now against the Day: The Generation before the Civil Rights Movement in the South.* Chapel Hill: University of North Carolina Press, 1995.

Executive Dept.–Communism, 1954, Allan Shivers Papers, Texas State Archives.

Executive Dept.–Communism 2, 1954, Allan Shivers Papers, Texas State Archives.

Gillette, Michael L. "Blacks Challenge the White University." *Southwestern Historical Quarterly* 86 (2): 322, 338–40.

Goodman, Walter. *The Committee: The Extraordinary Career of the House Committee on Un-American Activities*. New York: Farrar, Straus & Giroux, 1968.

Graham, Don. *No Name on the Bullet: A Biography of Audie Murphy*. New York: Viking, 1989.

Green, George Norris. *The Establishment in Texas Politics: The Primitive Years, 1938–1957*. Westport, CT: Greenwood Press, 1979.

Grieger, Roger, ed. *Perspectives on the History of Higher Education*. Vol. 24. New Brunswick, NJ: Transaction Publishers, 2005.

Handbook of Texas Online, Texas State Historical Association.

Hardeman, D. B. "Shivers of Texas: A Tragedy in Three Acts." *Harpers Magazine* (November 1956): 49–56.

Hatley, Allen G. *Texas Constables: A Frontier Heritage*. Lubbock: Texas Tech University Press, 1999.

Howarth, Shirley Reiff. *C. Paul Jennewein: Sculptor*. Tampa: The Tampa Museum, 1980.

Industrial Commission Folder, Allan Shivers Papers, Texas State Archives.

Jackson, H. Joaquin, with David Marion Wilkinson. *One Ranger: A Memoir*. Austin: University of Texas Press, 2005.

———, with Haley, James L. *One Ranger Returns*. Austin: University of Texas Press, 2008.

Kennedy, David M. *Freedom from Fear: The American People in Depression and War, 1929–1945*. New York: Oxford Press, 1999.

Kinch, Sam, and Stuart Long. *Allan Shivers: The Pied Piper of Texas Politics*. Austin: Shoal Creek Publishers, 1973.

Klehr, Harvey, *The Heyday of American Communism: The Depression Decade*. New York: Basic Books, 1984.

———, and John Earl Haynes. *The American Communist Movement: Storming Heaven Itself*. New York: Twayne Publishers, 1992.

Krammer, Arnold P. "When the Afrika Korps Came to Texas." *Southwestern Historical Quarterly* 80, no. 3 (January 1977): 255–56, 272.

Land Office Irregularities, Texas Department of Public Safety Records, Texas State Archives.

Malsch, Brownson. *Captain M. T. Gonzaullas, Lone Wolf: The Only Texas Ranger Captain of Spanish Descent*. Austin: Shoal Creek Publishers, 1980.

Marquart, James W., Sheldon Ekland Olson, and Jonathan R. Sorensen. *The Rope, the Chair, and the Needle: Capital Punishment in Texas, 1923–1990*. Austin: University of Texas Press, 1994.

McIntyre, Jennifer Toth. "Allegiance and Heritage: The German-Americans of Fredericksburg, Texas, in the Nazi Era, 1933–1945." Master's thesis, 2004. Texas Tech University.

McSwain, Ross, and Harold Byler. *Texas Politics and Greed: A Historical Story of the Veterans' Land Scandal in the 1950's*. Bloomington, Indiana: AuthorHouse, 2005.

Mooney, Booth. *Mister Texas: The Story of Coke Stevenson*. Dallas: Texas Printing House, 1947.

Newspapers. Fifty-seven published in Texas and seventeen published out of state.

Newton, Michael. *The Texarkana Moonlight Murders: The Unsolved Case of the 1946 Phantom Killer*. Jefferson, NC: McFarland, 2013.

Nieman, Robert. "Twentieth-Century Shining Star: Capt. Bob Crowder." *Texas Ranger Dispatch* 14 (Summer 2004). See http://www.texasranger.org/dispatch/Backissues/Dispatch_Issue_14.pdf

Ogden, August Raymond. *The Dies Committee: A Study of the Special House Committee for the Investigation of Un-American Activities, 1938–1944*. Westport, CT: Greenwood Press, 1984.

Olien, Roger M., and Diana Davids Olien. *Life in the Oil Fields.* Austin: Texas Monthly Press, 1986.

Pitre, Merline. *In Struggle against Jim Crow: Lulu B. White and the NAACP, 1900–1957*. College Station: Texas A&M University Press, 1999.

Proctor, Ben. *Just One Riot: Episodes of Texas Rangers in the 20th Century.* Austin: Eakin Press, 1991.

Ragsdale, Kenneth B. *The Year America Discovered Texas: Centennial '36*. College Station: Texas A&M University Press, 1987.

Reeves, Thomas C. *The Life and Times of Joe McCarthy: A Biography.* New York: Stern and Day, 1982.

Richardson, Susan. "Reds, Race, and Research: Homer P. Rainey and the Grand Texas Tradition of Political Interference, 1939–1944." In vol. 24 of Roger Geiger, ed. *Perspectives on the History of Higher Education.* New Brunswick, NJ: Transaction Publishers, 2005.

Richmond, Clint. *Fetch the Devil: The Sierra Diablo Murders and Nazi Espionage in America.* Lebanon, NH: University Press of New England, 2014.

Rigler, Lewis C., and Judyth Wagner Rigler. *In the Line of Duty: Reflections of a Texas Ranger Private.* Houston: Larksdale, 1984.

Sitton, Thad. *The Texas Sheriff: Lord of the County Line.* Norman: University of Oklahoma Press, 2000.

Spinks, S. E. *Law on the Last Frontier: Texas Ranger Arthur Hill.* Lubbock: Texas Tech University Press, 2007.

Stambaugh, J. Lee, and Lillian J. Stambaugh. *A History of Collin County, Texas.* Austin: Texas State Historical Association, 1958.

State of Pennsylvania v. Nelson, 350 U.S. 497 (1956), U.S. Supreme Court.

State of Texas v. Allen Murray, District Court Records, Denton County.

State of Texas v. Clyde Moore, District Court Records, Henderson County.

State of Texas v. Lester Orr, District Court Records, Hopkins County, Texas.

State of Texas v. Walter Radliff, District Court Records, Hopkins County, Texas.

State of Washington v. Richard Britton, Washington Supreme Court, March 13, 1947.

Stephens, Bob. "Manuel Trazazas 'Lone Wolf' Gonzaullas." *Texas Ranger Dispatch* 7 (Summer 2002). See http://www.texasranger.org/dispatch/Backissues/Dispatch_Issue_07.pdf

Stevenson, Coke, Papers (Addresses and Pamphlets), Center for American History, University of Texas at Austin.

Storey, John W., and Mary L. Kelley, eds. *Twentieth-Century Texas: A Social and Cultural History.* Denton: University of North Texas Press, 2008.

Swanson, Stanley. "Hat Fits a Killer." *Inside Detective* 25, no. 1 (January 1948): 41.

Taylor, Gregory S. *The History of the North Carolina Communist Party.* Columbia: University of South Carolina Press, 2009.

Texas A&M College Investigation, 1947, DPS Records, Texas State Archives.

Texas Communist Control Act, Art. 6889–3, Revised Civil Statutes of Texas.

Texas Department of Public Safety. *Annual Report*, September 1, 1936.

———. *Biennial Report for the Fiscal Years 1938–1939 and 1939–1940*.

Theft Prevention Handbook for the Texas Oil Industry. Dallas: Texas Mid-Continent Oil and Gas Association, 1944.

Thomas, J. D. "Death Parks a Clue." *Timely Detective Cases* 3, no. 3 (December 1946): 75.

Utley, Robert M. *Lone Star Lawmen: The Second Century of the Texas Rangers.* New York: Oxford University Press, 2007.

Walker, Richard P. *The Lone Star and the Swastika.* Austin: Eakin Press, 2001.

Woods, Jeff. *Black Struggle, Red Scare: Segregation and Anti-Communism in the South, 1948–1968.* Baton Rouge: Louisiana State University Press, 2004.

Wyatt, Frederica Burt, and Hooper Skelton. *Coke R. Stevenson: A Texas Legend.* Junction: Skelton Press, 1976.

INDEX

Abilene, Texas, 60
Acers, M. W., 79
Adams, B. A. "Jerry," 26–27
Addington, Wendell, 163–67, 169, 172
Aiken, Jr., A. M., 94, 135, 141
Aldrich, R. W., 16, 44
Alice, Texas, 55
Allee, Alfred Y., 13, 47, 71, 74, 153
Allen, Bill, 59
Allred, James V., 12, 25–27, 29, 37, 40, 46, 134, 137
Anderson, Albert A., 71, 73–74
Anderson, County, Texas, 20, 134
Anderson, Frank G., 143
Andrews, W. S., 139–40
Appelt, Ben, 44
Ardmore, Oklahoma, 108, 111
Army Air Corps, 4, 6, 145
Arnette, J. H., 36–39, 41–42, 47–48
Arnette, Jay, 59
Ashburn General Hospital, 87
Ashworth, Ray, 53
Atascosa County, Texas, 81
Aterberry, Tim, 121
Athens, Texas, 99
Aubrey, Texas, 95
Austin, Stephen F., 18
Austin American, 136, 143, 151–52, 189
Austin Statesman, 38, 42, 186, 189
Austin Tribune, 158
Austin, Texas, 35, 49, 54–55, 61, 63, 134, 144, 148, 150–51, 181, 187, 190

Bacchus, Joe, 57
Badgett, R. L., 88, 97, 113, 127, 129
Bagby, R. E., 63
Bailey, Lewis W., 88
Baldwin, Harry C., 67
Balmorhea, Texas, 69, 71
Baylor University, 169
Barber, Truett, 153
Barnes, Jack, 108
Barr, A. L., 47
Bartlett, Texas, 50
Bass, Everett G., 51
Bastrop County, Texas, 38–39, 86, 151
Battalion, The, 138, 143
Bead, Lugean "Shade," 128
Beaty, Larken Dudley, 84
Beaumont, Texas, 93–95, 158
Beeville, Texas, 84
Bell, John, 164, 188
Bell, Marshall, 165, 169–70
Bell, "Rabbit," 35
Bells, Texas, 107
Bergstrom Air Force Base, 154, 168
Berkeley, California, 69
Berkeley Daily Gazette, 74
Berry, K. L., 180
Berry, V. E. "Red," 114–16
Best, Ernest, 50, 53, 57, 59–61, 63
Biggerstaff, George, 106
Blue Ridge, Texas, 107
Blunt, Ralph "Peppy," 166
Boerne, Texas, 78
Bolton, Frank C., 142
Bone, Luther, 127
Bonham, Texas, 83, 90, 106, 110
Booker, Betty Jo, 125–26
Borum, Paul, 89, 107
Boutwell, James F., 186
Boyd, B. W., 96, 98
Bracewell, Searcy, 139
Brady, Texas, 61

Branch, Malcolm, 90, 106
Brandt, W. R., 68
Brazoria County, Texas, 67, 116
Bridgefarmer, Ethel, 110–11
Britton, H. M., 121
Britton, Homer, 120–22
Britton, Richard, 120–23, 126
Brooks, Homer, 158
Brooks, W. R., 65–66
Brown, Russell Morton, 56
Brownell, Herbert, 180
Brown, W. L., 130
Brownwood Bulletin, 61
Brownwood, Texas, 50, 58, 63
Bryan Army Air Field, 134
Bryan, Travis, 142, 144
Bullington, Orville, 159
Bullock, Tommie Spellman, 8, 9, 39, 47
Bureau of Intelligence, DPS, 13, 16, 18–19, 36, 45, 50, 101, 158
Burgunder, Robert, 72
Berkeley, California, 69
Burks, Alex, 106
Burnet, Texas, 59
Burns, Lee, 33
Burns, Sr., R. E., 63
Burns, Sr., L. B., 63
Butler, Naomi Jean, 74
Butler, R. B., 60
Button, W. E., 81, 95, 107, 110
Butts, Clyde, 68

Caldwell, Texas, 148–49
Cameron, Texas, 50, 146–49
Campbell, C. W., 65
Camp Howze, Texas, 85–86, 117
Camp Mabry, Texas, 14, 17–18, 35–37, 39, 48–49, 51, 104, 106, 110, 135, 142, 145, 148, 150
Camp Maxey, Texas, 83
Camp Swift, Texas, 86, 115
Camp Wolter, Texas, 83
Canady, O. L., 16
Canton, Texas, 117
Canyon, Texas, 57
Carmichael, Horace H., 13–14, 29, 37, 40, 72
Carney, Howard, 180
Carrizo Springs, Texas, 47–48, 71
Carson, David H., 41–42
Carthage, Texas, 77
Cason, III, Alex C., 55, 154, 186, 191
Celina, Texas, 95, 103
Centerville, Texas, 49
Chandler, Henry, 66
Charles, Micke, 68
Charney, Michael, 40–41
Christian, Fritz, 155–56, 192
Clark, F. C., 142–43, 145
Cleveland, Ohio, 10, 12
Cockran, C. D., 111
Cogburn, A. E., 120
Cogburn, E. "Hoss," 119
Coleman, Earl, 96
Coleman, Texas, 61
College Station, Texas, 136–37, 140, 142, 189
Collin County, Texas, 79, 95, 103, 106, 130
Collum, James Gordon, 83
Comanche, Texas, 61
Comfort, Texas, 60–61, 78
Commerce, Texas, 106
Communist Informant's Reports, 173–175, 178, 182, 188–89
Communist Party USA (CPUSA), 157, 162–66, 170, 172–75, 177, 179–80, 182–84, 189, 192
Connally, Tom, 93
Conroe, Texas, 45, 155
Cook, C. C., 84
Cooke County, Texas, 79, 86, 106, 108, 111
Cooper, Texas, 106
Corpus Christi Caller, 188
Corpus Christi, Texas, 53–55, 65–67, 82, 84, 153
Corsicana, Texas, 128
Coupland, Texas, 78
Cox, Mike, 106
Crane, Benjamin Joe, 38
Crawford, Pete, 71
Crook, Bill, 64
Cross Plains Review, 83
Cross Plains, Texas, 83
Crowder, Lucille, 19, 28, 42, 52
Crowder, Robert "Bob" Austin, 17–29, 31–32, 35, 40, 42, 52, 88, 97, 99, 113, 116–17, 187
Crystal City, Texas, 82
Cuero Record, 187–88
Cuero, Texas, 49, 187
Culbertson County, Texas, 71
Cullen, Hugh Roy, 169, 182

Daberko, Heinz, 86
Daily Courier Gazette (McKinney), 79
Daily Texan, 179, 181
Daily Worker, 162–63, 167, 169, 173, 178–79, 182, 186, 189
Dallas, B. E., 65
Dallas Morning News, 12, 74, 84, 89–90, 131, 143, 158, 164, 166, 169, 188
Dallas County, Texas, 97, 99–100, 103, 110
Dallas, Texas, 10, 12–13, 19, 33, 35, 38, 48–50, 57, 59, 79, 84–85, 87, 90, 103–105, 110, 116, 142, 160, 168, 178, 181
Daniel, Ernest, 59, 97, 99, 113
Daniel, Price, 154
Daniels, Leslie, 75
Darcy, T. E., 77
Darden, Ida, 168
Davenport, E. M. "Pappy," 46, 53–55
Davenport, Ida Mae, 55
Davies, Benton, 115
Davis, Paul, 30
Davis, T. A., 90
Davis, T. B., 96, 97–98
Dawson, County, Texas, 130
Dean, Stanley, 34
Deaton, Bobbie, 120
Deaton, Travis, 118
Decatur, Texas, 90, 106
Deering, John, 72
De Kalb, Texas, 128
Del Rio, Texas, 70, 87
Delta County, Texas, 106
Denison Herald, 49, 113
Denison, Texas, 83–84, 92, 103–104, 107, 109, 113, 117, 129
Denton County, Texas, 79, 89, 96–99, 106, 110, 134
Denton, S. H., 131–32
Denton, Texas, 83, 90–91, 95, 106
Desert. Texas, 107
Dickey, Ross, 93
Dies, Martin, 157–58
Dilley, Texas, 75
Dikes, Jimmy, 16
Distributive Processing and Office Workers Union (DPOWU), 178–79
Dixon, Annie May Elsdon, 1–3,
Dixon, Frederick William, 1, 3, 42–43
Dixon, Frederick Kemp, 39, 79, 126, 150
Dixon, Kenneth Ray, 51, 79, 126, 130, 150
Dixon, Leona Spellman, youth to Texas Centennial and death of Velma Ruth,1, 6–9, 12–13; living in Tyler, 18–19, 23, 27–28, 32, 35; in Austin and Goldthwaite, 37–41, 43, 46–48, 51–52, 54–55, 63; in McKinney, 87, 126, 130, 136, 144, 150; in Elgin, 154, 161; in Austin, 190, 192
Dixon, Norman Kemp, youth to Texas Centennial and death of Velma Ruth, 1–13; becomes a Ranger, 13–17; George Capps' disappearance, 20–22; E. H. Sojourner murder, 22–23; bank robber Harry Wells, 23–25; Land Commissioner W. H. McDonald investigation, 25–29; oil field theft rings, 30–35; crime lab, 36–42; bank robber Ralph Gresham, 43–45; Fred A. Pointer murder, 47–49; with E. M. "Pappy" Davenport, 53–55; cattle thefts, 60–62; John B. Harney case, 64–68; Frome murders, 69–75; un-American activities, 76–81; deserters, saboteurs, and POWs, 83–86; home front duties and sacrifices; Beaumont riot, 93–95; Allen Murray case, 95–99; Clyde Moore case, 99–100; communications, 104–106; Bridgefarmer murder, 110–11; Shilling swindle, 111–12; gambling crackdown, 113–16; capture of Walter Henry LeMay and C. M. Mershon, 116–17; Purcell murder and death of Carl Wilson, 118–20; Richard Britton case, 120–23; the Phantom Killer, 125–30; encounter with Audie Murphy, 131–32; Pardons and Parole Board investigation, 134–37; Texas A&M investigation, 137–45; Roy Hunt murder, 145–49; prison system investigation,154–56; investigations of Gays and Reds on the University of Texas campus, 157–61
Dixon, Ronald, 3, 9–12, 39–40, 62–63
Dixon, Velma Ruth, 10–11, 27
Dobie, J. Frank, 163
Doerner, Jr., F. W., 106, 109
Donahue, Lawrence, 81
Dos Passos, John, 159
Downs, W. W. "Woody," 64
DPS Chaparral, 151
Dunn, Earl, 53, 55

Durant, Oklahoma, 85, 108, 121–22
Duval County, Texas, 55

Eagle Pass, Texas, 71
Eastland County, Texas, 23
East Texas State College, 76
Edna, Texas, 55
Eldorado, Texas, 57
Eldread, Mead, 26–27
Elgin Courier, 151
Elgin, Texas, 150–51
Ellebracht, Chester, 50
Ellis, O. B., 154–56
El Paso County, Texas.70
El Paso, Texas, 37, 49, 69–72, 74
Embrey, Lester, 59
Embrey, Roy, 59
Estes, Fred, 169–70
Evans, A. B., 101
Everett, Brandon, 131–32

Fact Forum, 169
Faeke, Clarence, 121
Fannin County, Texas, 79, 92–93, 106, 111
Farmersville, Texas, 103, 131
FBI (Federal Bureau of Investigation), 45, 56, 79, 83–85, 101, 108, 111, 117, 127, 183, 189
Federal Communist Control Act, 170
Ferguson, Miriam "Ma," 134
Fields, Alton, 89–90
Fleming, Jr., Joe V., 151
Fletcher, Bill, 119
Fletcher, Joe, 153
Flippen, Jack,108
Floresville, Texas, 84
Flournoy, "Buck," 44–45
Floyd, "Pretty Boy," 108
Fort Bend County, Texas, 155
Ford, George, 89
Ford, Jon, 175
Fort Sam Houston, 6, 174, 176
Fort Worth, Texas, 73–74, 168
Fowler, Rex, 49
Fowler, Wick, 38, 158
Fox, Chris, 70–74
Fredericksburg, Texas, 40, 60, 78
Freeman, Dewey, and Eddie Freeman, 111–12
Frisco, Texas, 85, 103, 134
Fritz, J. W., 116–18
Frome, Hazel, 69–70, 73
Frome, Nancy, 69–70, 72–73
Frome, Weston G., 69–70
Furman v. Georgia, 100

Gafford, G. P., 121, 129
Gainesville, Texas, 59, 85, 89, 106, 108–109, 111, 117, 120, 132, 134
Galveston, Texas, 146–47, 162, 179, 181
Garner, G. W., 114
Garner, Howley, 114
Garner, Leroy, 114
Garrison, Homer, Jr., as DPS assistant director12–13, 16; DPS director through 1946, 40, 44, 48, 50, 54, 56–57, 59–61, 63, 65, 68–70, 73–74, 77, 79, 86, 101, 113–14, 132–33, 135, 144, 145, 148; as Norman Dixon's direct supervisor, 150, 152, 155–56, 158, 160–65, 169–70, 172, 181, 186, 189–92
Gary, Emmett C. "Pete," 117
Gault, Manny, 121, 146
Gebhard, Mary Lou, 155
Gentry, Sam, 134
Gerhardt, Raymond, 42
German-American Bund
Giddings, Texas, 38, 49
Gidley, W. E., 77
Gilbert, William, 138–39
Gilchrist, Gibb, 138–40, 142–45
Giles, Bascom, 187–88
Gillespie County, Texas, 78
Gill, M. R., 75
Gladewater, Texas, 18, 24, 116
Goldthwaite, Texas, 56–57, 59, 62, 78, 83, 85, 116, 150
Gonzales County, Texas, 6, 9
Gonzales, Texas, 55
Gonzalez, Polita, 54
Gonzaullas, Laura, 37, 39,101
Gonzaullas, Manuel Trazazas "Lone Wolf," as chief of the Bureau of Intelligence, 13–14, 16–19, 23, 27, 29, 34–39, 41; captain of Company B, 50, 59, 79–80, 83, 89, 92, 94–95, 97, 99–103, 107, 110–11, 113, 116–17, 121, 124, 126–27, 129–30, 133, 135, 146, 160
Goodman, Walter, 189
Gordon, Marvin, 23–24

Gorman, Texas, 83
Grabowski, Ruth, 109
Graves, Henry "Trotting Horse," 128
Grayson County, Texas, 48, 79, 84, 86, 92–93, 95, 103, 106, 108, 111, 121, 129
Green, James, 169
Greenville, Texas, 83, 106
Gregg County, Texas, 34, 105
Gresham, Ralph, 44–45
Griffin, Leonard, 55
Griffin, Richard L., 125
Grigsby, Louis, 39
Grisson, Mrs. Park, 131
Groesbeck, Texas, 117

Haag, Oberst Werner, 187
Hale County, Texas, 147
Halland, H. E., 64–66
Hallettsville, Texas, 44–46
Hall, Sam, 177, 179
Hall, Sylvia, 177
Hamer, Frank, 92
Hamilton, Texas, 59
Hamm, S. O., 49
Handley, Texas, 112
Hanna, Sam, 166
Harney, John B., 64–66, 68–69, 107
Harper, Major, 145
Harris, Charley, 34–35
Harris, Fred "Red," 136, 140–44
Harris, Hern, 56
Harrison, Duke, 106
Hart, Weldon, 143
Hatfield, Bonnie Price, 73–74
Hatfield, Charles, 73–74
Hatfield, Lois Van Court, 74
Hay, James, 174
Haynes, John Earl, 156, 167
Heard, Cyrus L., 66
Hergesheimer, Will A., 46
Heintze, Alvin, 44
Henderson County, Texas, 99
Henderson, Texas, 20, 32, 99
Hendrix, Luizye, 84
Henley, W. B., 106
Hester, Fred, 60
Higgins, Leroy, 46
Hill, Arthur, 57
Hill County, Texas, 117
Hillsboro, Texas, 117
Hill, Steel, 83
Hiss, Alger, 175
Holbrook, T. J., 25, 27
Holliday, R. W., 34
Hollis, Jimmy, 125
Home of the Brave, 167, 170
Honey Grove, Texas, 90, 92, 106
Hoover, J. Edgar, 56, 84
Horn, Emory, 118–20, 130, 134
House Un-American Activities Committee (HUAC), 159, 165, 178
Houston, Texas, 4, 27, 44, 46, 84, 87, 110, 128, 147–48, 163, 168–69, 178–79, 181–83
Howard County, Texas, 130
Howard, Mildred Faye, 86
Howarth, Shirley Reiff, 4
Howe, Texas, 59
Hubbard, Joe, 46
Hughes, George, 92
Humphries, Newt, 191
Hunt County, Texas, 79, 86, 106
Hunt, H. L., 169
Hunt, Roy, 145–49
Huntsville, Texas, 98–99, 135, 149, 155–56
Hutcheson, M.L., 98

Industrial Commission, 178–82
Inside Detective, 121
International Fur and Leather Workers, 178
International Union of Mine, Mill and Smelter Workers, 178
Ireland, Olen C., 41–42
Isaacs, S. J., 164
Ivy, F. M., 77

Jackson, Bill, 160
Jackson, Joaquin, 59, 74–75, 106
Jacksonville, Texas, 20
Jacobson, E. J., 175
James, Jesse, 160
Jameson, "Buck," 130
Jarrell, "Butch," 33
Jefferson, Texas, 24, 33
Jeffers, William M., 88
Jehovah's Witnesses, 81
Jennewein, C. Paul, 3–5
Jester, Beauford H., 100, 145, 147–49, 151, 155, 162

Jett, James, 100
Johnson, George, 92
Johnson, Harold V., 85
Johnston, Mrs. J. C., 128
Joiner, Columbus Marion "Dad," 25, 30
Jones, Gus T., 77
Jordan, A. W. "Bill," 154, 166, 168
Jung, Hans, 86
Jurecka, Adolph, 96

Karnes County, Texas, 9
Karnes City, Texas, 84
Kavanaugh, Bill, 186, 190, 192
Kazan, Phillip, 47
Keith, Amos, 58
Kelley, Edward, 38
Kelley, Mary L., 91
Kenedy, Texas, 81
Kennedy, M. Asher, 67
Kermit, Texas, 34–35
Kern, C. V. "Buster," 135, 169
Kerrville, Texas, 41, 50
Kilgore, Texas, 128
Kimble County, Texas, 61
King, William Henry, 64–65
Kingsland, Texas, 24
Kirchenbauer, Henry, 106, 108, 118
Kirk, W. A., 164
Klehr, Harvey, 156, 167
Klevenhagen, Johnny, 41
Klondike, Texas, 106
Klotz, H. L., 37, 39, 43
Knaggs, A. J., 47
Knickerbocker, Arthur B., 142
Kohut, Fred P., 135–36
Kreager, Mrs. N. O., 129
Kuhn, Fritz, 78

Laake, Adolph, 38
La Follette, Lelia, 110
Laird Hill, Texas, 72
Lambert, George, 109–110
Lamb County, Texas, 146
Lambert, "Slim," 114
Landman, E. A., 99
Lane, "Buck," 134
Laredo, Texas, 71
Larey, Mary Jeanne, 125
Lawrence, Harry, 67
Lawson, William J., 77
Leahy, John F., 186
Lee, Cecil, 3
LeMay, Walter Henry, 57, 116–17
Lewis, Abner, 135–37, 148
Lewis, Bennie Lee, 57–58
Lewis, Jess, 110
Lewisville, Texas, 90, 134
Limestone County, Texas, 117
Littlefield, Texas, 145–47
Llano, Texas, 49–50, 57–58, 149
Loftus, George, 154
Longview, Texas, 24–25, 32–34
Lowman, George, 53
Lowrey, John C., 83
Lowry, Todd, 170
Lozano, Jose, 66
Lubbock, Texas, 147, 163–64
Luckey, Mrs. G. W., 77
Lufkin, Texas, 40, 128
Luling, Texas, 24
Lupher, A. C., 59
Luther, J. T., 116–17

Majors Army Airfield, 86
Malkin, Maurice, 179
Mann, Gerald C., 65, 68
Mansell, E. E., 153
Mansfield, Texas, 146
Marlin, Texas, 112
Marsh, John W., 58
Marshall, Ed, 128
Marshall, Texas, 23, 85
Martin, Elbert M., 106–107
Martin, Paul, 125–26
Mash, Leon, 116–17
Mathews, Tommy, 55
Maverick County, Texas, 71
Maverick, Maury, 53
Massengale, J. B., 22–23
McAlister, Oklahoma, 85
McAllen, 183
McCormick, Bill, 139
McCarthy, Joseph, 167–69, 178, 182–84
McCrory, W. W., 115, 175
McDaniel, Jr., Robert L., 64–67
McDonald, William H., 25, 29, 187
McGraw, C. G., 13–14
McGuire, J. O., 45
McIntire, Fred, 174

McKinney, Texas, 79–80, 81, 83, 86–88, 90, 103, 106–107, 109–111, 124, 126, 129, 131–33, 144, 150, 160
McLaughlin, Glen, 97
McLinn, Marion, 152
McMurray, William, 20
McNeely, Ira, 121
McRorey, Elwin, 47
McRorey, Roe, 47–48
McRorey, Worth, 47
McSpadden, Earl Cliff, 128
McWilliams, Earl, 56–57
Meloy, Jr., Guy S., 138–39, 143
Merritt, L. E. "Red," 34, 39
Mershon, C. M., 116–17
Middlebrooks, T. E., 58
Midland, Texas, 34, 71
Milam County, Texas, 146
Milam, Jim, 69–71
Miller, Lee, 24, 41–42
Mills County, Texas, 56
Mills, Frank, 72
Millsap, Ernest, 129
Mineral Wells, Texas, 83, 111
Minute Women of the U.S.A., 168, 178
Mobile Register, 3
Mobley, Tom, 32, 34–35
Montague County, Texas, 79, 103, 111, 130
Montague, Texas 130
Moore, Clyde, 99–100
Moore, H. E., 99
Moore, Polly Ann, 125
Moore, Roy, 91, 95–96, 109, 134
Moreno, Jesse, 58
Moreno, Teodoro, 58
Morgan, M. B., 180
Morris, Marshall, 134–35
Morse, R. Emmett, 44
Moss, C. D., 119
Mull, Carl, 1, 6, 9
Mull, Gene Ellen, 6–7
Murchison, Clint, 169
Murphy, Audie, 131–32
Murray, Allen, 96–99
Murray, Sue, 127
Muskogee, Oklahoma, 112
Myres, Alfred, 81

National Maritime Union, 162
Naylor, W. E. "Dub," 25–27, 44, 63, 84, 114
Neal, Mrs. E. E., 83
Nelson, Paul, 89
Nevada, Texas, 83
New Braunfels, Texas, 78, 84
Newton, Michael, 128
Newton, Jr., William Roland, 145–48
Newton, Ruth, 146–47, 149
New York Times, 90, 183
Nichols, "Buster," 33
Nicholson, C. P., 96
Nipper, Cleo, 160
Nocona, Texas, 87
Norris, Pete, 107
Norstrum, A. J., 160
Northcutt, Lehman "Shug Moon," 154
North Gulch, Texas, 77
Nueces County, Texas, 64, 67, 107

O'Daniel, W. Lee "Pappy," 43, 60–61, 76–77, 81, 159
Odessa, Texas, 74, 183
Oklahoma City, Oklahoma, 89, 97–98
Oldham, Dick, 99
Oldham, Harold, 127
Olson, Fred, 50–51, 59–61, 114–15
O'Mary, Arthur, 59
One Ranger Returns, 59
Orr, Lester "Dutch," 32
Ott, Dan, 195
Owens, John Henry, 55

Pack, Leonard, 12
Paige, Texas, 38
Palestine, Texas, 30, 134–35
Parker County, Texas, 117
Parks, John Edmond, 118
Parks, Tommie Lee, 118
Passos, John Dos, 159
Peavy, Aleene, 128
Pecos, Texas, 73
Pennsylvania v. Nelson, 190–92
Perrin Field, Texas, 84, 86
Perry, Mrs. L. U., 28
Petsch, Alfred, 50
Pfeil, Edgar, 65–66
Phantom Killer, 124, 126–30
Phares, L. G., 14, 51
Phillips, Claude, 106
Phillips, N. F., 153

Phillips, Royal G., 50, 69, 73, 160
Pilot Point, Texas, 95–96
Pipes, Douglas, 59
Pipkin, "Red," 113, 115
Pitcock, George, 33
Plainview, Texas, 147
Plano, Texas, 103
Pointer, Fred A., 47–48
Port Arthur, Texas, 81, 178–79, 181, 185
Porter, Pleas, 48
Posey, J. B. 130
Robert Posey, 130
Powell, Fred L., 110–11
Presley, W. D. "Bill," 127, 129
Prestage, Fred, 121
Prewitt, Cecil, 145
Prince, Herschel, 59
Probst, Frank, 145
Procter, Les, 189
Progressive Party, 162, 165, 170
Purcell, Bill, 118–20
Purcell, Jr., Joe, 118
Purvis, Hardy B., 94

Radliff, Walter "Curly," 31–32
Rainey, Homer, 158–61
Rainey, M. L., 109–110
Randall County, Texas, 57
Ranger (magazine), 163–64
Rankin, Texas, 73
Ransom, Harry, 192
Ravenna, Texas, 83
Redwine, Norvell, 130
Reeves County, Texas, 73
Reeves, Jack, 73–74
Reeves, Thomas C., 168
Retrieve Prison Farm, 67–68, 116
Reyes, Severo, 68
Rhoades, Lonnie H., 56
Rice Institute, 4
Richardson, William H., 76
Riddle, Billy Joe, 100
Rigler, Lewis C., 19, 59, 103, 105
Riley, Frank, 128
Ritchie, Albert, 122
Roberts, Steve, 114
Robnett, D. C., 108–109, 111–12, 118, 121, 123
Rohatsch, R. F., 53
Rollins, John W., 138, 143
Roosevelt, Franklin D., 12, 88, 137, 158, 162, 167
Ross, Pat, 83
Rucker, Robert L., 154–56
Rusk County, Texas, 25, 30

Sammons, William L., 64
San Antonio Express, 53, 175
San Antonio Light, 42, 115
San Antonio, Texas, 6, 42, 50–51, 53, 55, 113, 115, 160, 168, 174–75, 178, 181
San Benito, Texas, 80–81
San Marcos, Texas, 77–78, 84
Schmidt, Smoot, 148
Schrobenhauser, Eugene, 77
Scott, Roy, 64
Seagoville, Texas, 81
Seattle, Washington, 120, 122, 126
Seay, Loron "Country," 89
Seay, Tully, 97, 116–17, 126
Seguin, Texas, 51, 84
Self, Harold, 108
Shearer, Thelmer, 63
Sheppard, John Ben, 178–79, 182, 188, 190
Sheriffs Association of Texas, 73, 112, 135
Sheriff's Association of Texas Magazine, 93
Sherman, Texas, 48, 79, 83, 85, 89, 92, 103, 106–108, 112–13, 121–22, 129, 132–33
Shilling, Mrs. Jose, 111
Shipley, Jess, 33, 35
Shivers, Allan, 135, 155, 169–70, 178, 180, 182, 184–88, 190–92
Short, Will Henry, 59
Shultz, Delbert V., 142–43
Sierra Blanca, Texas, 71
Simco, J. E., 73
Sinton, Texas, 153
Sisk, Tom, 45
Sitton, Thad, 58–59, 65
Smiley, Texas, 6–7, 10, 18, 54–55, 82, 160
Smith, Charles M., 66–68
Smith County, Texas, 32, 105
Smith, Doris, 166
Smith, Guy, 72
Smith, Harry, 121–22
Smith, Orbin Basil, 122–23
Smith, Roy, 7
Smith, Travis L., 141
Snow, Dewey, 32
Snow, Payne, 32

Sojourner, E. H., 22–23
Sons of the Republic of Texas, 182
Southern Methodist University (SMU), 164, 168
Southerland, W. I., 89
Southern Conservative, 168
Southern Methodist University, 76
Spain, B. F., 47, 53, 55
Spear, Franklin, 115
Spearman, Texas, 110
Spellman, Audley, 8
Spellman, Christian, 1, 6–9, 36–37
Spellman, Clyde, 7–8, 18
Spellman, Elna, 8, 9, 39
Spellman, Ethel, 8
Spellman, Frank, 9
Spellman, Gladys, 8, 39
Spellman, Laurance, 51
Spellman, Louis, 7
Spellman, Nora, 1, 6–7, 37, 39–40
Spellman, Robert "Bob," 51
Spellman, Rudolph, 9
Stamford, Texas, 58
Stanley, Stuart, 40, 126, 128
Stark, James "Raggedy Pappa," 89
Starks, Katy, 127
Starks, Virgil, 127
State of Texas v. Fred L. Powell, 110
Steadman, Jim, 158
Stevens, Howard, 118
Stevenson, Coke, 61, 74, 88, 93–94, 134–35
Stewart, Earl, 57, 59
Stewart, W. E., 35, 63
St. Johnston, Thomas Eric, 186
Stockberger, Clayton, 120, 123
Stone, Trueman, 114
Storey, John W., 91
Stout, A. R., 27–29
Stripling, Robert, 158
Sulphur Springs, Texas, 28, 31
Suran, R. C., 86
Sweatt, Heman, 163
Swisher, County, Texas, 147
Syracuse Post-Standard, 42

Tanner, Harold, 108
Taylor, James E., 76
Taylor, J. M., 51
Taylor, Texas, 78
Temple Daily Telegram, 60
Temple, Texas, 50
Texarkana Daily News, 129
Texarkana Moonlight Murders, The, 128
Texarkana, Texas, 93, 103, 107, 125–29
Texas A&M College, 76, 136–45, 150, 164
Texas Board of Pardons and Paroles, 99–100, 133–37, 145, 147–48
Texas Centennial Exposition, 10, 12
Texas Communist Control Act, 170, 172, 175
Texas Communist Party, 158, 162–64, 166, 168, 177
Texas Communist Suppression Act, 180–82
Texas Daily Sports News, 154
Texas Department of Public Safety (DPS), 12, 17, 29, 53, 57, 76, 82, 101, 104–105, 115, 144, 151, 153, 162, 165, 169–70, 172–74, 179–80, 182, 193
Texas General Land Office, 25, 29, 187–88
Texas Good Roads Association, 141, 150
Texas Highway Patrol, 14
Texas Liquor Control Board, 56
Texas Observer, 183
Texas Police Association, 183
Texas Public Employee,
Texas Ranger Hall of Fame and Museum,
Texas Sheriff, The, 58, 65
Texas State College for Women, 95
Texas Tech University, 163
Theft Prevention Handbook, 31–32
Thomas, Curtis, 93
Thomas, George D., 82
Thomas, Helen Darden, 168
Thomas, Jim, 146–49
Thomas, Johnny "Boy," 89
Thompson, Joe, 36–37, 39, 48, 126
Thorndale, Texas, 43, 45
Thurmond, Roy "Monk," 75
Tillotson College, 164, 166
Time, 166
Timely Detective Cases, 121
Time of the Rangers, 106
Tioga, Texas, 95–96
Towery, Roland Kenneth, 187–88
Townsend, Pearl. 113
Travis County, Texas, 82, 104
Trenton, Texas, 107
Tribble, Les, 89
Trotsky, Romano Nicholas, 72
Trower, "Dad," 32–35

Tuley, Martin Stover, 130–31
Tulia, Texas, 147
Tumlinson, Alonzo, 153
Turner, Andrew C., 155–56
Tyler Courier Times, 24
Tyler, Texas, 17–20, 23, 25, 28, 30–32, 35–36, 46–47, 116, 150

University of Florida, 3, 4, 82
University of Texas, 14, 15–16, 40, 76, 157–61, 164, 166, 172, 175, 177, 192
Utley, Robert M., 20, 40, 57, 81, 91

Van Alstyne, Texas, 107, 109, 121, 130
Vancuren, James Edward, 89
Van Horn, Texas, 69–70, 72–74, 103
Van Zandt County, Texas, 117
Veterans Land Act, 187–88
Veterans Land Board, 187–88
Vinson, Willie, 93

Wahler, Leo, 71
Walker, Willie Oscar, 83
Wallace, Frances, 81
Wallace, Henry, 162
Wallace, William Alfred, 81
Walton, T. O., 76, 141–42, 144
Waskom, Texas, 24
Waters, Raymond, 109, 121
Weatherford, Texas, 32, 35
Webb, V. L., 121
Wells, E. M., 16
Wells, Harry, 23–25
Wendland, Herman J., 64, 66
Westbrook, Dan, 50, 61
Westhoff, Texas, 6–7, 24
Wharton County, Texas,
Wharton, Texas, 44, 46
Whitten, Martin, 114
White, Bill, 58
White, Curtis, 9
White, Elna Spellman, 8
White, George, 138, 141
White, George Rollie., 216–20
Whitesboro, Texas, 95, 108
Whitlock, Ruby, 89–90
Whitsell, Dwight, 79, 132
Wichita Falls, Texas, 24, 168
Wilke, Geary, 152–53
Williams, Eugene, 164
Williams, Sam, 140
Wilson, Earl, 44, 46
Wilson, Carl, 106, 111, 118–19, 124
Winchester, Oleander A., 83–84
Winder, Ray, 120
Wise County, Texas, 79, 103, 106
Wofford, V. C. "Cotton," 32
Wolf, Bob, 130
Wolf, Frank, 106
Woodall, Ben, 55, 65
Woodrow, O. H., 89
Woodbury, Ruth, 2, 11
Wooley, Earl Gaddis, 136
Worcester, Chauncey, 71
Worcester, Hester, 71
Wray, Forest, 43, 46, 48
Wray, Mary, 43, 46 48
Wright City, Texas, 20, 30
Wyers, Robert Bruce, 89

Yarborough, Ralph, 184–85
York, Sam, 118
Yorktown, Texas, 6, 49
Young, "Blackie," 33
Young Progressives, of America, 165, 167, 170
Young, Walter Crowder, 100